# CONFIDENTIAL
# SECRETS

Publications International, Ltd.

# TABLE OF CONTENTS

# Chapter 1
# UNSOLVED MYSTERIES

## 9 OF HISTORY'S COLDEST CASES

They were gruesome crimes that shocked us with their brutality. But as time passed, we heard less and less about them until we forgot about the crime, not even realizing that the perpetrator remained among us. Yet the files remain open, and the families of the victims live on in a state of semi-paralysis. Here are some of the world's most famous cold cases.

**1. Elizabeth Short:** Elizabeth Short, also known as the Black Dahlia, was murdered in 1947. Like thousands of others, Elizabeth wanted to be a star. Unlike the bevy of blondes who trekked to Hollywood, this 22-year-old beauty from Massachusetts was dark and mysterious. She was last seen alive outside the Biltmore Hotel in Los Angeles on the evening of January 9, 1947.

Short's body was found on a vacant lot in Los Angeles. It had been cut in half at the waist and both parts had been drained of blood and then cleaned. Her body parts appeared to be surgically dissected, and her remains were suggestively posed. Despite receiving a number of false confessions and taunting letters that admonished police to "catch me if you can," the crime remains unsolved.

**2. The Zodiac Killer:** The Zodiac Killer was responsible for several murders in the San Francisco area in the 1960s and 1970s. His victims were shot, stabbed, and bludgeoned to death. After the first few kills, he began sending letters to the press in which he taunted police and made public threats, such as planning to blow up a school bus. In a letter sent to the *San Francisco Chronicle* two days after the murder of cabbie Paul Stine in October 1969, the killer, who called himself "The Zodiac," included in the package pieces of Stine's blood-soaked shirt. In the letters, which continued until 1978, he claimed a tally of 37 murders.

**3. Swedish Prime Minister Olof Palme:** On February 28, 1986, Swedish Prime Minister Olof Palme was gunned down on a Stockholm street as he and his wife strolled home from the movies unprotected around midnight. The prime minister was fatally shot in the back. His wife was seriously wounded but survived.

In 1988, a petty thief and drug addict named Christer Petterson was convicted of the murder because he was picked out of a lineup by Palme's widow. The conviction was later overturned on appeal when doubts were raised as to the reliability of Mrs. Palme's evidence. Despite many theories, the assassin remains at large.

**4. The Torso Killer:** In Cleveland, Ohio, during the 1930s, more than a dozen limbless torsos were found. Despite the efforts of famed crime fighter Eliot Ness, the torso killer was never found. The first two bodies, found in September 1935, were missing heads and had been horribly mutilated. Similar murders occurred during the next three years. Desperate to stop the killings, Ness ordered a raid on a run-down area known as Kingsbury's Run, where most of the victims were from. The place was torched, and hundreds of vagrants were taken into custody. After that, there were no more killings.

The key suspect in the murders was Frank Dolezal, a vagrant who lived in the area. He was a known bully with a fiery temper. Dolezal was arrested and subsequently confessed, but his confession was full of inaccuracies. He died shortly thereafter under suspicious circumstances.

**5. Bob Crane:** In 1978, Bob Crane, star of TV's *Hogan's Heroes*, was clubbed to death in his apartment. Crane shared a close friendship with John Carpenter, a pioneer in the development of video technology. The two shared an affinity for debauchery and sexual excesses, which were recorded on videotape. But by late 1978, Crane was tiring of Carpenter's dependence on him and had let him know that the friendship was over.

The following day, June 29, 1978, Crane was bludgeoned to death with a camera tripod in his Scottsdale, Arizona, apartment. Suspicion immediately fell on Carpenter, and a small spattering of blood was found in Carpenter's rental car, but police were unable to connect it to the crime. Examiners also found a tiny piece of human tissue in the car. Sixteen years after the killing, Carpenter finally went to trial, but he was acquitted due to lack of evidence.

**6. Tupac Shakur:** On September 7, 1996, successful rap artist Tupac Shakur was shot four times in a drive-by shooting in Las Vegas. He died six days later. Two years prior to that, Shakur had been shot five times in the lobby of a Manhattan recording studio the day before he was found guilty of sexual assault. He survived that attack, only to spend the next 11 months in jail. The 1994 shooting was a major catalyst for an East Coast-West Coast feud that would envelop the hip-hop industry and culminate in the deaths of both Shakur and Notorious B.I.G.(Christopher Wallace).

On the night of the fatal shooting, Shakur attended the Mike Tyson-Bruce Seldon fight at the MGM Grand in Las Vegas. After the fight, Shakur and his entourage got into a scuffle with a gang member. Shakur then headed for a nightclub, but he never made it. No one was ever arrested for the killing.

**7. Jack the Ripper:** In London in the late 1880s, a brutal killer known as Jack the Ripper preyed on local prostitutes. His first victim was 43-year-old Mary Ann Nichols, who was nearly decapitated during a savage knife attack. Days later, 47-year-old Annie Chapman had her organs removed from her abdomen before being left for dead. The press stirred up a wave of panic reporting that a serial killer was at large. Three weeks later, the killer was interrupted as he tore apart Swedish prostitute Elizabeth Stride. He managed to get away, only to strike again later that same night. This time the victim was Kate Eddowes. The killer, by now dubbed Jack the Ripper, removed a kidney in the process of hacking up Eddowes's body. His final kill was the most gruesome. On the night of November 9, 1888, Mary Kelly was methodically cut into pieces in an onslaught that must have lasted for several hours.

Dozens of potential Jacks have been implicated in the killings, including failed lawyer Montague John Druitt, whose body was fished out of the Thames River days after the last murder was committed. The nature of the bodily dissections has led many to conclude that Jack was a skilled physician with an advanced knowledge of anatomy. But more than a century after the savage attacks, the identity of Jack the Ripper remains a mystery.

**8. Jimmy Hoffa:** In 1975, labor leader Jimmy Hoffa disappeared on his way to a Detroit-area restaurant. Hoffa was the president of the Teamsters Union during the 1950s and 1960s. In 1964, he went to jail for bribing a grand juror investigating corruption in the union. In 1971, he was released on the condition that he not participate in any further union activity. Hoffa was preparing a legal challenge to that injunction when he disappeared on July 30, 1975. He was last seen in the parking lot of the Machus Red Fox Restaurant.

Hoffa had strong connections to the Mafia, and several mobsters have claimed that he met a grisly end on their say so.

Although his body has never been found, authorities officially declared him dead on July 30, 1982. As recently as November 2006, the FBI dug up farmland in Michigan hoping to turn up a corpse. So far, no luck.

**9. JonBenét Ramsey:** In the early hours of December 26, 1996, Patsy Ramsey reported that her six-year-old daughter, JonBenét, had been abducted from her Boulder, Colorado, home. Police rushed to the Ramsey home where, hours later, John Ramsey found his little girl dead in the basement. She had been battered, sexually assaulted, and strangled.

Police found several tantalizing bits of evidence—a number of footprints, a rope that did not belong on the premises, marks on the body that suggested the use of a stun gun, and DNA samples on the girl's body. The ransom note was also suspicious. Police found that it was written with a pen and pad of paper belonging to the Ramseys. The amount demanded, $118,000, was a surprisingly small amount, considering that John Ramsey was worth more than $6 million. It is also interesting to note that Mr. Ramsey had just received a year-end bonus of $118,117.50.

A number of suspects were considered, but one by one they were all cleared. Finally, the police zeroed in on the parents. For years, the Ramseys were put under intense pressure by authorities and the public alike to confess to Ramsey's murder. However, a grand jury investigation ended with no indictments. In 2003, a judge ruled that an intruder had killed JonBenét. Then, in August 2006, John Mark Karr confessed, claiming that he was with the girl when she died. However, Karr's DNA did not match that found on JonBenét. He was not charged, and the case has remained unsolved.

# THE MYSTERY OF THE MISSING COMMA

Legend implies that a punctuation error sparked one of history's greatest unsolved mysteries: Did Queen Isabella give the order for her husband's death, or was it a misunderstanding?

King Edward II of England is primarily remembered for his weakness for certain men and the way he died. He spent most of his life in submission to his alleged lovers, Piers Gaveston and, later, Hugh le Despenser, granting their every wish. When Edward married 12-year-old Princess Isabella of France in 1308, he politely greeted her upon her arrival in England—and then gave her wedding jewelry to Gaveston.

Isabella grew up as a queen accustomed to being pushed aside in favor of her husband's preferred companions. Even after Gaveston was murdered for being a bad influence on the king, Edward did not change, turning his affections to the greedy Despenser, whom the queen loathed and feared. When the opportunity arose for her to negotiate a treaty with her brother, the King of France, she took it, traveling to Paris and refusing to return.

## The Queen's Revenge

After nearly 20 years in an unhappy marriage, Isabella had had enough. Along with her lover, Roger Mortimer, she raised an army and led it into England in order to depose her husband. Once the king was in custody, the queen forced him to abdicate the throne to their 14-year-old son, Edward III, and proceeded to send a letter giving orders on how the deposed Edward should be treated in captivity.

## Conspiracy or Miscommunication?

Something very important was missing from Isabella's orders. In the letter, she wrote, "Edwardum occidere nolite timere bonum est." Many historians think she intended this to mean, "Do not kill Edward, it is good to fear." However, she neglected to write in a necessary comma. If the comma is inserted in a different place, the letter means "Do not be afraid to kill Edward; it is good." It's clear how Edward's jailers construed the message: Shortly after it was received, several men allegedly murdered Edward in his jail cell. Who knew that forgetting something as small as a comma could result in the murder of a king?

# VANISHED:
# THE LOST COLONY OF ROANOKE ISLAND

Twenty years before England established its first successful colony in the New World, an entire village of English colonists disappeared in what would later be known as North Carolina. Did these pioneers all perish? Did Native Americans capture them? Did they join a friendly tribe? Could they have left descendants who live among us today?

## Timing Is Everything

Talk about bad timing. As far as John White was concerned, England couldn't have picked a worse time to go to war. It was November 1587, and White had just arrived in England from the New World. He intended to gather relief supplies and immediately sail back to Roanoke Island, where he had left more than 100 colonists who were running short of food. Unfortunately, the English were gearing up to fight Spain. Every seaworthy ship, including White's, was pressed into naval service. No one could be spared for his return voyage.

## Nobody Home

When White returned three years later, he was dismayed to find that the colonists were nowhere to be found. Instead, he stumbled upon a mystery—one that has never been solved.

The village that White and company had founded in 1587 on Roanoke Island lay completely deserted. Houses had been dismantled (as if someone planned to move them), but the pieces lay in the long grass along with iron tools and farming equipment. A stout stockade made of logs stood empty.

White found no sign of his daughter Eleanor, her husband Ananias, or their daughter Virginia Dare—the first English child born in America. None of the 87 men, 17 women, and 11 children remained. No bodies or gravesites offered clues to their fate. The only clues—if they were clues—that White could find were the letters CRO carved into a tree and the word CROATOAN carved into a log of the abandoned fort.

## No Forwarding Address

All White could do was hope that the colonists had been taken in by friendly natives.

Croatoan—also spelled "Croatan"—was the name of a barrier island to the south and also the name of a tribe of Native Americans that lived on that island. Unlike other area tribes, the Croatoans had been friendly to English newcomers, and one of them, Manteo, had traveled to England with earlier explorers and returned to act as interpreter for the Roanoke colony. Had the colonists, with Manteo's help, moved to Croatoan? Were they safe among friends?

White tried to find out, but his timing was rotten once again. He had arrived on the Carolina coast as a hurricane bore down on the region. The storm hit before he could mount a search. His ship was blown past Croatoan Island and out to sea. Although the ship and crew survived the storm and made it back to England, White was stuck again. He tried repeatedly but failed to raise money for another search party.

No one has ever learned the fate of the Roanoke Island colonists, but there is no shortage of theories as to what happened to them. A small sailing vessel and other boats that White had left with them were gone when he returned. It's possible that the colonists used the vessels to travel to another island or to the mainland. White had talked with others before he left about possibly moving the settlement to a more secure location inland. It's even possible that the colonists tired of waiting for White's return and tried to sail back to England. If so, they would have perished at sea. Yet there are at least a few shreds of hearsay evidence that the colonists survived in America.

## Rumors of Survivors

In 1607, Captain John Smith and company established the first successful English settlement in North America at Jamestown, Virginia. The colony's secretary, William Strachey, wrote four years later about hearing a report of four Englishmen, two boys, and one young woman who had been sighted south of Jamestown at a settlement of the Eno tribe, where they were being used as slaves. If the report was true, who else could these English have been but Roanoke survivors?

For a century after the disappearance, stories emerged of gray-eyed Native Americans and English-speaking villages in North Carolina and Virginia. In 1709, an English surveyor said members of the Hatteras tribe living on North Carolina's Outer Banks—some of them with light-colored eyes—claimed to be descendants of white people. It's possible that the Hatteras were the same people that the 1587 colonists called Croatoan.

In the intervening centuries, many of the individual tribes of the region have disappeared. Some died out. Others were absorbed into larger groups such as the Tuscarora. One surviving group, the Lumbee, has also been called Croatoan. The Lumbee, who still live in North Carolina, often have Caucasian features. Could they be descendants of

Roanoke colonists? Many among the Lumbee dismiss the notion as fanciful, but the tribe has long been thought to be of mixed heritage and has been speaking English so long that none among them know what language preceded it.

# WHO DOWNED THE RED BARON? THE MYSTERY OF MANFRED VON RICHTHOFEN

He was the most successful flying ace of World War I—the conflict that introduced the airplane as a weapon of war. Yet his demise has been credited to a number of likely opponents, both in the sky and on the ground.

## Precious Little Prussian

Manfred Von Richthofen was born in Silesia, Prussia (now part of Poland), in May 1892. Coming from a family steeped in nobility, the young von Richthofen decided he would follow in his father's footsteps and become a career soldier. At 11 years old, he enrolled in the cadet corps and, upon completion, became a member of a Prussian cavalry unit.

## Up, Up, and Away

The Germans were at the forefront in using aircraft as offensive weapons against the British, French, and Russians during World War I. Von Richthofen was recruited into a flying unit as an "observer"—the second occupant of a two-seat plane who would direct the pilot over areas to gather intelligence. By 1915, von Richthofen decided to become a pilot himself, having already downed an enemy aircraft as an observer.

The young and green pilot joined a prestigious flying squad, one of the premier German *jagdstaffeln*—literally "hunting squadrons." In late 1916, von Richthofen's aggressive style brought him face-to-face with Britain's greatest fighter pilot,

Major Lanoe Hawker. After a spirited battle in the sky, the German brought Hawker down in a tailspin, killing him. Von Richthofen called Hawker "a brave man and a sportsman." He later mounted the machine gun from the British plane over the door of his family home as a tribute to Hawker. The bold flying ace often showed a great deal of respect and affinity for his foes, once referring to his English dogfight opponents as "waltzing partners." Yet, he remained ruthless, even carrying with him a photograph of an Allied pilot he had viciously blown apart.

## Creating an Identity

Von Richthofen quickly became the most feared, and re-spected, pilot in the skies. As he sought faster and more nimble aircraft, he decided he needed to be instantly recognizable. He ordered his plane to be painted bright red, with the German Iron Cross emblazoned on the fuselage. The "Red Baron" was born.

## The End—But at Whose Hands?

By the spring of 1918, the Red Baron had shot down an amazing 80 Allied airplanes. This feat earned him the dis-tinguished "Blue Max" award, and he assembled his own squadron of crack-shot pilots known as "the Flying Circus." But the celebrated pilot was not without his failures.

Von Richthofen suffered a head wound during an air battle in July 1917, which may have left an open wound exposing a small portion of his skull until his death. There are theories that this injury resulted in brain damage—if so, it would have caused the Red Baron to make some serious errors in judg-ment that may have led to his death on April 21, 1918.

On that day, von Richthofen was embroiled in a deadly dog-fight with British Royal Air Force Sopwith Camels. As the Red Baron trained his machine-gun sights on a young pilot, enemy fire came seemingly from nowhere, striking his red Fokker.

Von Richthofen crashed in an area of France occupied by Australian and Canadian allies. He was buried with full military honors by a respectful British Royal Air Force (RAF).

However, questions remain to this day as to who exactly killed von Richthofen. He suffered a fatal bullet wound through his chest. The RAF credited one of their pilots, but another story tells of Canadian soldiers who pounced on the plane crash and literally murdered the Red Baron. Still other tales claim von Richthofen was shot from the ground by rifle or machine gun fire as he flew overhead.

The answer remains lost, perhaps forever. But there is no question as to the identity of the greatest flying ace of the First World War. That honor belongs to the Red Baron.

# THE LIZZIE BORDEN MURDER MYSTERY

Most people know the rhyme that begins, "Lizzie Borden took an axe and gave her mother 40 whacks." In reality, approximately 20 hatchet chops cut down Abby Borden, but no matter the number, Lizzie's stepmother was very much dead on that sultry August morning in 1892. Lizzie's father was killed about an hour later. His life was cut short by about a dozen hatchet chops to the head. No one knows who was guilty of these murders, but Lizzie has always carried the burden of suspicion.

## Andrew Borden, an American "Scrooge"

Andrew Jackson Borden had been one of the richest men in Fall River, Massachusetts, with a net worth of nearly half a million dollars. In 1892, that was enormous wealth. Andrew was a shrewd businessman: At the time of his death, he was the president of the Union Savings Bank and director of another bank plus several profitable cotton mills.

Despite his wealth, Andrew was miserly. Though some of his neighbors' homes had running hot water, the three-story Borden home had just two cold-water taps. There was no water available above the first floor. The Bordens' only latrine was in the cellar, so they generally used chamber pots that were either dumped on the lawn behind the house or emptied into the cellar toilet. And, although most wealthy people used gas lighting, the Bordens lit their house with inexpensive kerosene lamps.

Worst of all, for many years, Andrew was an undertaker who offered some of the lowest prices in town. He worked on the bodies in the basement of the Borden home, and allegedly, he bent the knees of the deceased—and in some cases, cut off their feet—to fit the bodies into smaller, less expensive coffins in order to increase his business.

So, despite the brutality of Andrew's murder, it seems few people mourned his loss. The question wasn't why he was killed, but who did it.

## Lizzie vs. William

In 1997, when psychic Jane Doherty visited the murder site, she uncovered several clues about the Lizzie Borden case. Doherty felt that the real murderer was someone named "Willie." There is no real evidence to support this claim, but some say Andrew had an illegitimate son named William, who may have spent time as an inmate in an insane asylum. His constant companion was reportedly his hatchet. He talked to it as though it were a friend. Also, at least one witness reportedly saw William at the Borden house on the day of the murders. William was supposedly there to challenge Andrew about his new will.

Was William the killer? A few years after the murders, William took poison and then hung himself in the woods. Near his swinging body, he'd reportedly left his hatchet on the ground. So, with William dead and Lizzie already acquitted, the Borden murder case was put to rest.

## Lizzie's Forbidden Romance

One of the most curious explanations for the murder involves the Bordens' servant Bridget Sullivan. Her participation has always raised questions. Like the other members of the Borden household, Bridget had suffered from apparent food poisoning the night before the murders. She claimed to have been ill in the backyard of the Borden home.

During the time Abby was being murdered, Bridget was apparently washing windows in the back of the house. Later, when Andrew was killed, Bridget was resting in her room upstairs. Why didn't she hear two people being butchered?

According to some theories, Lizzie and Bridget had been romantically involved. In this version of the story, their relationship was discovered shortly before the murders. Around this same time, Andrew was reportedly rewriting his will. His wife was now "Mrs. Borden," to Lizzie, not "Mother," as Lizzie had called her stepmother for many years. The reason for the estrangement was never clear.

Lizzie also had a strange relationship with her father and had given him her high school ring, as though he were her sweetheart. He wore the ring on his pinky and was buried with it.

Just a day before the murders, Lizzie had been attempting to purchase prussic acid—a deadly poison—and the family came down with "food poisoning" that night. Some speculate that Bridget was Lizzie's accomplice in the murders and helped clean up the blood afterward. This theory was bolstered when, a few years after the murders, Lizzie became involved with actress Nance O'Neil. For two years, Lizzie and the statuesque actress were inseparable. This prompted Emma Borden, Lizzie's sister, to move out of their home.

At the time, the rift between the sisters sparked rumors that either Lizzie or Emma might reveal more about the other's role in the 1892 murders. However, neither of them said anything new about the killings.

## Whodunit?

Most people believe that Lizzie was the killer. She was the only one accused of the crime, with good reason. Lizzie appeared to be the only one in the house at the time, other than Bridget. She showed no signs of grief when the murders were discovered. During questioning, Lizzie changed her story several times. The evidence was entirely circumstantial, but it was compelling enough to go to trial. Ultimately, the jury accepted her attorney's closing argument, that the murders were "morally and physically impossible for this young woman defendant." In other words, Lizzie had to be innocent because she was petite and well bred. In nineteenth century New England, that seemed like a logical and persuasive defense. Lizzie went free, and no one else was charged with the crimes.

But Lizzie wasn't the only one with motive, means, and opportunity. The most likely suspects were family members, working alone or with other relatives. Only a few had solid alibis, and—like Lizzie—many changed their stories during police questioning. But there was never enough evidence to officially accuse anyone other than Lizzie.

So, whether or not Lizzie Borden "took an ax" and killed her parents, she's the one best remembered for the crime.

## Lizzie Borden Bed and Breakfast

The Borden house has been sold several times over the years, but today it is a bed-and-breakfast—the main draw, of course, being the building's macabre history. The Victorian residence has been restored to reflect the details of the

**19**

Borden home at the time of the murders, including the couch on which Andrew lay, his skull hideously smashed.

As a guest, you can stay in one of six rooms, even the one in which Abby was murdered. Then, after a good night's sleep, you'll be treated to a breakfast reminiscent of the one the Bordens had on their final morning in 1892. That is, if you get to sleep at all. (They say the place is haunted.) As with all good morbid attractions, the proprietors at the Lizzie Borden B&B don't take themselves too seriously. Before you leave, you can stop by the gift shop and pick up a pair of hatchet earrings or an ax-wielding Lizzie Borden bobble-head doll.

# Thomas Ince:
# A Boating Excursion Turns Deadly

Film mogul Thomas Ince joins other Hollywood notables for a weekend celebration in 1924 and ends up dead. Was it natural causes or one of the biggest cover-ups in Hollywood history?

The movie industry has been rocked by scandal throughout its history, but few incidents have matched the controversy and secrecy surrounding the death of Thomas Ince, a high-profile producer and director of many successful silent films. During the 1910s, he set up his own studio in California where he built a sprawling complex of small homes, sweeping mansions, and other buildings that were used as sets for his movies. Known as Inceville, the studio covered several thousand acres, and it was there that Ince perfected the idea of the studio system—a factory-style setup that used a division of labor amongst large teams of costumers, carpenters, electricians, and other film professionals who moved from project to project as needed. This system, which allowed for the mass production of movies with the producer in creative and financial control, would later be adopted by all major Hollywood film companies.

Down on his luck by the 1920s, Ince still had many influential friends and associates. In November 1924, newspaper magnate William Randolph Hearst offered to host a weekend birthday celebration for the struggling producer aboard his luxury yacht the *Oneida*. Several Hollywood luminaries attended, including Charlie Chaplin and Marion Davies, as well Louella Parsons, then a junior writer for one of Hearst's East Coast newspapers. But at the end of the cruise, Ince was carried off the ship on a medical gurney and rushed home, where he died two days later. A hastily scribbled death certificate blamed heart failure.

## The Rumors Fly

Almost immediately, the rumor mill churned out shocking and sordid versions of the incident. The stories were sensational, and very different from the official line. A Chaplin employee, who was waiting at the docks when the boat returned, reportedly claimed that Ince was suffering from a gunshot wound to the head when he was taken off the *Oneida*. Could he have been the victim of a careless accident at the hands of a partying Hollywood celeb? Perhaps, but film industry insiders knew of complex and passionate relationships among those on board, and a convoluted and bizarre scenario soon emerged and has persisted to this day. As it turns out, Davies was Hearst's longtime mistress, despite being almost 34 years his junior. She was also a close friend of the notorious womanizer Chaplin. Many speculate that Hearst, enraged over the attention that Chaplin was paying to the young ingenue, set out to kill him but shot the hapless Ince by mistake.

Certain events after Ince's death helped the rumors gain traction. Ince's body was cremated, so no autopsy could be performed. And his grieving widow was whisked offto Europe for several months courtesy of Hearst—conveniently away from the reach of the American press. Louella Parsons was also elevated within the Hearst organization, gaining a lifetime contract and the plum assignment as his number-one celebrity gossip columnist, which she parlayed into a noto-riously self-serving enterprise. Conspiracy theorists believe that she wrangled the deal with Hearst to buy her silence about the true cause of Ince's death.

## Lingering Mystery

Was Ince the victim of an errant gunshot and subsequent cover-up? If anyone in 1920s California had the power to hush witnesses and bend officials to his will in order to get away with murder, it was the super-rich and powerful Hearst. But no clear evidence of foul play has emerged after all these decades. Still, the story has persisted and even served as the subject for *The Cat's Meow*, a 2002 film directed by Peter Bogdanovich, which starred Kirsten Dunst as Davies and Cary Elwes as the doomed Ince.

# THELMA TODD: SUICIDE OR MURDER?

During her nine-year film career, Thelma Todd appeared in dozens of classic comedies with the likes of Harry Langdon, Laurel and Hardy, and the Marx Brothers. Today, however, the "Ice Cream Blonde," as she was known, is best remem-bered for her bizarre death, which remains one of Holly-wood's most enduring mysteries. Let's explore what could have happened.

## Sins Indulged

Todd was born in Lawrence, Massachu-setts, in 1906 and arrived in Hollywood at age 20 via the beauty pageant circuit. Pretty and vivacious, she quickly became a hot commodity and fell headlong into Tinseltown's anything-goes party scene. In 1932, she married Pasquale "Pat" DiCicco, an agent of sorts who was also associated with gangster Charles "Lucky" Luciano. Their marriage was plagued by drunken fights, and they divorced two years later.

For solace, Todd turned to director Roland West, who didn't approve of her drinking and drug use, but was apparently unable to stop her. With his help, Todd opened a roadhouse called Thelma Todd's Sidewalk Café, located on the Pacific Coast Highway, and the actress moved into a spacious apartment above the restaurant. Shortly after, Todd began a relationship with gangster "Lucky" Luciano, who tried to get her to let him use a room at the Sidewalk Café for illegal gambling. Todd repeatedly refused.

On the morning of December 16, 1935, Todd was found dead in the front seat of her 1934 Lincoln Phaeton convertible, which was parked in the two-car garage she shared with West. The apparent cause of death was carbon monoxide poisoning, though whether Todd was the victim of an accident, suicide, or murder remains a mystery.

Little evidence supports the suicide theory, outside the mode of death and the fact that Todd led a fast-paced lifestyle that sometimes got the better of her. Indeed, her career was going remarkably well, and she had purchased Christmas presents and was looking forward to a New Year's Eve party. So, suicide does not seem a viable cause, though it is still mentioned as a probable one in many accounts.

## The Accident Theory

However, an accidental death is also a possibility. The key to her car was in the "on" position, and the motor was dead when Todd was discovered by her maid. West suggested to investigators that the actress turned on the car to get warm, passed out because she was drunk, and then succumbed to carbon monoxide poisoning. Todd also had a heart condition, according to West, and this may have contributed to her death.

Nonetheless, the notion of foul play is suggested by several incongruities found at the scene. Spots of blood were discovered on and in Todd's car and on her mouth, and her nose was broken, leading some to believe she was knocked out then placed in the car to make it look like a suicide. (Police attributed the injuries to Todd falling unconscious and striking her head on the steering wheel.)

In addition, Todd's blood alcohol content was extremely high—high enough to stupefy her so that someone could carry her without her fighting back—and her high-heeled shoes were clean and unscuffed, even though she would have had to ascend a flight of outdoor, concrete stairs to reach the garage, which was a 271-step climb behind the restaurant. Investigators also found an unidentified smudged handprint on the left side of the vehicle.

## Two with Motive

If Todd was murdered, as some have suggested, who had motive? Because of her wild and reckless lifestyle, there are several potential suspects, most notably Pasquale DiCicco, who was known to have a violent temper, and "Lucky" Luciano, who was angry at Todd for refusing to let him use her restaurant for illegal activities.

Despite the many questions raised by the evidence found at the scene, a grand jury ruled Todd's death accidental. The investigation had been hampered by altered and destroyed evidence, threats to witnesses, and cover-ups, making it impossible to ever learn what really happened.

An open-casket service was held at Forest Lawn Memorial Park, where the public viewed the actress bedecked in yellow roses. After the service, Todd was cremated, eliminating the possibility of a second autopsy. Later, when her mother, Alice Todd, died, the actress's ashes were placed in her mother's casket so they could be buried together in Massachusetts.

# WILLIAM DESMOND TAYLOR

The murder of actor/director William Desmond Taylor was like something out of an Agatha Christie novel, complete with a handsome, debonair victim and multiple suspects, each with a motive. But unlike Christie's novels, in which the murderer was always unmasked, Taylor's death remains unsolved nearly 100 years later.

On the evening of February 1, 1922, Taylor was shot in the back by an unknown assailant; his body was discovered the next morning by a servant, Henry Peavey. News of Taylor's demise spread quickly, and several individuals, including officials from Paramount Studios, where Taylor was employed, raced to the dead man's home to clear it of anything incriminating, such as illegal liquor, evidence of drug use, illicit correspondence, and signs of sexual indiscretion. However, no one called the police until later in the morning.

## Numerous Suspects

Soon an eclectic array of potential suspects came to light, including Taylor's criminally inclined former butler, Edward F. Sands, who had gone missing just before the murder; popular movie comedienne Mabel Normand, whom Taylor had entertained the evening of his death; actress Mary Miles Minter, who had a passionate crush on the handsome director who was 28 years her senior; and Charlotte Shelby,

Minter's mother, who often wielded a loaded gun to protect her daughter's tarnished honor.

Taylor's murder was the last thing Hollywood needed at the time, coming as it did on the heels of rape allegations against popular film comedian Fatty Arbuckle. Scandals brought undue attention on Hollywood, and the Arbuckle story had taken its toll. Officials at Paramount tried to keep a lid on the Taylor story, but the tabloid press had a field day. A variety of personal foibles were made public in the weeks that followed, and both Normand and Minter saw their careers come to a screeching halt as a result. Taylor's own indiscretions were also revealed, such as the fact that he kept a special souvenir, usually lingerie, from every woman he bedded.

## Little Evidence

Police interviewed many of Taylor's friends and colleagues, including all potential suspects. However, there was no evidence to incriminate anyone specifically, and no one was formally charged.

Investigators and amateur sleuths pursued the case for years. Sands was long a prime suspect, based on his criminal past and his estrangement from the victim. But it was later revealed that on the day of the murder, Sands had signed in for work at a lumberyard in Oakland, California—some 400 miles away—and thus could not have committed the crime. Coming in second was Shelby, whose temper and threats were legendary. Shelby's own acting career had fizzled out early, and all of her hopes for stardom were pinned on her daughter. She threatened many men who tried to woo Mary.

In the mid-1990s, another possible suspect surfaced—a long-forgotten silent film actress named Margaret Gibson. According to Bruce Long, author of *William Desmond Taylor: A Dossier*, Gibson confessed to a friend on her deathbed in 1964 that years before she had killed a man named William Desmond Taylor. However, the woman to whom Gibson cleared her conscience didn't know who Taylor was and thought nothing more about it.

## The Mystery Continues

Could Margaret Gibson (aka Pat Lewis) be Taylor's murderer? She had acted with Taylor in Hollywood in the early 1910s, and she may even have been one of his many sexual conquests. She also had a criminal past, including charges of blackmail, drug use, and prostitution, so it's entirely conceivable that she was a member of a group trying to extort money from the director, a popular theory among investigators. But according to an earlier book, *A Cast of Killers* by Sidney D. Kirkpatrick, veteran Hollywood director King Vidor had investigated the murder as material for a film script and through his research believed Shelby was the murderer. But out of respect for Minter, he never did anything about it.

Ultimately, however, we may never know for certain who killed William Desmond Taylor, or why. The case has long grown cold, and anyone with specific knowledge of the murder is likely dead. Unlike a Hollywood thriller, in which the killer is revealed at the end, Taylor's death is a macabre puzzle that likely will never be solved.

# MYSTERIOUS MARILYN

Marilyn Monroe's life story has been exposed and analyzed countless times. The problem is that each version seems to contradict the others, making it difficult to sort out even the simplest details of her complicated life.

The iconic film star whose work includes classics such as *How to Marry a Millionaire* and *Some Like It Hot* continues to be the subject of intense scrutiny. But despite all of the books and movies made about Marilyn Monroe, misconceptions about her life abound, including the following:

**Myth:** Marilyn was illegitimate.

**Fact:** According to Marilyn's birth certificate, her mother's estranged husband, Martin Edward Mortensen, was her father, but Marilyn never believed this. Her mother, Gladys, abandoned Mortensen after several months of marriage and proceeded to have a series of affairs, most notably with Stanley Gifford, an employee at the film lab where she worked. Mortensen, who had never met Marilyn, always claimed that he was her real father. After his death in 1981, a copy of Marilyn's birth certificate was found in his effects, and it is now widely believed that he was telling the truth.

**Myth:** Marilyn was born blonde.

**Fact:** Marilyn Monroe's natural hair color was brown. In 1946, she was offered a job modeling for a series of Lustre Cream shampoo ads on the condition that she trade her flowing brunette curls for a straightened blonde hairstyle. It is said that she strongly resisted coloring her hair but ultimately relented under pressure. She was 20 years old at the time and would remain a blonde for the rest of her life.

**Myth:** Marilyn personified the dumb blonde.

**Fact:** Marilyn Monroe rose to stardom playing the "dumb blonde" and was considered a master of this Hollywood archetype. But was she actually featherbrained? She definitely played up that image for the public, but her private pursuits were surprisingly intellectual. She wasn't interested in vapid romance novels; instead, she was often observed on her movie sets absorbed in classic works such as Thomas Paine's *The Rights of Man*. Her library was filled with titles by Willa Cather, Dorothy Parker, and Carson McCullers, among many other notable authors. In one famous photo-graph, she is sitting in front of her book collection reading a copy of *Poetry and Prose: Heinrich Heine.*

Marilyn also took her work as an actress very seriously and insisted that every take be perfect, which often resulted in her being perceived as difficult to work with. Her 1955 departure from Hollywood to study with Lee Strasberg at the Actors Studio in New York City was a bold attempt to take control of her career. She even went so far as to start her own production company, which enabled her to reject any director or script of which she did not approve.

**Myth:** Marilyn committed suicide.

**Fact:** On August 5, 1962, Marilyn was found deceased in her home in Brentwood, California. The Los Angeles County coroner's office classified her death as "probable suicide," but many people, especially those closest to her, never believed it. During the summer of 1962, things were looking up for Marilyn. She had just achieved a major publicity coup with a cover story in *Life* magazine. Her contract with 20th Century Fox studios had been successfully renegotiated, and several projects were in the pipeline, including a film version of the Broadway musical *A Tree Grows in Brooklyn.* She was busy planning renovations of her new house, the first she had ever purchased (albeit with a little help from her ex-husband Joe DiMaggio). To those who knew her well, it did not make sense that she would take her own life, and there are even conspiracy theorists who claim that President John F. Kennedy had a hand in her death. But given the fact that her long-term addiction to sleeping pills had led to near-overdoses in the past, the most logical explanation is that her death was an accident.

# A Superior Tragedy:
# The *Edmund Fitzgerald*

Many ships have been lost to storms on the Great Lakes, but few incidents have fascinated the world like the sinking of the *Edmund Fitzgerald* off the shores of northern Michigan on November 10, 1975. The mysterious circumstances of the tragedy, which took 29 lives—all memorialized in a 1976 song by Gordon Lightfoot—have kept the story fresh to this day. The fateful journey began in Wisconsin.

## Least Likely to Sink

The 729-foot-long *Edmund Fitzgerald* was considered as unsinkable as any steamer. At its christening in June 1958, it was the Great Lakes' largest and most expensive freighter. Its name honored Edmund Fitzgerald, the president of Northwestern Mutual Insurance Company of Milwaukee, who commissioned the boat.

During the christening, a few incidents occurred that some saw as bad omens. As a crowd of more than 10,000 watched, it took Mrs. Fitzgerald three tries to shatter the bottle of champagne. Then, when the ship was released into the water, it hit the surface at the wrong angle, causing a wave that splattered the entire ceremonial area with lake water and knocking the ship into a nearby dock. One spectator died on the spot of a heart attack.

## The Last Launch

The weather was unseasonably pleasant the morning of November 9, 1975, so much so that the crew of 29 men who set sail from Superior, Wisconsin, that day were unlikely to have been concerned about their routine trip to Zug Island on the Detroit River. But the captain, Ernest McSorley, knew a storm was in the forecast.

McSorley, a 44-year veteran of the lakes, had captained the *Fitzgerald* since 1972. He paid close attention to the gale warnings issued that afternoon, but no one suspected they would yield a "once-in-a-lifetime storm." However, when the weather report was upgraded to a full storm warning, McSorley changed the ship's course to follow a safer route closer to the Canadian shore.

Following the *Fitzgerald* was another freighter, the *Arthur Anderson*. The two captains stayed in touch as they traveled through winds measuring up to 50 knots (about 58 miles per hour) with waves 12 feet or higher. On November 10, around 1:00 p.m., McSorley told Captain Cooper of the *Anderson* that the *Fitzgerald* was "rolling." By about 2:45 p.m., as the *Anderson* moved to avoid a dangerous shoal near Caribou Island, a crewman sighted the *Fitzgerald* about 16 miles ahead, closer to the shoal than Cooper thought safe.

About 3:30 p.m., McSorley reported to Cooper that the *Fitzgerald* had sustained some minor damage and was beginning to roll to one side. The ships were still 16 to 17 miles apart. At 4:10 p.m., with waves now 18 feet high, McSorley radioed that his ship had lost radar. The two ships stayed in radio contact until about 7:00 p.m. when the *Fitzgerald* crew told the *Anderson* they were "holding [their] own." After that, radio contact was lost, and the *Fitzgerald* dropped offthe radar. Around 8:30 p.m., Cooper told the Coast Guard at Sault Ste. Marie that the *Fitzgerald* seemed to be missing.

Evidently, the *Fitzgerald* sank sometime after 7:10 p.m., just 17 miles from the shore of Whitefish Point, Michigan. Despite a massive search effort, it wasn't until November 14 that a navy flyer detected a magnetic anomaly that turned out to be the wreck. The only other evidence of the disaster to surface was a handful of lifeboats, life jackets, and some oars, tools, and propane tanks. A robotic vehicle was used to thoroughly photograph the wreck in May 1976.

## One Mysterious Body

One odd aspect of the tragedy was that no bodies were found. In most temperate waters, corpses rise to the surface as decomposition forms gas. But the Great Lakes are so cold that decomposition is inhibited, causing bodies to stay on the bottom.

In 1994, a Michigan businessman named Frederick Shannon took a submarine equipped with a full array of modern surveillance equipment to the site, hoping to film a documentary about the ship. His crew discovered a body on the lake bottom near the bow of the wreck, covered by cork sections of a decayed canvas life vest. However, this body may not be associated with the *Fitzgerald*. Two French vessels were lost nearby in 1918, and none of those bodies had been recovered either. A sailor from one of them could have been preserved by the lake's frigid water and heavy pressure.

## What Sank the Mighty Fitz?

One theory is that the *Fitzgerald* got too close to the dangerous Six-Fathom Shoal near Caribou Island and scraped over it, damaging the hull. Another is that the ship's hatch covers were either faulty or improperly clamped, which allowed water in. Wave height may also have played a part, with the storm producing a series of huge swells known as the "Three Sisters"—a trio of lightning-fast waves that pound a vessel—the first washes over the deck, the second hits the deck again so fast that the first has not had time to clear itself, and the third quickly adds another heavy wash, piling thousands of gallons of water on the ship. Few ships can withstand this.

## For Whom the Bell Tolls

On July 4, 1995, the bell of the *Edmund Fitzgerald* was retrieved and laid to rest in the Great Lakes Shipwreck Historical Museum in Whitefish Bay, Michigan. A replica bell, symbolizing the ship's "spirit," was left with the wreckage. Every year on November 10, during a memorial service, the original, 200-pound bronze bell is rung 29 times—once for each crew member who perished.

# WHAT REALLY KILLED JOHN WAYNE?

*The Conqueror* (1956) wasn't exactly John Wayne's master-piece. According to "The Duke" himself, the film was actually written with Marlon Brando in mind for the lead role, and this historical drama has been criticized for miscasting Wayne in the part. However, *The Conqueror* has been connected to far worse things than box office failure: Some say the movie is to blame for Wayne's death from stomach cancer two decades after its debut. What's more, Wayne isn't the only person believed to have died as a result of the project. Was a nearby nuclear testing site to blame?

## Radiation Exposure

The questions surrounding *The Conqueror* come as a result of its filming location: It was shot near St. George and Snow Canyon, Utah, an area close to a nuclear testing site. In the early 1950s, the U.S. military set off nearly a dozen atomic bombs just miles from the location, sending clouds of ra-dioactive dust into St. George and Snow Canyon. Work on *The Conqueror* began two years later, even though the film company knew about the radiation. To make matters worse, after the location work had wrapped, the film's crew trans-ported dirt from the area back to Hollywood to help recreate the setting for in-studio shooting. (At the time, the effects of radiation exposure were not as well documented as they are now.)

In the years following the filming of *The Conqueror*, nu-merous members of the cast and crew developed cancer.

Aside from Wayne, at least 45 people from the group died from causes related to the disease, including actress Agnes Moorehead, who died in 1974 from uterine cancer; actress Susan Hayward, who died from brain and skin cancer at age 57 in 1975; and director Dick Powell, who, in 1963, passed away at age 58 from lymphatic cancer. Actors Pedro Armendariz and John Hoyt both took their own lives after learning of their diagnoses.

An article published in *People* magazine in 1980 stated that 41 percent of those who worked on the movie—91 out of 220 people—later developed cancer. That figure reportedly didn't include the hundreds of Utah-based actors who worked as extras. Still, the numbers far exceeded any statistical normality for a given group of individuals. A scientist with the Pentagon's Defense Nuclear Agency was quoted in the article as saying: "Please, God, don't let us have killed John Wayne."

## Broader Findings

While many of the actors were heavy smokers—Wayne included—the strange circumstances surrounding the filming of *The Conqueror* have turned into an underground scandal of sorts. And the general findings from the city of St. George certainly don't help quell the concerns.

In 1997, a study by the National Cancer Institute found that children who lived in the St. George area during the 1950s were exposed to as much as 70 times the amount of radiation than was originally reported because of contaminated milk taken from exposed animals. Consequently, the study reported that the children had elevated risks for cancer development. The report further stated that the government "knew from the beginning that a Western test site would spread contamination across most of the country" and that the exposure could have easily been avoided.

The government eventually passed an act called the Radiation Exposure Compensation Act, which provided $50,000 to people who lived downwind of the nuclear testing site near St. George and had been exposed to radiation. At least 40,000 people are thought to have been exposed in Utah alone. While John Wayne is the most famous of them, the true cause of his cancer may never be definitively known.

# ANYTHING BUT SPLENDOR: NATALIE WOOD

The official account of Natalie Wood's tragic death is riddled with holes. For this reason, cover-up theorists continue to run hog-wild with conjecture. Here's a sampling of the questions, facts, and assertions surrounding the case.

## A Life in Pictures

There are those who will forever recall Natalie Wood as the adorable child actress from *Miracle on 34th Street* (1947) and those who remember her as the sexy but wholesome grown-up star of movies such as *West Side Story* (1961), *Splendor in the Grass* (1961), and *Bob & Carol & Ted & Alice* (1969). Both groups generally agree that Wood had uncommon beauty and talent. At the time of her death, Natalie Wood's future was bright.

Wood appeared in her very first film, *Happy Land* (1943), in a bit part alongside other people from her hometown of Santa Rosa, California, where the film was shot. She stood out to the director, who remembered her later when he needed to cast a child in another film. Wood was uncommonly mature and professional for a child actress, which helped her make a relatively smooth transition to ingénue roles.

Although Wood befriended James Dean and Sal Mineo—her troubled young costars from *Rebel Without a Cause* (1955)—and she briefly dated Elvis Presley, she preferred to move in established Hollywood circles. By the time she was 20, she was married to Robert Wagner and was costarring with Frank Sinatra in *Kings Go Forth* (1958), which firmly ensconced her in the Hollywood establishment. The early 1960s represent the high point of Wood's career, and she specialized in playing high-spirited characters with determination and spunk.

She added a couple more Oscar nominations to the one she received for Rebel and racked up five Golden Globe nominations for Best Actress. This period would also prove to be personally turbulent for Wood, as she suffered through a failed marriage to Wagner and another to Richard Gregson. After taking time off to raise her children, she remarried Wagner and returned to her acting career.

## Shocking News

And so, on November 29, 1981, the headline hit the newswires much like an out-of-control car hits a brick wall. Natalie Wood, the beautiful, vivacious 43-year-old star of stage and screen, had drowned after falling from her yacht the *Splendour*, which was anchored off California's Santa Catalina Island. Wood had been on the boat during a break from her latest film, *Brainstorm*, and was accompanied by Wagner and *Brainstorm* costar Christopher Walken. Skipper Dennis Davern was at the helm. Foul play was not suspected.

## In My Esteemed Opinion

After a short investigation, Chief Medical Examiner Dr. Thomas Noguchi listed Wood's death as an accidental drowning. Tests revealed that she had consumed "seven or eight" glasses of wine, and the coroner contended that in her intoxicated state Wood had probably stumbled and fallen overboard while attempting to untie the yacht's rubber dinghy.

He also stated that cuts and bruises on her body could have occurred when she fell from the boat.

## Doubting Thomases

To this day, many people question Wood's mysterious demise and believe that the accidental drowning theory sounds a bit too convenient. Pointed questions have led to many rumors: Does someone know more about Wood's final moments than they're letting on?

Was her drowning really an accident, or did someone intentionally or accidentally *help* her overboard? Could this be why she sustained substantial bruising on her face and the back of her legs? Why was Wagner so reluctant to publicly discuss the incident? Were Christopher Walken and Wood an item as had been rumored? With this possibility in mind, could a booze-fueled fight have erupted between the two men? Could Wood have then tried to intervene, only to be knocked overboard for her efforts? And why did authorities declare Wood's death accidental so quickly? Would such a hasty ruling have been issued had the principals not been famous, wealthy, and influential?

## Ripples

At the time of Wood's death, she and Wagner were seven years into their second marriage to each other. Whether Wood was carrying on an affair with Walken, as was alleged, may be immaterial, even if it made for interesting tabloid fodder. But Wagner's perception of their relationship could certainly be a factor. If nothing else, it might better explain the argument that ensued between Wagner and Walken that fateful night.

## Case Closed?

Further information about Wood's death is sparse because no eyewitnesses have come forward. However, a businesswoman whose boat was anchored nearby testified that she heard a woman shouting for help, and then a voice responding, "We'll be over to get you," so the woman went back to bed. Just after dawn, Wood's body was found floating a mile away from the *Splendour*, approximately 200 yards offshore. The dinghy was found nearby; its only cargo was a stack of lifejackets.

In 2008, after 27 years of silence, Robert Wagner recalled in his autobiography, *Pieces of My Heart: A Life*, that he and Walken had engaged in a heated argument during supper after Walken had suggested that Wood star in more films, effectively keeping her away from their children. Wagner and Walken then headed topside to cool down.

Sometime around midnight, Wagner said he returned to his cabin and discovered that his wife was missing. He soon realized that the yacht's dinghy was gone as well. In his book, he surmised that Wood may have gone to secure the dinghy that had been noisily slapping against the boat. Then, tipsy from the wine, she probably fell into the ocean and drowned. Walken notified the authorities.

Was Natalie Wood's demise the result of a deadly mix of wine and saltwater as the coroner's report suggests? This certainly could be the case. But why would she leave her warm cabin to tend to a loose rubber dinghy in the dark of night? Could an errant rubber boat really make such a commotion?

Perhaps we'll never know what happened that fateful night, but an interview conducted shortly before Wood's death proved prophetic: "I'm frightened to death of the water," said Wood about a long-held fear. "I can swim a little bit, but I'm afraid of water that is dark."

# Chapter 2

# PECULIAR LOCATIONS

## Europe's Most Haunted Hotels

Many of Europe's haunted hotels are located in Britain and Ireland, where ghosts are often considered as friends or even members of the family, and are given the same respect as any living person—or even more. Other European cultures aren't as comfortable with ghosts—opting to tear down haunted hotels instead of coexisting with spirits—but there are still a few places in Europe where ghost hunters can explore.

### Comlongon Castle, Dumfries, Scotland

Lady Marion Carruthers haunts Scotland's beautiful Comlongon Castle. On September 25, 1570, Lady Marion leaped to her death from the castle's lookout tower rather than submit to an arranged marriage. Visitors can easily find the exact spot where she landed; for more than 400 years, it's been difficult to grow grass there. Because Lady Marion's death was a suicide, she was denied a Christian burial, and it seems her spirit is unable to rest in peace. Dressed in green, her ghost wanders around the castle and its grounds.

### Ettington Park Hotel, Alderminister, England

You may feel chills when you see the Ettington Park Hotel, where the classic 1963 horror movie *The Haunting* was filmed. It was an apt choice for the movie locale because the hotel features several ghosts.

The Shirley family rebuilt this Victorian Gothic structure in the mid-1800s, and the ghost of the "Lady in Gray" has appeared on the staircase regularly since that time. Her identity is unknown, unlike the phantom "Lady in White," who was supposedly a former governess named Lady Emma. The voices of crying children are probably the two Shirley children who drowned nearby in the River Stour; they're buried by the church tower.

Watch out for poltergeists in the Library Bar, where books fly across the room. And don't be alarmed if you hear a late-night snooker game when no one is in the room—it's just the ghosts having fun.

## Ye Olde Black Bear, Tewkesbury, England

If you're looking for headless ghosts dragging clanking chains, Ye Olde Black Bear is just the place. Built in the early 1300s, the structure is the oldest inn in Gloucestershire. The hotel's headless ghost may be one individual or several—without a head, it's difficult to tell. However, the ghost's uniform suggests that he was a soldier killed in a battle around the 1470s. Those who've seen the figure at the hotel suspect he doesn't realize he's dead—Ye Olde Black Bear was supposedly a favorite hangout for soldiers during his era.

## Renvyle House Hotel, Galway, Ireland

Renvyle House Hotel is not old by haunted hotel standards. The site has been built on, destroyed, built again, destroyed again—once by a fire set by the IRA—and so on, until the current hotel was erected in the 1930s. But its ghosts have an impressive pedigree, dating back to a sixteenth century Irish pirate queen, Gráinne O'Malley. A redheaded boy is a more recent spirit, possibly a son of the Blake family who owned the site in the nineteenth century. The hotel is haunted by so many spirits that it was regularly visited by celebrities, such as poet W. B. Yeats, who conducted séances there. Today, Renvyle House Hotel is still a favorite destination for ghost hunters, and it is included in many "haunted hotel" tours.

## Royal Lion Hotel, Lyme Regis, England

The Royal Lion Hotel was built in 1601 as a coaching inn, but some of its ghosts may be visiting from across the street, where executions allegedly took place. Other misty, ghostly figures around the hotel may be the spirits of pirates who sailed into the port, or they could be some of the rebels who were hung and quartered on the nearby beach after trying to overthrow King James II in 1685. Waterfront hotels are often haunted due to their association with pirates and wrecked ships. However, with several dozen different spirits, this site reports more ghosts than most.

## Dragsholm Slot Hotel, Nekselø Bay, Denmark

In Danish, the word slot means "castle," and the Dragsholm is one of the world's great haunted castle hotels. According to legend, Dragsholm's "Gray Lady"—a twelfth century maid who loved working at the hotel—visits on most nights. She silently checks on guests to be sure they are comfortable. The "White Lady" haunts the corridors nightly. She may be the young woman who was allegedly walled up inside the castle; her ancient corpse was found during nineteenth century renovations.

James Hepburn, the Fourth Earl of Bothwell, is the castle's most famous ghost. Hepburn became the third husband of Mary, Queen of Scots, after he helped murder her previous spouse. For his role in that crime, Bothwell spent the last ten years of his life chained to a pillar in Dragsholm. If you think you've seen his ghostly apparition, you can compare it to his mummified body in a nearby church in Faarevejle.

## Hotel Scandinavia, Venice, Italy

The Hotel Scandinavia is in a building dating back to the year 1000, and it's surrounded by stories of ghosts and apparitions. In the fifteenth century, the apparition of a wealthy (and rather buxom) Madonna first appeared close to the hotel's palazzo. Witnesses report hearing sounds from the sorrowful ghosts of condemned prisoners who long ago crossed the nearby Bridge of Sighs. This famous bridge was where convicts caught a final glimpse of Venice before being imprisoned. These spirits apparently visit the hotel, and their voices are most often heard in the lobby. Because of the location's unique ghosts and how often they're heard, the Hotel Scandinavia is consistently ranked as one of the world's top five haunted hotels.

# WELCOME TO HELL TOWN

Looking for a scary adventure in Ohio? Then dare to travel to Hell Town in Summit County. According to local legend, it's a sinister place where a host of nefarious characters partner with the U.S. government to protect dark secrets.

Stanford road, the only road into the once prosperous town of Boston Mills, is chained off at both ends. Throughout the town, conspicuous "U.S. PROPERTY–NO TRESPASSING" signs are affixed on abandoned houses. At night, local law enforcement officials curtly order loiterers to move on during regular patrols.

This is a place known throughout large parts of Ohio as Hell Town. According to local legend, it's an evil and foreboding place that holds dark secrets—and though it may seem quiet, danger is all around.

From all the signs posted, conspiracy theorists have jumped to the conclusion that the government doesn't want people hanging around. Supposedly, it's all part of an elaborate scheme to cover up a disastrous chemical spill that turned town residents into disfigured mutants. The urban myth goes on to say that most were evacuated and never seen again, but some still lurk about, snatching those who unwittingly wander into the town.

## Cults, Ghosts, and Lunatics

The legend maintains that the government cover-up is only part of the story. A lot of weird stuff is said to happen in Hell Town, all of which is perpetrated by a host of dark, sinister characters. In short, it's not just chemically altered mutants out to get you in Hell Town:

**A Satanic cult now calls Boston Mills home!** Satanists have chained Stanford Road to keep people out and their devilish activities a secret. Devil-worshipping congregations hold candlelit black masses at the old Mother of Sorrows church, which is marked by Satanic symbols of upside-down crosses, and practice other nefarious rituals in the abandoned funeral home (also called the old slaughterhouse) near the Boston Cemetery.

**The Highway to Hell!** An evil paranormal force compels cars to crash or veer off of Stanford Road, dubbed the "Highway to Hell." Passengers then fall prey to swarms of cult members who suddenly emerge from the woods—or the ruthless axe murderer who lives in the woods and continues to elude capture by the police.

**The marauding hearse!** If they somehow manage to dodge the cult members and axe murderer on Stanford Road, visitors who reach town should beware a creepy man driving an old funeral hearse with one working headlight. If they try chasing him down, he and his ghoulish wheels will simply vanish.

**The haunted cemetery!** The grounds of the old Boston Cemetery are haunted by a specter that sits on a bench and stares into the distance, and they are also guarded by Satanists who mystically maneuver the trees from one spot to another to scare people away.

**Get on the bus of death!** An old abandoned school bus sits in the town, a reminder of a grisly incident in which the last children to ride on it were slaughtered in the woods by an escaped mental patient (or a serial killer or the Satanists again) after the bus ran out of gas on a secluded road. There are no seats in the bus, but at night, the kids can be seen sitting on the bus in their spots—sometimes they're calm, other times they're crying and screaming. Sitting in the back of the bus is an eerie ghostlike man smoking a cigarette. All attempts to remove the bus have ended in tragic misfortune, so now it's left to sit.

**The church cellar dweller!** An evil old man dwells in the basement of the Boston Community Church. Once a re-spected member of the community, he now hides his face when spotted through the basement windows, ashamed of his secretive past as the leader of a clandestine Satanic cult.

## And Now, the Real Story:

The federal government did force residents to leave Boston Mills, but not because of a disfiguring chemical spill. In the mid-1970s, the National Park Service appropriated hundreds of properties in the area to create national parkland—and most homeowners were compelled to sell and move from the area. It was all done rather quickly, thus making it seem as if the locals had vanished overnight. The government slapped its signs on the houses; some were demolished, some were boarded up and left untouched, and a few were used for firefighting training.

Abandoned and burned-out houses, closed roads, government signs, police patrols—and not a soul for miles. It's all given rise to rumors of sinister happenings at Boston Mills. For the record, there never was a chemical spill at Boston Mills; the local municipality closed Stanford Road because it's in a state of disrepair. The cops on patrol are merely there to ward off the increased numbers of vandals and trespassers as the town grows in infamy. While they make for a great story, the legends surrounding the town—and the attention they generate—are of serious detriment to the few residents who elected to stay.

# Labor of Love: The Taj Mahal

Known as one of the Wonders of the World, the Taj Mahal was a shrine to love and one man's obsession. Today an average of three million tourists a year travel to see what the United Nations has declared a World Heritage site.

## Taj Mahal: Foundations

The mughal (or "Mogul") Empire occupied India from the mid-1500s to the early 1800s. At the height of its success, this imperial power controlled most of the Indian subcontinent and much of what is now Afghanistan, containing a population of around 150 million people.

During this era, a young prince named Khurram took the throne in 1628, succeeding his father. Six years prior, after a military victory Khurram was given the title Shah Jahan by his emperor father. Now, with much of the subcontinent at his feet, the title was apt: Shah Jahan is Persian for "King of the World."

Peculiar Locations

# When Khurram Met Arjumand

Being shah had a lot of fringe benefits—banquets, treasures, and multiple wives, among other things. Shah Jahan did have several wives, but one woman stood out from the rest. When he was age 15, he was betrothed to 14-year-old Arjumand Banu Begam. Her beauty and compassion knocked the emperor-to-be off his feet; five years later, they were married. The bride took the title of *Mumtaz Mahal*, which means, according to various translations, "Chosen One of the Palace," "Exalted One of the Palace," or "Beloved Ornament of the Palace."

Court historians recorded the couple's close friendship and intimate relationship. They traveled extensively together, Mumtaz often accompanying her husband on his military jaunts. But tragedy struck in 1631, when on one of these trips, Mumtaz died giving birth to what would have been their fourteenth child.

# Breaking Ground

Devastated, Shah Jahan began work that year on what would become the Taj Mahal, a monument to his wife and their everlasting love. While there were surely many hands on deck for the planning of the Taj, the architect who is most often credited is Ustad Ahmad Lahori. The project took until 1648 to complete and enlisted the labor of 20,000 workers and 1,000 elephants. The structure and surrounding grounds covers 42 acres. Here are the basic parts of Mumtaz's giant mausoleum.

**The Gardens:** To get to the structural parts of the Taj Mahal, one must cross the enormous gardens surrounding it. Following classic Persian garden design, the grounds to the south of the buildings are made up of four sections divided by marble canals (reflecting pools) with adjacent pathways. The gardens stretch from the main gateway to the foot of the Taj.

**The Main Gateway:** Made of red sandstone and standing 100 feet high and 150 feet wide, it is composed of a central arch with towers attached to each of its corners. The walls are richly adorned with calligraphy and arabesques inlaid with gemstones.

**The Tomb:** Unlike most Mughal mausoleums, Mumtaz's tomb is placed at the north end of the Taj Mahal, above the river and in between the mosque and the guesthouse. The tomb is entirely sheathed in white marble with an exterior dome that is almost 250 feet above ground level. The effect is impressive: Depending on the light at various times of the day, the tomb can appear pink, white, or brilliant gold.

**The Mosque and the Jawab:** On either side of the great tomb lie two smaller buildings. One is a mosque, and the other is called the jawab, or "answer." The mosque was used as a place of worship; the jawab was often used as a guest-house. Both buildings are made of red sandstone so as not to take away too much from the grandeur of the tomb. The shah's monument to the love of his life still stands, and still awes, more than 360 years later.

# SHOICHI YOKOI: LOST SOLDIER, FOUND

Shoichi Yokoi fled from the Americans invading Guam in 1944 and was not captured until 1972. Repatriated to Japan, he quickly became a sensation—for better or worse.

On the night of July 21, 1944, Sergeant Shoichi Yokoi of the Japanese Imperial Army was engaged in a desperate fight with advancing Americans whose tanks were ripping apart his regiment. As the situation became increasingly dire, Yokoi chose to flee rather than be killed, or worse, captured alive. He was not alone: More than 1,000 Japanese soldiers were hiding in the jungles of Guam when Americans secured the island; nearly all were killed or captured soon afterward. Only Yokoi and eight other soldiers remained undiscovered in the dense depths of the jungle.

By 1964, his companions had either surrendered or died, and Yokoi was alone. He knew the war was over but he chose to remain hidden. "We Japanese soldiers were told to prefer death to the disgrace of getting captured alive," he later said. Certainly, Yokoi had another strong motive for remaining hidden. The Japanese army had been cruel to the native Guam population and Yokoi feared that he would be killed in reparation. So, he hid and survived alone for another eight years—a remarkable 28 years total.

## How Did He Do It?

**Clothing:** Before the war, Yokoi had been a tailor's apprentice. Though his skills with fabric were of no help against American tanks, they proved very useful in the jungle. By pounding tree bark, Yokoi was able to make fiber that he used to fashion three suits of clothes. He reworked a piece of brass to make a sewing needle and repurposed plastic to make buttons.

**Food:** While hiding in the jungles of Guam, Yokoi ate snails, rats, eels, pigeons, mangoes, nuts, crabs, and prawns. Occasionally he'd have wild hog. Although he boiled all the water he drank, and cooked the meat thoroughly, he once became ill for a month after eating a cow.

**Shelter:** Surviving in the jungle for 28 years is one thing. Surviving undetected in the jungle is quite another. Yokoi went to great lengths to disguise his shelters. His most permanent dwelling was a tunnel-like cave, hand-dug using a piece of artillery shell. At one end of the three-foot-high shelter, a latrine emptied down an embankment into a river;

at the other end a small kitchen contained some shelves, a cooking pot, and a coconut shell lantern.

**"It is with much embarrassment that I have returned alive"**

The Japanese word *ganbaru* refers to the positive character traits associated with sticking to one's task during tough times. For many Japanese who survived the war, Yokoi was the living embodiment of ganbaru. However, for the young people of Japan's increasingly Western culture, Yokoi was an embarrassing reminder of the previous generations' blind fealty to the Emperor that had caused Japan's disgrace. Though he longed to see the Emperor and wrote a letter to apologize for having survived the war, Yokoi was never granted an audience.

## Reassimilation

Millions of television viewers across Japan watched Yokoi's return trip to his native village where a gravestone listed his death as September 1944. From those who considered him a hero, Yokoi received gifts of money totaling more than $80,000 and many marriage offers.

He purchased a modest home and married Mihoko Hatashin, who he described as a "nice, old-fashioned" girl, unlike the modern Japanese girls whom he described as "monsters whose virtue is all but gone from them, and who screech like apes."

Though horrified by the Westernization of his homeland, Yokoi prospered as a lecturer on survival techniques. He unsuccessfully ran for Parliament on a platform that stressed simplicity and discipline and included such measures as enforced composting and converting golf courses into bean fields. On September 22, 1997, Yokoi died of heart failure at age 82.

# HISTORY'S GRIM PLACES OF QUARANTINE

Life has never been easy for lepers. Throughout history, they've been stigmatized, feared, and cast out by society. Such reactions—though undeniably heartless—were perhaps understandable because the disease was thought to be rampantly contagious. Anyone suspected of leprosy was forced into quarantine and left to die.

Leprosy has affected humanity since at least 600 BC. This miserable disease, now known as Hansen's disease, attacks the nervous system primarily in the hands, feet, and face and causes disfiguring skin sores, nerve damage, and progressive debilitation. Medical science had no understanding of leprosy until the late 1800s and no effective treatment for it until the 1940s. Prior to that point, lepers faced a slow, painful, and certain demise.

Misinterpretations of Biblical references to leprosy in Leviticus 13:45–46, which labeled lepers as "unclean" and dictated that sufferers must "dwell apart . . . outside the camp," didn't help matters. (The "leprosy" cited in Leviticus referred to several skin conditions, but Hansen's disease was not one of them.) It's really no surprise that society's less-than-compassionate response to the disease was the leper colony.

## Cast Out in Misery and Despair

The first leper colonies were isolated spots in the wilderness where the afflicted were driven, forgotten, and left to die. The practice of exiling lepers continued well into the twentieth century. In Crete, for instance, lepers were banished to mountainside caves, where they survived by eating scraps left by wolves. More humane measures were adopted in 1903 when lepers were corralled into the Spinalonga Island leper colony and given food and shelter and cared for by priests and nuns. However, once you entered, you never left, and it remained that way until the colony's last resident died in 1957.

Still, joining a leper colony sometimes beat living among the healthy. It wasn't much fun wandering from town to town while wearing signs or ringing bells to warn of one's affliction. And you were always susceptible to violence from townsfolk gripped by irrational fear—as when lepers were blamed for epidemic outbreaks and thrown into bonfires as punishment.

## Life in the American Colony

American attitudes toward lepers weren't more enlightened. One of modern time's most notorious leper colonies was on the Hawaiian island of Molokai, which was established in 1866. Hawaiian kings and American officials banished lepers to a peninsula ringed by jagged rock and sea cliffs. Molokai became one of the world's largest leper colonies—its population peaked in 1890 at 1,174—and over 8,000 people were forcibly confined there before the practice was ended in 1969.

The early days of Molokai were horrible. The banished were abandoned in a lawless place where they received minimal care and had to fight with others for food, water, blankets, and shelter. Public condemnation led to improved conditions, but residents later became freaks on display as Hollywood celebrities flocked to the colony on macabre sightseeing tours.

## A Leper Haven in Louisiana

While sufferers of leprosy were being humiliated in Hawaii, they were being helped in Louisiana. In 1894, the Louisiana Leper House, which billed itself as "a place of treatment and research, not detention," opened in Carville. In 1920, it was transferred to federal authority and renamed the National Leprosarium of the United States. Known today as the National Hansen's Disease (leprosy) Program (NHDP), the facility became a leading research and rehabilitation center, pioneering treatments that form the basis of multidrug therapies currently prescribed by the World Health Organization (WHO) for the treatment of Hansen's disease.

It was here that researchers enlisted a common Louisiana critter—the armadillo—in the fight against the disease. It had always been difficult to study Hansen's disease. Human nerves are seldom biopsied, so direct data on nerve damage from Hansen's was minimal. But in the 1960s, NHDP researchers theorized that armadillos might be susceptible to the germ because of their low body temperature. They began inoculating armadillos with it and discovered that the animals could develop the disease systemically. Now the armadillo is used to develop infected nerves for research worldwide.

## A Thing of the Past?

In 1985, leprosy was still considered a public health problem in 122 countries. In fact, the last remaining leper colony, located in Croatia, didn't close until 2002. However, WHO has made great strides toward eradicating the disease and indicated in 2000 that the rate of infection had dropped by 90 percent. The therapies currently prescribed for the treatment of leprosy are available to all patients for free via WHO. Approximately four million patients have been cured since 2000.

# THE MYSTERY OF EASTER ISLAND

On Easter Sunday in 1722, a Dutch ship landed on a small island 2,300 miles from the coast of South America. Polynesian explorers had preceded them by a thousand years or more, and the Europeans found the descendants of those early visitors still living on the island. They also found a strange collection of almost 900 enormous stone heads, or moai, standing with their backs to the sea, gazing across the island with eyes hewn out of coral. The image of those faces haunts visitors to this day.

## Ancestors at the End of the Land

Easter Island legend tells of the great Chief Hotu Matu'a, the Great Parent, striking out from Polynesia in a canoe, taking his family on a voyage across the trackless ocean in search of a new home. He made landfall on Te-Pito-te-Henua, the End of the Land, sometime between AD 400 and 700. Finding the island well-suited to habitation, his descendants spread out to cover much of the island, living off the natural bounty of the land and sea.

With their survival assured, they built *ahu*—ceremonial sites featuring a large stone mound—and on them erected moai, which were representations of notable chieftains who led the island over the centuries. The moai weren't literal depictions of their ancestors, but rather embodied their spirit, or mana, and conferred blessings and protection on the islanders.

The construction of these moai was quite a project. A hereditary class of sculptors oversaw the main quarry, located near one of the volcanic mountains on the island. Groups of people would request a moai for their local ahu, and the sculptors would go to work, their efforts supported by gifts of food and other goods. Over time, they created 887 of the stone moai, averaging just over 13 feet tall and weighing around 14 tons, but ranging from one extreme of just under four feet tall to a behemoth that towered 71 feet. The moai were then transported across the island by a mechanism that still remains in doubt, but that may have involved rolling them on the trunks of palm trees felled for that purpose— a technique that was to have terrible repercussions for the islanders.

When Europeans first made landfall on Easter Island, they found an island full of standing moai. Fifty-two years later, James Cook reported that many of the statues had been toppled, and by the 1830s none were left standing. What's more, the statues hadn't just been knocked over; many of them had boulders placed at strategic locations, with the intention of decapitating the moai when they were pulled down. What was going on?

## A Culture on the Brink

It turns out the original Dutch explorers had encountered a culture on the rebound. At the time of their arrival, they found two or three thousand living on the island, but some estimates put the population as high as 15,000 a century before. The story of the islanders' decline is one in which many authors find a cautionary tale: The people simply consumed natural resources to the point where their land could no longer support them. For a millennium, the islanders simply took what they needed: They fished, collected bird eggs, and chopped down trees to pursue their obsession with building moai. By the 1600s, life had changed: The last forests on the island disappeared, and the islanders' traditional foodstuffs disappeared from the archaeological record. Local tradition tells of a time of famine and even rumored cannibalism, and it is from this time that island history reveals the appearance of the spear. Tellingly, the Polynesian words for "wood" begin to take on a connotation of wealth, a meaning found nowhere else that shares the language. Perhaps worst

of all, with their forests gone, the islanders had no material to make the canoes that would have allowed them to leave their island in search of resources. They were trapped, and they turned on one another.

The Europeans found a reduced society that had just emerged from this time of terror. The respite was short-lived, however. The arrival of the foreigners seems to have come at a critical moment in the history of Easter Island. Either coincidentally or spurred on by the strangers, a warrior class seized power across the island, and different groups vied for power. Villages were burned, their resources taken by the victors, and the defeated left to starve. The warfare also led to the toppling of an enemy's moai—whether to capture their mana or simply prevent it from being used against the opposing faction. In the end, none of the moai remained standing.

## Downfall and Rebound

The troubles of Easter Island weren't limited to self-inflicted chaos. The arrival of the white man also introduced smallpox and syphilis; the islanders, with little natural immunity to the exotic diseases, fared no better than native populations elsewhere. As if that weren't enough, other ships arrived, collecting slaves for work in South America. The internal fighting and external pressure combined to reduce the number of native islanders to little more than a hundred by 1877—the last survivors of a people who once enjoyed a tropical paradise.

Easter Island, or Rapa Nui, was annexed by Chile in 1888. As of 2009, there are 4,781 people living on the island. There are projects underway to raise the fallen moai. As of today, approximately 50 have been returned to their former glory.

# FUGITIVE NAZIS IN SOUTH AMERICA

Nazi leaders were sentenced to death after the war, but a few managed to escape the grip of Nuremberg and sneak into South America.

In July 1972, an old man complaining of intense abdominal pain checked himself into a hospital in Sao Paulo, Brazil. The admitting physician noted that the man, obviously a foreigner, looked much older than the 46 years listed on his identity card but accepted the excuse that the date was misprinted. The man had an intestinal blockage: He had a nervous habit of chewing the ends of his walrus mustache, and over the years the bits of hair had accumulated in his digestive tract. The man had good reason to be nervous. He was Josef Mengele, a Nazi war criminal, who had been hiding in South America since the end of the Second World War.

After the war, many Nazi war criminals escaped to start new lives in non-extraditing countries like Argentina, Brazil, Uruguay, Chile, and Paraguay. They lived in constant danger of discovery, though in several cases, friendly dictatorships turned a blind eye in exchange for services. Many were found and kidnapped by the Israeli Mossad, tried, and sentenced for their crimes. Some, including Mengele, the cruel concentration camp doctor, eluded capture until their deaths. Mengele died by accidental drowning in 1979.

South America was a refuge from the net of international justice that swept Europe at war's end. Several of the countries had enjoyed friendly prewar relations with the Reich—Argentina, in particular, was sympathetic to the plight of the fugitive Nazis. Many found positions in Argentina's Fascist government, controlled by Juan Perón. His wife, Evita, later traveled to Europe, ostensibly on a goodwill tour. However, she was actually raising funds for the safe passage of war criminals.

In Argentina, Uruguay, Chile, Bolivia, and Paraguay, scores of Nazis found familiar traditions of elitism and militarism. Perhaps most importantly, corruption in those countries made it easy to obtain false identification papers through bribery.

## Nazis Who Slipped Overseas

• Walter Rauff invented the Auschwitz "death trucks" that killed more than half a million prisoners. Rauff was arrested in Santiago, Chile, in 1963, but the Chilean authorities released him after three months in jail. Many believe that Rauff designed the concentration camps where Chilean political prisoners were killed under the Pinochet regime.

• Paul Schäfer served in the Hitler Youth. Years later, he was arrested for pedophile activities while working at an orphan-age in postwar Germany. Schaefer fled to Chile where he established a settlement known as Colonia Dignida, in which abuse, torture, and drugs were used to control followers. The adults were taught to call Schaefer "Führer"; the colony's children called him "Uncle." Schaefer sexually abused hundreds of children in the decades that followed. The colony prospered and, despite information from escaped members, it remained in operation until 1993 when Schaeffer went into hiding. He managed to escape justice until 2006 when he was sentenced to 20 years in prison.

• Klaus Barbie, the notorious "Butcher of Lyon," became a counterintelligence officer for the U.S. military which helped him to flee to Bolivia soon after the war. In 1971, he assisted in a military coup that brought the brutal General Hugo Banzar to power. Barbie went on to head the South American cocaine ring called Amadeus that generated funds for political activity friendly to U.S. interests in the region. When a more moderate government came to power in 1983, Barbie was deported to France, where he was tried and convicted of war crimes. He died of cancer after spending four years in prison.

## Nueva Germania

German colonists had settled in South America long before the start of the Second World War. One of the more outlandish attempts occurred in the late-nineteenth century when Elisabeth Nietzsche-Forster and her husband Bernhard Forster led a group of 14 families to Paraguay. They founded a utopian village dedicated to anti-Semitism and an "authentic rebirth of racial feeling." They called their remote settlement Nueva Germania. Within two years, many of the colonists had died of disease, Bernhard drank himself to death, and Elisabeth returned to Europe where she successfully worked to have her husband's writings adopted as the favorite philosophy of the Nazi Party. After the Second World War, many fugitive Nazis were rumored to have sheltered in Nueva Germania, including Josef Mengele.

## Submarines Full of Nazi Gold

Despite evidence suggesting that Hitler's secretary, Martin Bormann, died in the streets of Berlin in 1945, rumors persist about his escape to South America. According to the same accounts, Bormann witnessed his Führer's suicide and then followed prearranged orders to escape to Argentina, where he had been transporting large amounts of Reich gold and money using submarines. In the final days of the war, go the stories, Bormann and dozens of other Nazi officials left Germany in 10 submarines, five of which arrived safely in Argentina. Waiting for them was a friendly government and the stolen wealth of Europe, safely deposited by the Peróns in Swiss bank accounts. Some estimates place the accumulated wealth at $800 million.

# Reward: One Lost Island

Did the legendary island of Atlantis ever really exist? Or did Plato make the whole thing up?

It's hard to believe that Plato, an early Greek philosopher, was the type to start rumors. But in two of his dialogues, *Timaeus* and *Critias*, he refers to what has become one of the most famous legends of all time: the doomed island of Atlantis.

In *Timaeus*, Plato uses a story told by Critias to describe where Atlantis existed, explaining that it "came forth out of the Atlantic Ocean, for in those days the Atlantic was navigable; and there was an island situated in front of the straits which are by you called the Pillars of Heracles; the island was larger than Libya and Asia put together, and was the way to other islands." Not only that, but Plato also divulges the details of its fate: "afterwards there occurred violent earthquakes and floods; and in a single day and night of misfortune all your warlike men in a body sank into the earth, and the island of Atlantis in like manner disappeared in the depths of the sea. For which reason the sea in those parts is impassable and impenetrable, because there is a shoal of mud in the way; and this was caused by the subsidence of the island." In *Critias*, the story revolves around Poseidon, the mythical god of the sea, and how the kingdom of Atlantis attempted to conquer Athens.

Although many ascribe Plato's myth to his desire for a way to emphasize his own political theories, historians and writers perpetuated the idea of the mythical island for centuries, both in fiction and nonfiction. After the Middle Ages, the story of the doomed civilization was revisited by such writers as Francis Bacon, who published *The New Atlantis* in 1627. In 1870, Jules Verne published his classic *Twenty Thousand Leagues Under the Sea*, which includes a visit to sunken Atlantis aboard Captain Nemo's submarine Nautilus. And in 1882, *Atlantis: The Antediluvian World* by Ignatius Donnelly was written to prove that Atlantis did exist—initiating much of the Atlantis mania that has occurred since that time.

The legendary Atlantis continues to surface in today's science fiction, romantic fantasy, and even mystery stories.

More recently, historians and geologists have attempted to link Atlantis to the island of Santorini (also called Thera) in the Aegean Sea. About 3,600 years ago, one of the largest eruptions ever witnessed by humans occurred at the site of Santorini: the Minoa, or Thera, eruption. This caused the volcano to collapse, creating a huge caldera or "hole" at the top of the volcanic mountain. Historians believe the eruption caused the end of the Minoan civilization on Thera and the nearby island of Crete, most likely because a tsunami resulted from the massive explosion. Since that time, most of the islands, which are actually a complex of overlapping shield volcanoes, grew from subsequent volcanic eruptions around the caldera, creating what is now the volcanic archipelago of islands called the Cycladic group.

Could this tourist hot spot truly be the site of the mythological island Atlantis? Some say that Plato's description of the palace and surroundings at Atlantis were similar to those at Knossos, the central ceremonial and cultural center of the Minoan civilization. On the scientific end, geologists know that eruptions such as the one at Santorini can pump huge volumes of material into the air and slump other parts of a volcanic island into the oceans. To the ancient peoples, such an event could literally be translated as an island quickly sinking into the ocean. But even after centuries of study, excavation, and speculation, the mystery of Atlantis remains unsolved.

Dan Brown's blockbuster novel *The Da Vinci Code* reignited public interest in Atlantis in a roundabout way. Brown's story referenced the Knights Templar, an early Christian military order with a dramatic history that involved bloodshed, exile, and secrets—one of which was that they were carriers of ancient wisdom from the lost city of Atlantis.

# Why Didn't the Vikings Stay in North America?

According to ancient Norse sagas that were written in the thirteenth century, Leif Eriksson was the first Viking to set foot in North America. After wintering at the place we now call Newfoundland in the year 1000, Leif went home. In 1004, his brother Thorvald led the next expedition, composed of 30 men, and met the natives for the first time. The Vikings attacked and killed eight of the nine native men they encountered. A greater force retaliated, and Thorvald was killed. His men then returned home.

Six years later, a larger expedition of Viking men, women, and various livestock set up shop in North America. They lasted two years, according to the sagas. The Vikings traded with the locals initially, but they soon started fighting with them and were driven off. There may have been one further attempt at a Newfoundland settlement by Leif and Thorvald's sister, Freydis.

In 1960, Norse ruins of the appropriate age were found in L'Anse aux Meadows, Newfoundland, by Norwegian couple Helge and Anne Stine Ingstad. The Vikings had been there, all right.

Excavations over the next seven years uncovered large houses and ironworks where nails and rivets were made, as well as woodworking areas. Also found were spindlewhorls, weights that were used when spinning thread; this implies that women were present, which suggests the settlement was more than a vacation camp. The ruins don't reveal why the Vikings left, but they do confirm what the old sagas claimed: the Vikings were in North America.

The sagas say that the settlers fought with the local *Skraelings*, a Norse word meaning "natives," until the *Skraelings* came at them in large enough numbers to force the Vikings out.

This sounds plausible, given the reputation of the Vikings— they'd been raiding Europe for centuries—and the Eriksson family's history of violence. Erik the Red, the father of Leif, founded a Greenland colony because he'd been thrown out of Iceland for murder, and Erik's father had been expelled from Norway for the same reason. Would you want people like that as your neighbors?

# TOP-SECRET LOCATIONS YOU CAN VISIT

There are plenty of stories of secret government facilities hidden in plain sight. Places where all sorts of strange tests take place, far away from the general public. Many of the North American top-secret government places have been (at least partially) declassified, allowing average Joes to visit. We've listed some locations where you can play Men in Black.

## Titan Missile Silo

Just a little south of Tucson, Arizona, lies the Sonoran Desert, a barren, desolate area where nothing seems to be happening. That's exactly why, during the Cold War, the U.S. government hid an underground Titan Missile silo there.

Inside the missile silo, one of dozens that once littered the area, a Titan 2 Missile could be armed and launched in just under 90 seconds. Until it was finally abandoned in the 1990s, the government manned the silo 24 hours a day, with every member being trained to "turn the key" and launch the missile at a moment's notice. Today, the silo is open to the public as the Titan Missile Museum. Visitors can take a look at one of the few remaining Titan 2 missiles in existence, still sitting on the launch pad (relax, it's been disarmed). Folks with extra dough can also spend the night inside the silo and play the role of one of the crew members assigned to prepare to launch the missile at a moment's notice.

## Peanut Island

You wouldn't think a sunny place called Peanut Island, located near Palm Beach, Florida, could hold many secrets. Yet in December 1961, the U.S. Navy came to the island on a secret mission to create a fallout shelter for President John F. Kennedy and his family. The shelter was completed, but it was never used and was all but forgotten when the Cold War ended. Today, it is maintained by the Palm Beach Maritime Museum, which conducts weekend tours of the space.

## Wright-Patterson Air Force Base

If you believe that aliens crash-landed in Roswell, New Mexico, in the summer of 1947, then you need to make a trip out to Ohio's Wright-Patterson Air Force Base. That's because, according to legend, the UFO crash debris and possibly the aliens (both alive and dead) were shipped to the base as part of a government cover-up. Some say all that debris is still there, hidden away in an underground bunker beneath the mysterious Hanger 18.

While most of the Air Force Base is off-limits to the general public, you can go on a portion of the base to visit the National Museum of the U.S. Air Force, filled with amazing artifacts tracing the history of flight. But don't bother to ask any of the museum personnel how to get to Hanger 18—the official word is that the hanger does not exist.

## Los Alamos National Laboratory

Until recently, the U.S. government refused to acknowledge the Los Alamos National Laboratory's existence. But in the early 1940s, the lab was created near Los Alamos,

New Mexico, to develop the first nuclear weapons in what would become known as the Manhattan Project. Back then, the facility was so top secret it didn't even have a name. It was simply referred to as Site Y. No matter what it was called, the lab produced two nuclear bombs, nicknamed Little Boy and Fat Man—bombs that would be dropped on Hiroshima and Nagasaki, effectively ending World War II. Today, tours of portions of the facility can be arranged through the Lab's Public Affairs Department.

## Nevada Test Site

If you've ever seen one of those old black-and-white educational films of nuclear bombs being tested, chances are it was filmed at the Nevada Test Site, often referred to as the Most Bombed Place in the World.

Located about an hour north of Las Vegas, the Nevada Test Site was created in 1951 as a secret place for the government to conduct nuclear experiments and tests in an outdoor laboratory that is actually larger than Rhode Island. Out there, scientists blew everything up from mannequins to entire buildings.

Those curious to take a peek inside the facility can sign up for a daylong tour. Of course, before they let you set foot on the base, visitors must submit to a background check and sign paperwork promising not to attempt to photograph, videotape, or take soil samples from the site.

# WHO BUILT THE PYRAMIDS?

The Great Pyramids of Egypt have maintained their mystery through the eons, and there's still a lot we don't know about them. But we do know that slaves, particularly the ancient Hebrew slaves, did not build these grand structures.

It's easy to see why people think slaves built the pyramids. Most ancient societies kept slaves, and the Egyptians were no exception. And Hebrew slaves did build other Egyptian monuments during their 400 years of captivity, according to the Old Testament. Even ancient scholars such as the Greek historian Herodotus (fifth century BC) and the Jewish historian Josephus (first century AD) believed that the Egyptians used slave labor in the construction of the pyramids.

Based on the lifestyles of these builders, however, researchers have discredited the notion that they were slaves (Nubians, Assyrians, or Hebrews, among others) who were forced to work. They had more likely willingly labored, both for grain (or other foodstuffs) and to ensure their place in the afterlife. What's more, we now know that the Great Pyramids were built more than a thousand years before the era of the Hebrews (who actually became enslaved during Egypt's New Kingdom).

Archaeologists have determined that many of the people who built the pyramids were conscripted farmers and peasants who lived in the countryside during the Old Kingdom. Archaeologist Mark Lehner of the Semitic Museum at Harvard University has spent more than a decade studying the workers' villages that existed close to the Giza plateau, where the pyramids were built. He has confirmed that the people who built the pyramids were not slaves—rather, they were skilled laborers and "ordinary men and women."

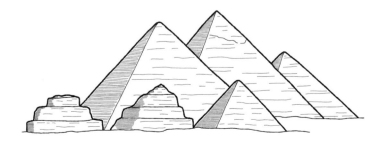

# Chapter 3
# SPORTING TRIVIA

## ODDITIES SURROUNDING THE 1900 OLYMPICS

The second modern Olympic Games were held in 1900 in Paris and were billed as part of the Exposition Universelle Internationale, the world's fair that featured the unveiling of the Eiffel Tower. It was the first Olympiad to be held outside of Greece, and there were plenty of other firsts to it as well.

• Despite the fact that nearly a thousand athletes competed in the 1900 Olympics, spectator attendance was low. The press preferred to focus on the Paris Exposition and seldom referred to the games as actual Olympic events. Instead, they were reported variously as "International Championships," "Paris Championships," "World Championships," and even "Grand Prix of the Paris Exposition." The founder of the International Olympic Committee, Baron Pierre de Coubertin, later said: "It's a miracle that the Olympic movement survived that celebration."

• The Olympic status of the athletes was equally downplayed, to the extent that many competitors never actually knew they were participating in the Olympics. Margaret Ives Abbott, a student from Chicago who won the nine-hole women's golf tournament, died in 1955 without realizing she was America's first female Olympic champion.

• Because the Olympics were held in conjunction with the Paris Exhibition, the scheduling and locations of the sporting events were often absurd. The fencing competition, for instance, was held as a sort of sideshow in the exhibition's cutlery area, and swimmers were forced to battle the polluted waters and strong currents of the Seine.

• After preliminary rounds, Myer Prinstein (from Syracuse University) had a clear lead in the long-jump competition and seemed poised to win. But when the final jump was scheduled on a Sunday, the official in charge of U.S. athletes disapproved of their competing on the Christian Sabbath. The athletes gave their word not to participate; Prinstein, who was Jewish, reluctantly agreed as well. On Sunday, however, Prinstein's main rival, Alvin Kraenzlein (University of Pennsylvania), broke his promise and competed, beating Prinstein's qualifying jump by a centimeter and winning the gold. Allegedly, Prinstein was so angry that he punched Kraenzlein in the face.

• Alvin Kraenzlein also won the 110-meter hurdles, the 220-meter hurdles, and the 60-meter dash—and he did it in three days. He was the first track-and-field athlete to accomplish the feat of winning four gold medals in individual events at a single Olympics.

• Women made their first appearance in the 1900 Games, albeit in small numbers: Of the thousand or so athletes participating, only 22 were women. The first female Olympic champion was Charlotte Cooper of Great Britain, who won the tennis singles and the mixed doubles. Female athletes wore the ankle-length skirts and dresses typical of the time.

• Ray Ewry of Indiana won the gold in three champion-ships—standing high jump, standing long jump, and standing triple jump—all on the same day. A remarkable feat for any man, these victories amounted to Olympic heroism for Ewry, who had spent his childhood confined to a wheelchair because of polio.

- After the French won both gold and silver medals in the marathon, three runners from the United States contested the results, accusing the winners of taking a short cut. As proof, they submitted their observation that the new champions were the only contestants not splattered with mud. Although the objection was not sustained, the celebratory spirit had been soured.

# THE DOUBLEDAY MYTH

It's a great story that's been passed from one generation to the next. It's also a work of fiction.

"The first scheme for playing Baseball, according to the best evidence available to date, was devised by Abner Doubleday at Cooperstown, N.Y. in 1839."

That finding, announced after a three-year study by the Mills Commission in 1907, is the main reason the tiny central New York hamlet was chosen to be the home of the National Baseball Hall of Fame and Museum. This "creation myth" has since been debunked from so many angles it seems positively ridiculous now, but it was accepted as truth back then.

Had Abner Doubleday truly invented baseball in 1839 in Cooperstown, New York, as so many generations of children have been told over the years, pundits could answer the question "Why Cooperstown?" in far fewer words. As it stands, the response requires a little more explanation.

So why Cooperstown? "The answer involves a commission, a tattered baseball, a philanthropist, and a centennial celebration," describes the Hall of Fame in its official statement. The commission was the brainchild of sporting goods magnate Albert G. Spalding in 1905, in response to a story that baseball had evolved from the British game of rounders. The baseball in question was an old, tattered, homemade ball discovered in a dusty attic trunk in a farmhouse near Cooperstown in 1934. It became known as the "Double-day Ball," and it served to support the commission's 1907 findings. Singer sewing machine magnate Stephen C. Clark purchased the "Doubleday ball" for $5 in 1935 and pushed for the formation of the Hall of Fame. The museum's opening was planned to coincide with a "century of baseball" cele-bration set to take place in Cooperstown in 1939. Thanks largely to Clark and his family, the Hall of Fame opened its doors in June of that year.

Even before the Hall of Fame opened, many people ques-tioned the findings of the Mills Commission, which said that Doubleday, a West Point cadet and Union general in the Civil War, had set down rules for a game of "town ball" for a group of Cooperstown boys to take on those from a neigh-boring town. The tale was based largely on the testimony of Abner Graves, a retired mining engineer who claimed to have witnessed the event. But historians later learned that Graves's testimony was questionable at best (he spent his final years in an insane asylum) and that baseball's presumed "founding father" was likely not in or even near Cooperstown in 1839.

Abner Doubleday's credibility as the inventor of baseball wasn't helped by the dozens of diaries he wrote after retir-ing from the U.S. Army in 1873. Neither the diaries nor the Doubleday obituary that appeared in *The New York Times* 20 years later include any mention of baseball.

In fact, the Hall of Fame plaque of Alexander Cartwright credits him as the "Father of Modern Base Ball." Cartwright, a New York bank teller and talented draftsman, organized the first regular team, which he called the New York Knick-erbockers. Rather than play "town ball," where scores could

**69**          Sporting Trivia

top 100, Cartwright devised rules for a game that would feature bases 90 feet apart on a diamond-shape infield, nine players per side, a three-strikes-and-you're-out policy, and "force outs" at first base if the ball got to the infielder before the runner—all rules that have stood the test of time. The first game under Cartwright's rules was played at the Elysian Fields in Hoboken, New Jersey, on June 19, 1846.

# The Sad Saga of Sonny Liston

Climbing up from utter poverty, this world heavyweight champ found controversial success in the boxing ring but couldn't maintain his balance on the outside.

Charles "Sonny" Liston was born the son of an impoverished sharecropper in rural Arkansas, probably on May 8, but the year of his birth is unknown. This is the first of many mysteries in the life of a complicated, impenetrable man. Though many who knew him said he was born in 1927, Liston himself claimed he was born in 1932, and contemporary documents seem to back him up. Emotionally and physically abused, young Liston was not unhappy when his miserable parents split up and his mother moved to St. Louis—in fact, he followed her there as soon as he could.

## The Hard Time

Liston was only in his early teens when he made his way north, and like everyone else in his family, he was illiterate. He had his imposing build going for him, however, and this led local organized crime to recruit him as a debt collector. As long as Liston stuck to breaking kneecaps, he was to some degree under the mob's protection from law enforcement. But when he struck out on his own, robbing two gas stations and a restaurant with other youths in 1950, the police caught up to him, and he was busted. Liston pleaded

guilty to two counts of robbery and two counts of larceny—
he was lucky to be sentenced to concurrent prison terms
that ran only five years.

In the penitentiary, a Roman Catholic priest noticed Liston's
remarkable physique and urged him to take up boxing. Liston
followed that advice, and after serving only two years of his
time, he was paroled to a team of "handlers" who worked
for St. Louis mobster John Vitale. Vitale set Liston up in the
boxing world and controlled his contract for six years before
selling it to Frankie Carbo and Blinky Palermo, underworld
figures on the East Coast. Eventually, Liston's criminal ties
would lead him all the way to the U.S. Senate, where in
1960 he testified before a subcommittee investigating organized crime's control of boxing.

## The Big Time

Liston's first professional fight lasted only 33 seconds—he
took out Don Smith with only one punch. His first five fights
were in St. Louis, but his sixth was in Detroit. In that nation-
ally televised bout, he won an eight-round decision against
John Summerlin. The odds had been long, so the fight
garnered the young upstart a lot of attention. He suffered his
first professional defeat from his next opponent, when Marty
Marshall broke his jaw. Nevertheless, Liston moved steadi-
ly up the ranks, and finally, at Chicago's Comiskey Park in
1962, he became the heavyweight champion of the world by
knocking out Floyd Patterson in the first round.

Fighting success did not keep him out of trouble with the
law, however. A total of 19 arrests and a second jail sentence made Liston an unpopular figure on the American
sports scene. Many of his fights were thought to be fixed,
and some considered him a puppet of the mob. Unfortunately for him, Liston's most famous moment was one of defeat:
his knockout by Muhammad Ali on May 25, 1965. In one of
the most famous sports photos ever taken, *Sports Illustrated*

photographer Neil Leifer shot Liston sprawled on the mat with a menacing, screaming Ali towering over him. Some claim that Ali's punch was a "phantom punch" that never connected and that Liston had taken a dive because he feared the Nation of Islam.

## Strange Death

On January 5, 1971, he was found dead in his Las Vegas home by his wife, Geraldine, who had been out of town. Though the coroner ruled that he had died from heart failure and lung congestion, Liston's body was in a state of decomposition, and there was much speculation that Liston had been murdered by unsavory associates. The man who came into the world so anonymously that his birth year was not really known left it in fame, but with just as many unan-swered questions.

# FRAN'S FATHER

It is said that the death of Fran Tarkenton's father was caused by officiating miscues in the 1975 playoff game be-tween Minnesota and Dallas. Tarkenton's father did die during the game, but it was before the referees made their blunders.

One must approach such a macabre myth delicately, which is more than can be said for the perpetrators of this tall tale, who were probably the same lunatics who plunked an on-field official with a whiskey bottle during the tumul-tuous NFL contest that was played on December 28, 1975.

That year, the Minnesota Vikings had pillaged their way through the regular season, posting a 12–2 record. Bolstered by quarterback Fran Tarkenton, the Vikings were not expected to have any trouble subduing the Dallas Cowboys when they clashed in Minnesota on that solemn Sunday. Less than six minutes remained on the clock when the men in stripes began their football follies.

The first questionable call came when Dallas receiver Drew Pearson appeared to step out of bounds before snagging a do-or-die pass on a fourth-and-sixteen play. The officials ruled that Pearson had kept both feet in play. With only a handful of ticks left in the game and Dallas still trailing 14–10, Roger Staubach pitched a prayer toward the end zone before disappearing under a mound of Minnesota muscle. Pearson caught the ball, but he appeared to push Viking defender Nate Wright to the ground before grabbing the toss. Once again, the on-field zebras ignored the malfeasance and signaled a touchdown.

A shower of debris rained onto the field, including the well-flung bottle that bopped field judge Armen Terzian. After the contest, Tarkenton learned that his father had suffered a fatal heart attack during the third quarter of the game, long before the tables had turned. Staubach's miracle missile was later described as a "Hail Mary," the first time that divine designation was applied to a flying football.

# Brains and Brawn

The Olympic Games haven't always featured athletics alone. Relive the era when pens carried as much weight as the pentathlon and a gold medal performance was measured in both breaststrokes and brushstrokes.

Today's Olympic games feature sports exclusively, but there was a time when artists competed for gold medals alongside runners, swimmers, and discus throwers. Cultural events ran side-by-side with athletics during both the ancient and modern Olympics. But because the most recent edition of these "brain" games took place just prior to the television era, knowledge of them is limited.

## Herodotus the Hurtler?

Records are scarce, but it appears that the first competitor in this artistic free-for-all was the writer Herodotus. Competing in 444 BC at Olympia, Greece, the athlete participated in both writing and sporting contests. His pairing of brains and brawn would represent the ideal throughout much of the ancient era.

After a 1,500-plus-year hiatus, the Olympics made a comeback in 1896. International Olympic Committee founder Pierre de Coubertin lobbied to reinstate the cultural element into the modern games. His wish became reality at the Stockholm Olympics in 1912.

## A Slow Start

The roster of events at that meet included architecture, painting, sculpture, music, and literature. Despite its historic nature, turnout was disappointing—only 35 artists actually entered the competition.

The 1928 Amsterdam Olympics represented the height of artistic participation. More than 1,000 works of art were entered, and organizers permitted artists to sell them at the competition's end. This move, though well intended, violated the IOC's stance on amateurism. Following the 1948 games, an IOC report concluded that most artistic contestants were receiving money for their works and recommended that such competition be abolished.

# Who's Too Old for the Olympics?

Think of the average Olympic athlete, and the following images likely come to mind: physical perfection, drive, determination—and youth? Not necessarily. It could be just a matter of time before the AARP holds its own Olympic trials.

**Hilde Pedersen.** When Norway's Pedersen took home the bronze in the 10-kilometer cross-country skiing event at the 2006 Turin Winter Olympics, she became the oldest woman to win a Winter Games Olympic medal. It was an impressive achievement for the 41-year-old, but as she and other "older" competitors have proved in the past, age is no barrier to claiming an Olympic medal.

**Oscar Swahn.** Swedish shooter Swahn participated in three Olympic Games. At age 60, he won two gold medals and a bronze at his first Olympics, which took place in London in 1908. Four years later, at the Sweden Games, he won a gold in the single shot running deer team, making him the world's oldest gold medalist. Swahn returned to the Olympics in 1920 at age 72 and managed to win a silver medal in the double shot running deer competition.

**Anders Haugen.** Even at the ripe age of 72, Swahn is not the oldest person to have won an Olympic medal. At the first Winter Olympic Games in Chamonix, France (1924), U.S. ski jumper Anders Haugen placed fourth with a score of 17.916 points. Third-place winner, Norway's Thorlief Haug, received a score of 18.000 points. Fifty years later, a sports historian determined that Haug's score had been miscalculated and that he should have finished behind Haugen. At a special ceremony in Oslo, Haugen was finally awarded the bronze medal when he was 83 years old, making him the "eldest" recipient of an Olympic medal and the only American to ever win a medal in the ski jump event.

# THE TRAMPOLINE:
## A NEW SPORT SPRINGS TO LIFE

The trampoline has become a fixture in backyards and gymnasiums as a source of recreation. But can its origin really be traced to Alaska?

If postcards sold in the Anchorage, Alaska, airport are to be believed, the genesis of the trampoline can be traced all the way to the Arctic Circle. The tourist tokens show Eskimos stretching a piece of walrus skin and using the taut tarp to toss each other in the air. It's a good story, but it's not true. It was actually an athlete and coach from the University of Iowa who created the first manufactured version of the rebounding rig known as the trampoline.

During the winter of 1934, George Nissen, a tumbler on the college gymnastics team, and Larry Griswold, his assistant coach, were discussing ways to add some flair to their rather staid sport. The two men were intrigued by the possibilities presented by the buoyant nature of the safety nets used by trapeze artists. Griswold and Nissen constructed an iron frame and covered it with a large canvas, using springs to connect the cloth to the frame. The apparatus was an effective training device and a popular attraction among the kids who flocked to the local YMCA to watch Nissen perform his routines. The pair of cocreators eventually formed the Griswold-Nissen Trampoline & Tumbling Company and started producing the first commercially available and affordable trampolines.

Nissen can also claim fame for attaching a name to his pliant production. While on a tour of Mexico in the late 1930s,

Nissen discovered the Spanish word for springboard was *el trampolin*. Intrigued by the sound of the word, he Anglicized the spelling, and the trampoline was born. In 2000, trampolining graduated from acrobatic activity to certified athletic achievement when it was officially recognized as a medal-worthy Olympic sport.

# HOW THE MARATHON DIDN'T GET STARTED

The primary connection between the modern race and the ancient messenger lies in a nineteenth century poem that gets the details wrong.

## The Basic Legend

Almost everyone has heard it: The Athenians paddled the Persians in the Battle of Marathon (490 BC), saving Greece from becoming a Persian province. Afterward, Pheidippides the messenger ran all the way to Athens to announce the elating news, then fell dead. Thereafter, a distance-racing sport called the Pheidippidaion became popular.

Okay, that wasn't its name. Can you imagine the "Boston Pheidippidaion"? It sounds like a tongue twister. And "Pheidippi-de-doo-dah" would never have caught on.

Did the run happen? We can't know for sure; it isn't impossible. Did the run inspire an ancient sport? No. Evidently, distance running was already an ancient sport if we believe Herodotus, since he clearly calls Pheidippides a professional distance runner. The longest race at the ancient Olympics was the well-documented dolichos, which literally means "long race" and was anywhere from 7 to 24 stades, or 1,400 to 4,800 meters. Pheidippides probably ran this race.

## Ancient Sources

For those not steeped in the ancient world, Herodotus is revered as the "father of history"; antiquarians do not casually dismiss him. The story about Pheidippides usually gets pinned on Herodotus, but people garble what the great man actually wrote. Pheidippides (others name him "Philippides" or "Phidippides") was a professional runner sent to Sparta (which was also in for a stomping if Persia won) to ask for help.

Pheidippides returned, saying that the god Pan had waylaid him. "How come you ungrateful Athenians never worship Me? After all I do for you, too. I hear you have a battle coming up; planned to pitch in there as well. The least you could do is throw Me a decent bash now and then," whined the deity. (Herodotus digresses that the Athenians responded to this come-to-Pan meeting by initiating annual ceremonies and a torch-race honoring him, mindful of his help in the battle.)

As for Spartan aid, Pheidippides relayed their lame excuse: Spartan law forbade them to march until the moon was full. That's a heck of a note for someone who purportedly just ran 135 miles in two days, then returned at the same pace. Gods only knew how quickly Pheidippides might have arrived had he not stopped to listen to Pan complain.

Herodotus says nothing of a messenger to Athens after the battle. (One wonders just how the Athenians had managed to reach 490 BC without acquiring a horse.) A few later Greek sources refer to the event, but none ever met living witnesses to this Marathon. Herodotus may well have met some elderly survivors, writing nearly half a century after the events.

## More Recently

As with numerous popular legends, this one owes its modern currency to a poet. In 1879, Robert Browning published "Pheidippides," in which the runner makes the run to Sparta and back à la Herodotus' histories, then the run to Athens where he announces Athens' salvation before keeling over.

People believed this, as they are apt to believe nearly any legend embellished by a poet. What's more, a philhellenic era was about to revive the ancient Olympics in modern form, minus the prostitutes and blood sports. In 1896, the modern Olympics restarted and included a marathon for men. It took 88 more years to include one for women. Marathon lengths have varied over the years but not by much. The modern distance is 26.22 miles.

Today, of course, "marathon" has come to mean either an endurance footrace or any ultra-long event, such as an 18-inning baseball game or an office meeting that lasts until nearly every bladder present is about to rupture.

# BEEFED UP

You're probably familiar with the terms "juiced," "roid-raged," "hyped," and "pumped"—all used to describe the effects of anabolic steroids. For better or for worse, steroids have invaded the worlds of professional and amateur sports, and even show business.

## Better Living Through Chemistry

Anabolic steroids (also called anabolic-androgenic steroids or AAS) are a specific class of hormones that are related to the male hormone testosterone. Steroids have been used for thousands of years in traditional medicine to promote healing in diseases such as cancer and AIDS. French neurologist Charles-Édouard Brown-Séquard was one of the first physicians to report its healing properties after injecting himself with an extract of guinea pig testicles in 1889. In 1935, two German scientists applied for the first steroid-use patent and were offered the 1939 Nobel Prize for Chemistry, but they were forced to decline the honor by the Nazi government.

Interest in steroids continued during World War II. Third Reich scientists experimented on concentration camp inmates to treat symptoms of chronic wasting as well as to test its effects on heightened aggression in German soldiers. Even Adolf Hitler was injected with steroids to treat his endless list of maladies.

## Giving Athletes a Helping Hand

The first reference to steroid use for performance enhancement in sports dates back to a 1938 *Strength and Health* magazine letter to the editor, inquiring how steroids could improve performance in weightlifting and bodybuilding.

During the 1940s, the Soviet Union and a number of Eastern Bloc countries built aggressive steroid programs designed to improve the performance of Olympic and amateur weight lifters. The program was so successful that U.S. Olympic team physicians worked with American chemists to design Dianabol, which they administered to U.S. athletes.

Since their early development, steroids have gradually crept into the world of professional and amateur sports. The use of steroids have become commonplace in baseball, football, cycling, track—even golf and cricket. In the 2006 *Monitor the Future* survey, steroid use was measured in eighth-, tenth-, and twelfth-grade students; a little more than 2 percent of male high school seniors admitted to using steroids during the past year, largely because of their steroid-using role models in professional sports.

Steroids have a number of performance enhancement perks for athletes, such as promoting cell growth, protein synthesis from amino acids, increasing appetite, bone strengthening, and the stimulation of bone marrow and production of red blood cells. Of course, there are a few "minor" side effects to contend with as well: shrinking testicles, reduced sperm count, infertility, acne, high blood pressure, blood clotting, liver damage, headaches, aching joints, nausea, vomiting, diarrhea, loss of sleep, severe mood swings, paranoia, panic attacks, depression, male pattern baldness, the cessation of menstruation in women, and an increased risk of prostate cancer—small compromises in the name of athletic achievement, right?

While many countries have banned the sale of anabolic steroids for non-medical applications, they are still legal in Mexico and Thailand. In the United States, steroids are classified as a Schedule III controlled substance, which makes their possession a federal crime, punishable by prison time. But that hasn't deterred athletes from looking for that extra edge. And there are thousands of black market vendors willing to sell more than 50 different varieties of steroids. Largely produced in countries where they are legal, steroids are smuggled across international borders. Their existence has spawned a new industry for creating counterfeit drugs that are often diluted, cut with fillers, or made from vegetable oil or toxic substances. They are sold through the mail, the internet, in gyms, and at competitions. Many of these drugs are veterinary-grade steroids.

## Impact on Sports and Entertainment

Since invading the world of amateur and professional sports, steroid use has become a point of contention, gathering supporters both for and against their use. Arnold Schwarzenegger, the famous bodybuilder, actor, and politician, freely admits to using anabolic steroids while they were still legal. "Steroids were helpful to me in maintaining muscle size while on a strict diet in preparation for a contest," says Schwarzenegger, who held the Mr. Olympia bodybuilding title for seven years. "I did not use them for muscle growth, but rather for muscle maintenance when cutting up."

Lyle Alzado, the colorful, record-setting defensive tackle for the Los Angeles Raiders, Cleveland Browns, and Denver Broncos admitted to taking steroids to stay competitive but acknowledged their risks. "Ninety percent of the athletes I know are on the stuff. We're not born to be 300 lbs. or jump 30 ft. But all the time I was taking steroids, I knew they were making me play better," he said. "I became very violent on the field and off it. I did things only crazy people do. Now look at me. My hair's gone, I wobble when I walk and have to hold on to someone for support and I have trouble remembering things. My last wish? That no one else ever dies this way."

Recently, a few show business celebrities have come under scrutiny for their involvement with steroids and other banned substances. In 2008, 61-year-old *Rambo* star Sylvester Stallone paid $10,600 to settle a criminal drug possession charge for smuggling 48 vials of Human Growth Hormone (HGH) into the country. HGH is popularly used for its anti-aging benefits.

"Everyone over 40 years old would be wise to investigate it (HGH and testosterone use) because it increases the quality of your life," says Stallone.

"If you're an actor in Hollywood and you're over 40, you are doing HGH. Period," said one Hollywood cosmetic surgeon. "Why wouldn't you? It makes your skin look better, your hair, your fingernails. Everything."

# When Bicycles Ruled
# the (Sporting) World

What sport lasted a day longer than the ancient Olympics, broke the race barrier before baseball, and caused more injuries than modern football? Turn-of-the-century bicycle racing, of course.

## Blood, Guts, and Determination

In 1900, the most popular sport in North America was the grueling phenomenon known as the six-day bicycle race. Usually held on indoor velodromes with wooden tracks, teams of two would compete for 144 hours, taking turns accruing laps and competing in sprinting events. These six-day events were not a sport for the faint of heart. At a race, as many as 70,000 fans would thrill to the sight of these riders sustaining serious, often fatal, injuries and pushing themselves to the limits of endurance. Here are some of the sport's major players.

## Reggie McNamara (1887–1970)

Dubbed the "Iron Man" of cycling, Australian Reggie Mc-Namara had a seemingly inhuman capacity for the punishment and exertion that defined the six-day events. On the fourth day of a competition in Melbourne, McNamara underwent an emergency trackside operation without anesthesia to remove a large abscess "from his side." Though he lost a considerable amount of blood, he rose from the dust and, ignoring the entreaties of his trainer and doctor, resumed the race. In fact, his injuries on the track put him in the hospital so often that he wound up marrying an American nurse after a 1913 competition in New York. He achieved several world records and defeated the French champions so soundly that they refused to ride against him.

## Bobby Walthour (1878–1949)

During his career, bicycling champion Bobby Walthour of Atlanta, Georgia, suffered nearly 50 collarbone fractures and was twice assumed to be dead on the track—only to rise and continue riding. By the time he was age 18, he was the undisputed champion of the South; soon he held the title of international champion and kept it for several years. In addition to making himself and cycling familiar to people all over the world, Walthour brought a great deal of prominence to his native Atlanta. Invigorated by his accomplishments, Atlanta built the Coliseum, one of the world's preeminent velodromes at the time.

## Marshall "Major" Taylor (1879–1932)

African American cyclist Major Taylor, the son of an Indianapolis coach driver, proved that endurance bicycling was a sport in which individual talent could not be denied. In an era of overt racism and discrimination, he rose through the cycling ranks to become one of the highest paid athletes of his time. After relocating to the somewhat more race-tolerant Worcester, Massachusetts, Taylor began to rack up a string of impressive victories in the six-day and sprinting competitions. Dubbed the "Worcester Whirlwind," Taylor toured the world, defeated Europe's best riders, and set several world records during his professional career.

## Enter the Machines

Like modern stock car racing, six-day cycling events used pacing vehicles. Originally, these were bicycles powered by two to five riders. But in 1895, English races began using primitive motorcycles. These new pace vehicles allowed the cyclists to travel faster, owing to the aerodynamic draft produced by the machines. Crowds thrilled to the speed and noise of these mechanical monsters, which weighed about 300 pounds each. It took two men to operate the motorcycles, one to steer and one to control the engine. They were also quite dangerous: A tandem pacer forced off the track in Waltham, Massachusetts on May 30, 1900, killed both riders and injured several fans. The advent of motorcycles increased the popularity of the six-day races for a time, but it waned with the arrival of a new vehicle spectators preferred over bicycles: the automobile.

# WHY IS A FOOTBALL SHAPED THAT WAY?

Would you rather call it a bladder? Because that's what footballs were made of before mass-produced rubber or leather balls became the norm.

The origins of the ball and the game can be traced back to the ancient Greeks, who played something called *harpaston*. As in football, players scored by kicking, passing, or running over the opposition's goal line. The ball in harpaston was often made of a pig's bladder. This is because pigs' bladders were easy to find, roundish in shape, relatively simple to inflate and seal, and fairly durable. (If you think playing ball with an internal organ is gross, consider what the pig's bladder replaced: a human head.)

Harpaston evolved into European rugby, which evolved into American football. By the time the first "official" football game was played at Rutgers University in New Jersey in the fall of 1869, the ball had evolved, too. To make the ball more durable and consistently shaped, it was covered with a protective layer that was usually made of leather.

Still, the extra protection didn't help the pig's bladder stay permanently inflated, and there was a continuous need to reinflate the ball. Whenever play was stopped, the referee unlocked the ball—yes, there was a little lock on it to help keep it inflated—and a player would pump it up.

Footballs back then were meant to be round, but the sphere was imperfect for a couple reasons. First, the bladder lent itself more to an oval shape; even the most perfectly stitched leather covering couldn't force the bladder to remain circular. Second, as a game wore on, players got tired and were less enthused about reinflating the ball. As a result, the ball would flatten out and take on more of an oblong shape. The ball was easier to grip in that shape, and the form slowly gained popularity, particularly after the forward pass was introduced in 1906.

Through a series of rule changes relating to its shape, the football became slimmer and ultimately developed its current look. And although it's been many decades since pigs' bladders were relieved of their duties, the football's nickname—a "pigskin"—lives on.

## WHY ISN'T A BOXING RING ROUND?

Boxing has been around for ages because, when you get down to it, humans like to pummel each other. The ancient Greeks were the ones who decided to make it into a legitimate sport: Boxing was introduced as an Olympic event in 688 BC. The competitors wrapped pieces of soft leather around their hands and proceeded to fight.

The Romans took it a little further, adding bits of metal to the leather. No wonder those guys ruled most of the known world for so long! Fast forward to England in the eighteenth century. Boxing was popular—and it was violent. The fighters battled each other inside a ring of rope that was lined with—and sometimes held up by—spectators. That's right, a *ring*.

These spectators couldn't be counted on to be sober and often raucously crowded the boxers—the rope ring would get smaller and smaller until the onlookers were practically on top of the fighters. Often the spectators would have a go at it with the boxers themselves.

Naturally, the fighters got a bit testy about this. Jack Broughton, a heavyweight champion, came up with a set of rules to protect his fellow boxers in 1743. These included a chalked-off square inside which boxers would fight. Event organizers attached rope to stakes that were pounded into the ground, which prevented the fighting area from changing sizes and from being invaded. Why a square? Because it was easy to make.

Broughton's rules were eventually revised to formalize the square shape. By 1853, the rules stated that matches had to take place in a 24-foot square "ring" that was enclosed by ropes. That, good reader, is the origin of what boxing aficionados call "the squared circle."

## How Do Corked Bats Help Cheating Baseball Players Hit the Ball Farther?

In this age of performance-enhancing drugs, it's almost refreshing when a hitter gets caught cheating the old-fashioned way. Corked bats somehow recall a more innocent time.

There are different ways to cork a wooden baseball bat, but the basic procedure goes like this: Drill a hole into the top of the bat, about an inch in diameter and 12 inches deep; fill the hole with cork—in rolled sheets or ground up—and close the top with a wooden plug that matches the bat; finally, carefully stain and finish the top of the bat so that the plug blends in.

The supposed benefits of a corked bat involve weight and bat speed. Cork is lighter than wood, which enables a player to generate more speed when swinging the bat. The quicker the swing, the greater the force upon contact with the ball—and the farther that ball flies. The lighter weight allows a batter more time to evaluate a pitch, since he can make up the difference with his quicker swing; this extra time amounts to only a fraction of a second, but it can be the difference between a hit and an out at the major league level.

Following the logic we've set forth, replacing the wood in the bat with nothing at all would make for an even lighter bat and, thus, provide more of an advantage. The problem here is that an empty core would increase the likelihood that the bat would break; at the very least, it would cause a suspicious, hollow sound upon contact with the ball. The cork fills in the hollow area, and does so in a lightweight way.

Not everyone believes that a corked bat provides an advantage; some tests have indicated that the decreased bat density actually diminishes the force applied to the ball. But Dr. Robert Watts, a mechanical engineer at Tulane University who studies sports science, sees things differently. He concluded that corking a bat increases the speed of the swing by about 2.5 percent; consequently, the ball might travel an extra 15 to 20 feet, a distance that would add numerous home runs to a player's total over the course of his career.

## WHY DO GOLFERS WEAR SUCH SILLY CLOTHES?

In most of the major sports, athletes don't have much choice when it comes to what they wear. Basketball, football, baseball, and hockey teams all have uniforms. But other athletes aren't so lucky (and neither are their fans). Golfers, for example, are allowed to choose their own garb, leading to a parade of "uniforms" that sometimes look as if they were stitched together by a band of deranged clowns.

Why big-time golfers wear such hideous clothes is a source of bewilderment. Some apologists blame it on the Scots. Golf, after all, was supposedly invented by shepherds in Scotland back in the twelfth century, and it almost goes without saying that a sport born in a country where manskirts are considered fashionable is doomed from the start. We'd like to point out that we are no longer in twelfth century Scotland—let's move on, people.

But history may indeed play a role in golf's repeated fashion disasters. Kings and queens were reputed to have hit the links in the sixteenth and seventeenth centuries, and by the late nineteenth century, golf was a popular pastime amongst the nobility of England and Scotland.

The nobility, however, wasn't exactly known for its athletic prowess. The other "sports" many of these noblemen participated in were activities like steeplechase (which has its own awful fashion), and so most early golfers had no idea what types of clothes would be appropriate for an athletic endeavor. Early golfers simply took to the links wearing the fashionable attire of the day—attire that, unfortunately, included breeches and ruffled cravats (these were like neckties).

The tradition of wearing stuffy, silly attire continued into the twentieth century (as did the tradition of wealthy, paunchy white guys playing the sport), with awful sweaters, loud patterns, and polyester pants replacing the ruffled cravats and knee-length knickers. Yet, remarkably, modern golfers take umbrage at the stereotype that duffers have no sense of fashion. According to one golf wag, the knock on golfers for being the

Sporting Trivia

world's worst-dressed athletes is unfair because nowadays almost everybody wears Dockers and polo shirts.

# How Come Nobody Else Calls It Soccer?

Millions of kids across the United States grow up playing a game that their parents hardly know, a game that virtually everyone else in the world calls football. It's soccer to us, of course, and although Americans might be ridiculed for calling it this, the corruption is actually British in origin.

Soccer—football, as the Brits and others insist—has an ancient history. Evidence of games resembling soccer has been found in cultures that date to the third century BC. The Greeks had a version that they called *episkyro*. The Romans brought their version of the sport along when they colonized what is now England and Ireland. Over the next millennium, the game evolved into a freewheeling, roughneck competition—matches often involved kicking, shoving, and punching.

In England and Ireland, the sport was referred to as football; local and regional rules varied widely. Two different games—football and rugby—slowly emerged from this disorganized mess. The Football Association was formed in 1863 to standardize the rules of football and to separate it from rugby. The term "soccer" most likely is derived from the association's work.

During the late nineteenth century, the Brits developed the linguistic habit of shortening words and adding "-ers" or "-er." (We suffer this quirk to this day in expressions like "preggers." A red card to the Brits on this one.) One popular theory holds that given the trend, it was natural that those playing "Assoc." football were playing "assoccers" or "soccer." The term died out in England, but was revived in the United States in the early part of the twentieth century to separate the imported sport with the round white ball from the American sport with the oblong brown ball.

Soccer has long struggled to catch on as a major spectator sport in the United States. For most Americans, there just isn't enough scoring or action. In fact, many Yanks have their own word for soccer: boring.

# How Did the Biathlon Become an Olympic Event?

It's one thing to ski through the frozen countryside; it's quite another to interrupt that heart-pounding exertion and muster up the calm and concentration needed to hit a target that's a few centimeters wide with a .22-caliber bolt-action rifle.

Yes, the biathlon is an odd sport. Cross-country skiing combined with rifle marksmanship? Why not curling and long jump? Figure skating and weight lifting? In actuality, however, the two skills that make up the biathlon have a history of going hand in hand, so combining them as an Olympic event makes perfect sense.

It's no surprise that the inspiration for the biathlon came from the frigid expanses of northern Europe, where there's not much to do in the winter besides ski around and drink aquavit. Cross-country skiing provides a quick and efficient way to travel over the snowy ground, so northern cultures mastered the technique early—and it was especially useful when it came time to hunt for winter food. People on skis were killing deer with bows and arrows long before such an activity was considered a sport.

But skiing and shooting (with guns, eventually) evolved from an act of survival into a competition. The earliest biathlon competitions were held in 1767 as informal contests between Swedish and Norwegian border patrols. The sport spread through Scandinavia in the nineteenth century as sharpshooting skiers formed biathlon clubs. In 1924, it was included as a demonstration sport in the Winter Olympics in Chamonix, France, although it was called military patrol.

In 1948, the Union Internationale de Pentathlon Moderne et Biathlon—the first international governing body for the sport—was formed. The official rules for what would come to be the modern biathlon were hammered out over the next several years.

During the 1960 Olympics at Squaw Valley Ski Resort in California, a biathlon was contested as an official Olympic event for the first time. The sport has evolved over the decades—it now features smaller-caliber rifles, different distances, various types of relays, and the participation of women. (A women's biathlon was first staged as an Olympic event in 1992 in Albertville, France.)

Today, biathlon clubs and organizations are active all over the world, and there are versions of the sport for summer in which running replaces skiing. Still, the biathlon's popularity remains strongest in its European birthplace.

## JEU DE PAUME, ANYONE?

Ever watch people playing handball and wonder, "Ow! Isn't that hell on their hands?" Well, it can be. That's why some players decided to take a different approach to handball, and used a racket instead. Here's more on the origins of tennis.

# Tennis: Sport of Monks

Interestingly, no one is quite sure exactly when tennis was invented. Some folks believe it's an ancient sport, but there's no credible evidence that tennis existed before AD 1000. Whenever the time period, most people can agree that tennis descends from handball.

The first reliable accounts of tennis come from tales of eleventh century French monks who needed to add a little entertainment to their days spent praying, repenting, and working.

They played a game called *jeu de paume* ("palm game," that is, handball) off the walls or over a stretched rope. The main item separating tennis from handball—a racket—evolved within these French monasteries. (The first rackets were actually used in ancient Greece, in a game called *sphairistike* and then in *tchigan*, played in Persia.) The monks had the time and means to develop these early forms of the tennis racquet: Initially, webbed gloves were used for hand protection, then paddles, and finally a paddle with webbing. The first balls were made from leather or cloth stuffed with hair, wool, or cork.

# Banned by the Pope

Once outside the cloister, the game's popularity spread across the country with the speed of an Amélie Mauresmo backhand. According to some sources, by the thirteenth century, France had more than 1,800 tennis courts. Most of the enthusiasts were from the upper classes. In fact, the sport became such a craze that some leaders, including kings and the pope, tried to discourage or ban the game as too distracting. Not to be torn from their beloved game, the people played on. It didn't take long for tennis to reach merry olde England.

There the game developed a similar following, counting kings Henry VII and Henry VIII among its fans. Even The Bard,

William Shakespeare, refers to the game in his play *Henry V*. At England's Hampton Court Palace, research suggests that the first tennis court was built there between 1526 and 1529. Later, another court was built, The Royal Tennis Court, which was last refurbished in 1628 and is still in use.

## 15-Love!

Those who believe that tennis originated in ancient Egypt argue that the word "tennis" derives from the Egyptian town of Tinnis. It is also possible that the term comes from the French cry of "*Tenez!*" which in this context could mean, "take this!" or "here it comes!" using the formal address. A similar version would be "Tiens!" As with any living language, French pronunciation has evolved, so it's difficult to know precisely whether the word actually grew out of French monastery trash-talk—but it's quite plausible.

Ever wonder what's up with tennis's weird scoring system? And what does any of it mean, anyway? Here are a few tennis pointers.

The term "Love," meaning a score of zero, may descend from *L'Oeuf*, which means "the egg"—much like "goose egg" means zero in American sports slang.

Evidently, the scoring once went by 15s (0, 15, 30, 45, and Game). But for some reason, it was decided that the numbers should have the same number of syllables. Hence, the "5" got dropped from the French word *quarante-cinq* (45), leaving just *quarante* (40), which is in use today.

The term "Deuce" (when the game ties 40–40 and is reset to 30–30) likely comes from "À Deux!" which loosely translates as "two to win!" This is because in tennis, one must win by two.

# DRIBBLING DRIVEL

There are numerous rules on how to properly dribble a basketball, but bouncing the ball with such force that it bounds over the head of the ball handler is not illegal.

Although it might fun-up the standard NBA game to see players drumming dribbles with the exaggerated effort of the Harlem Globetrotters, it wouldn't do anything to move the game along. And contrary to popular belief, there is no restriction on how high a player may bounce the ball, provided the ball does not come to rest in the player's hand.

Anyone who has dribbled a basketball can attest to the fact it takes a heave of some heft to give the globe enough momentum to lift itself even to eye-level height. Yet, the myth about dribbling does have some connection to reality. When Dr. James Naismith first drafted the rules for the game that eventually became known as basketball, the dribble wasn't an accepted method of moving the ball. In the game's infancy, the ball was advanced from teammate to teammate through passing. When a player was trapped by a defender, it was common practice for the ball carrier to slap the sphere over the head of his rival, cut around the befuddled opponent, reacquire possession of the ball, and then pass it up court. This innovation was known as the overhead dribble, and it was an accepted way to maneuver the ball until the early part of the twentieth century. The art of "putting the ball on the floor" and bouncing it was used first as a defensive weapon to evade opposing players.

By the way, there is absolutely no credence to wry comments made by courtside pundits that the "above the head" rule was introduced because every dribble that former NBA point guard Muggsy Bogues took seemed to bounce beyond the upper reaches of his diminutive frame.

# Chapter 4
# ART HAPPENINGS

## 7 Notorious Art Thefts

Some people just can't keep their hands off of other people's things—including the world's greatest art. Art thieves take their loot from museums, places of worship, and private residences. Because they would have trouble selling the fruits of their labor on the open market—auction houses and galleries tend to avoid stolen works—art burglars often either keep the art for themselves or try to ransom the hot property back to the original owner. Among the major robberies in the past hundred years are these daring thefts of very expensive art (values estimated at the time of the theft).

**1. Boston, March 1990:** $300 million: Two men dressed as police officers visited the Isabella Stewart Gardner Museum in the wee hours of the morning. After overpowering two guards and grabbing the security system's surveillance tape, they collected Rembrandt's only seascape, *Storm on the Sea of Galilee*, as well as Vermeer's *The Concert*, Manet's *Chez Tortoni*, and several other works. Authorities have yet to find the criminals despite investigating everyone from the Irish Republican Army to a Boston mob boss.

**2. Oslo, August 2004:** $120 million: Two armed and masked thieves threatened workers at the Munch Museum during a daring daylight theft. They stole a pair of Edvard Munch paintings, *The Scream* and *The Madonna*, estimated at a combined value of 100 million euros. In May 2006, authorities convicted three men who received between four and eight years in jail. The paintings were recovered three months later.

**3. Paris, August 1911:** $100 million: In the world's most notorious art theft to date, Vincenzo Peruggia, an employee of the Louvre, stole Leonardo da Vinci's *Mona Lisa* from the storied museum in the heart of Paris. Peruggia simply hid in a closet, grabbed the painting once alone in the room, hid it under his long smock, and walked out of the famed museum after it had closed. The theft turned the moderately popular *Mona Lisa* into the best-known painting in the world. Police questioned Pablo Picasso and French poet Guillaume Apollinaire about the crime, but they found the real thief—and the *Mona Lisa*—two years later when Peruggia tried to sell it to an art dealer in Florence.

**4. Oslo, February 1994:** $60–75 million: *The Scream* has been a popular target for thieves in Norway. On the day the 1994 Winter Olympics began in Lillehammer, a different version of Munch's famous work—he painted four—was taken from Oslo's National Art Museum. In less than one minute, the crooks came in through a window, cut the wires holding up the painting, and left through the same window. They attempted to ransom the painting to the Norwegian government, but they had left a piece of the frame at a bus stop—a clue that helped authorities recover the painting within a few months. Four men were convicted of the crime in January 1996.

**5. Scotland, August 2003:** $65 million: Blending in apparently has its advantages for art thieves. Two men joined a tour of Scotland's Drumlanrig Castle, subdued a guard, and made off with Leonardo da Vinci's *Madonna of the Yarnwinder*. Alarms around the art were not set during the day, and the thieves dissuaded tourists from intervening, reportedly telling them: "Don't worry . . . we're the police. This is just practice." The painting was recovered in 2007, and four men were arrested.

**6. Stockholm, December 2000:** $30 million: Caught! Eight criminals each got up to six and half years behind bars for conspiring to take a Rembrandt and two Renoirs—all of them eventually recovered—from Stockholm's National Museum. You have to give the three masked men who actually grabbed the paintings credit for a dramatic exit. In a scene reminiscent of an action movie, they fled the scene by motorboat. Police unraveled the plot after recovering one of the paintings during an unrelated drug investigation four months after the theft.

**7. Amsterdam, December 2002:** $30 million: Robbers used a ladder to get onto the roof of the Van Gogh Museum, broke in, and stole two of the Dutch master's paintings, *View of the Sea at Scheveningen and Congregation Leaving the Reformed Church in Nuenen*, together worth $30 million. Police reported that the thieves worked so quickly that, despite setting off the alarms, they had disappeared before police could get there. Authorities in the Netherlands arrested two men in 2003, based on DNA from hair inside two hats left at the scene, but they have been unable to recover the paintings, which the men deny taking.

# THE VANISHING TREASURE ROOM

In the Age of Enlightenment, kings and emperors built immense palaces to outdo one another—each one bigger and more gilded and bejeweled than the last. But one of Russia's greatest eighteenth century treasures became one of the twentieth century's greatest unsolved mysteries.

The storied history of the Amber Room begins in 1701, when it was commissioned by Frederick I of Prussia. Considered by admirers and artists alike to be the "Eighth Wonder of the World," the sparkling, honey-gold room consisted of a series of wall panels inlaid with prehistoric amber, finely carved and illuminated by candles and mirrors. In 1716, Prussian King Freidrich Wilhelm I made a gift of the panels to his then-ally Russian Tsar Peter the Great to ornament the imperial palace at his new capital, St. Petersburg.

After sitting at the Winter Palace for four decades, the Amber Room was relocated to Tsarskoye Selo, the Romanov palace just south of St. Petersburg. During the mid-eighteenth century, Prussia's King Frederick the Great sent Russia's Empress Elizabeth more of the amber material from his Baltic holdings, and Elizabeth ordered her court's great Italian architect, Bartolomeo Rastrelli, to expand the Amber Room into an 11-foot-square masterpiece.

The golden room was not finished until 1770, under the reign of Catherine the Great. Incorporating more than six tons of amber and accented with semiprecious stones, the fabled room became not only a prized imperial showpiece of the Russian empire, but a symbol of the long-standing alliance between Prussia and Russia.

## From Peace to War

Two centuries after the Amber Room was removed to the Catherine Palace, the world was a much darker place. Prussia and Russia, formerly faithful allies, were locked in a deadly struggle that would bring down both imperial houses. By 1941, the former dominions of Frederick and Peter were ruled by Adolf Hitler and Joseph Stalin.

In a surprise attack, Hitler's armies advanced across the Soviet border in June 1941 to launch the most destructive war in history. German panzers rumbled from the Polish frontier to the gates of Moscow in a harrowing six-month campaign, laying waste to some of the most fertile, productive territory in Eastern Europe.

One of the unfortunate cities in the path of the Nazi on-slaught was St. Petersburg, renamed Leningrad by its communist conquerors. Frantic palace curators desperately tried to remove the Amber Room's antique panels, but the fragile prehistoric resin began to crack and crumble as the panels were detached. Faced with probable destruction of one of Russia's greatest treasures or its abandonment to the Nazis, the curators attempted to hide the room's precious panels by covering them with gauze and wallpaper.

Although Leningrad withstood a long, bloody siege, German troops swept through the city's suburbs, capturing Tsarskoye Selo intact in October 1941. Soldiers discovered the treasure hidden behind the wallpaper, and German troops disassembled the room's panels over a 36-hour period, packed them in 27 crates, and shipped them back to Königsberg, in East Prussia.

The fabled Amber Room panels were put on display in Königsberg's castle museum. They remained there for two years—until the Third Reich began to crumble before the weight of Soviet and Anglo-American military forces. At some point in 1944, the room's panels were allegedly dismantled and packed into crates, to prevent damage by British and Soviet bombers. In January 1945, Hitler permitted the westward movement of cultural treasures, including the Italo-Russo-German masterpiece.

And from there, the Amber Room was lost to history.

## The Great Treasure Hunt

The world was left to speculate about the fate of the famous imperial room, and dozens of theories have been spawned about the room's whereabouts. Some claim the Amber Room was lost—sunk aboard a submarine, bombed to pieces, or perhaps burned in Königsberg itself. This last conclusion was finally accepted by Alexander Brusov, a Soviet investigator sent to find the Amber Room shortly after the war's end. Referring to the destruction of Königsberg Castle by Red Army forces on April 9, 1945, he concluded: "Summarizing all the facts, we can say that the Amber Room was destroyed between 9 and 11 April 1945."

An in-depth hunt by two British investigative journalists pieced together the last days of the Amber Room and concluded that its fate was sealed when Soviet troops accidentally set fire to the castle compound during the last month of combat, destroying the brittle jewels and obscuring their location.

Other treasure hunters, however, claim the room still sits in an abandoned mine shaft or some long-forgotten Nazi bunker beneath the outskirts of Königsberg. One German investigator claimed former SS officers told him the room's panels were packed up and hidden in an abandoned silver mine near Berlin; a Lithuanian official claimed witnesses saw SS troops hiding the panels in a local swamp. Neither has been able to prove his claims.

## The Trail Goes Cold

The hunt for the Amber Room has been made more difficult because its last witnesses are gone—several under mysterious circumstances. The Nazi curator in charge of the room died of typhus the day before he was scheduled to be interviewed by the KGB, and a Soviet intelligence officer who spoke to a journalist about the room's whereabouts died the following day in a car crash. In 1987, Georg Stein, a former German soldier who had devoted his life to searching for the Amber Room, was found murdered in a forest, his stomach slit open by a scalpel.

In 1997, the world got a tantalizing glimpse of the long-lost treasure when German police raided the office of a Bremen lawyer who was attempting to sell an amber mosaic worth

$2.5 million on behalf of one of his clients, the son of a former German lieutenant. The small mosaic—inlaid with jade and onyx as well as amber—had been stolen from the Amber Room by a German officer and was separated from the main panels. After its seizure, this last true remnant of the legendary tsarist treasure made its way back to Russia in April 2000.

Decades of searches by German and Soviet investigators have come up empty. The fate of the fabled room—worth over $250 million in today's currency—has remained an elusive ghost for treasure seekers, mystery writers, and investigators looking for the Holy Grail of Russian baroque artwork.

## Picking up the Pieces

In 1979, the Soviet government, with help from a donation made by a German gas firm, began amassing old photographs of the Amber Room and pieces of the rare amber to create a reconstructed room worthy of its predecessor. Carefully rebuilt at a cost exceeding $7 million, the reconstructed room was dedicated by the Russian president and German chancellor at a ceremony in 2003, marking the tricentennial of St. Petersburg's founding. The dazzling Amber Room is now on display for the thousands of tourists who come to Tsarskoye Selo to view the playground of one of Europe's great dynasties.

# CRACKING THE CODE OF DA VINCI'S MASTERPIECE

After centuries of beguiling viewers—and maddening artists and scientists who tried to uncover its secrets—Leonardo da Vinci's Mona Lisa may have finally revealed her secret code.

The renaissance genius began his portrait of Lisa del Gio-condo, a Florentine gentlewoman, in 1503 and is believed to have finished the painting just before his death in 1519. Using a process of brushwork he called *sfumato* (from the Italian fumo, meaning smoke), da Vinci said his technique created a painting "without lines or borders, in the manner of smoke or beyond the focus plane." Although he left many notes on his other projects, Leonardo never explained how the subtle effects of light and shadow that give his master-work an unworldly, three-dimensional quality.

Although the painting has been studied extensively over the centuries, even the most modern scientific instruments have been unable to uncover its secrets. Much of the brushwork on the portrait's face and hands is too small to be stud-ied by X-ray or microscope. French artist and art historian Jacques Franck, however, believes he has discovered da Vinci's methods through his own trial and error. According to Franck, after completing a conventional sketch of his sub-ject, da Vinci applied a base coat of pale yellow imprimatu-ra—a diluted semi-opaque wash—then began one of history's greatest creative marathons. Using minute crosshatching techniques, da Vinci spent more than 15 years brushing on 30 successive layers of paint. Apparently requiring a magni-fying glass, the process took 30 to 40 small dots of oil paint smaller than the head of a pin to cover one square millimeter of canvas. Franck believes da Vinci applied additional layers of imprimatura between each layer of paint to further soften lines and blend colors, creating successively finer layers of shading and tones.

Although Franck's conclusions have been disputed by some art historians, he has convincingly reproduced the effects with his own copies of small sections of the painting. A re-cent exhibit at the Uffizi Gallery in Florence displayed six panels by Franck recreating one of Mona Lisa's eyes, illustrating the step-by-step process of how Leonardo may have worked. Though his artistic sleuthing remains controversial, Franck points out that the use of minute dots of paint—similar to the pointillism developed by modern artists—had been used since Roman times and is clearly evident in some of da Vinci's earlier paintings. With the Mona Lisa, Leonardo apparently took the technique to an unmatched level of virtuosity.

## JOHN MYATT, MASTER FORGER

When people hear the word forgery, they usually think of money. But legal currency isn't the only thing that can be faked.

"Monet, Monet, Monet. Sometimes I get truly fed up doing Monet. Bloody haystacks." John Myatt's humorous lament sounds curiously Monty Pythonesque, until you realize that he can do Monet—and Chagall, Klee, Le Corbusier, Ben Nicholson, and almost any other painter you can name, great or obscure. Myatt, an artist of some ability, was probably the world's greatest art forger. He took part in an eight-year forgery scam in the 1980s and 1990s that shook the foundations of the art world.

Despite what one might expect, art forgery is not a victimless crime. Many of Myatt's paintings—bought in good faith as the work of renowned masters—went for extremely high sums. One "Giacometti" sold at auction in New York for $300,000, and as many as 120 of his counterfeits are still out there, confusing and distressing the art world. But Myatt never set out to break the law.

Initially, Myatt would paint an unknown work in the style of one of the cubist, surrealist, or impressionist masters, and he seriously duplicated both style and subject. For a time, he gave them to friends or sold them as acknowledged fakes. Then he ran afoul of John Drewe.

## The Scheme Begins

Drewe was a London-based collector who had bought a dozen of Myatt's fakes over two years. Personable and charming, he ingratiated himself with Myatt by posing as a rich aristocrat. But one day he called and told Myatt that a cubist work the artist had done in the style of Albert Gleizes had just sold at Christies for £25,000 ($40,000)—as a genuine Gleizes. Drewe offered half of that money to Myatt.

The struggling artist was poor and taking care of his two children. The lure of Drewe's promise of easy money was irresistible. So the scheme developed that he would create a "newly discovered" work by a famous painter and pass it along to Drewe, who would sell the painting and then pay Myatt his cut—usually only about 10 percent. It would take Myatt two or three months to turn out a single fake, and he was only making about £13,000 a year (roughly $21,000)— hardly worthy of a master criminal.

One of the amazing things about this scam was Myatt's materials. Most art forgers take great pains to duplicate the exact pigments used by the original artists, but Myatt mixed cheap emulsion house paint with a lubricating gel to get the colors he needed. One benefit is that his mix dried faster than oil paints.

## The Inside Man

But Drewe was just as much of a master forger, himself. The consummate con man, he inveigled his way into the art world through donations, talking his way into the archives of the Tate Gallery and learning every trick of *provenance*, the authentication of artwork. He faked letters from experts and, on one occasion, even inserted a phony catalog into the archives with pictures of Myatt's latest fakes as genuine.

But as the years went by, Myatt became increasingly worried about getting caught and going to prison, so at last he told Drewe he wanted out. Drewe refused to let him leave, and Myatt realized that his partner wasn't just in it for the money. He loved conning people.

## The Jig Is Up

The scam was not to last, of course. Drewe's ex-wife went to the police with incriminating documents, and when the trail led to Myatt's cottage in Staffordshire, he confessed.

Myatt served four months of a yearlong sentence, and when he came out of prison, Detective Superintendent Jonathan Searle of the Metropolitan Police was waiting for him. Searle suggested that since Myatt was now infamous, many people would love to own a real John Myatt fake. As a result, Myatt and his second wife Rosemary set up a tidy business out of their cottage. His paintings regularly sell for as much as £45,000 ($72,000), and Hollywood has shown interest in a movie—about the real John Myatt.

# A Portrait of Oils

The unique characteristics of oil paint contributed to the accomplishments of the Renaissance—and still inspire artists today.

Paintings are among the most ancient of artworks. More than 30,000 years ago, Neolithic painters decorated caves with patterns and images of animals. All paints include two elements: pigment and a liquid binder. Pigments from charred wood and colored minerals are ground into a fine powder. Then they are mixed into the binder; linseed oil is the most popular, but other oils, including walnut oil, are common.

The idea of using oil as a binder for pigment is very old, but oil paints as we know them are relatively modern. In the twelfth century, a German monk named Theophilus wrote about oil paint in his *Schoedula Diversarum Artium* and warned against paint recipes using olive oil because they required excessively long drying times. The Italian painter and writer Cennino Cennini described the technique of oil painting in his encyclopedic *Book of Art*. Oil paints came into general use in northern Europe, in the area of the Netherlands, by the fifteenth century and, from there, spread southward into Italy. Oils remained the medium of choice for most painters until the mid-twentieth century.

Oil paintings are usually done on wood panels or canvas, although paintings on stone and specialty paper are not uncommon. In any case, the support material is usually prepared with a ground to which oil paint easily adheres. Oil paints dry slowly, an advantage to artists, who adjust their compositions as they work. When the painting is done, a protective layer of varnish is often applied. In the nineteenth century, oil paint in tubes simplified the painter's work. A rainbow of innovative, synthetic colors contributed to the emergence of new approaches to art and, in particular, modern abstract painting.

# WHO INVENTED THE PRINTING PRESS?

Sure, Johannes Gutenberg's development of the printing press in fifteenth century Germany led to mass-market publishing. But innovations in printing technology were around long before Gutenberg revolutionized the industry.

Art Happenings

# The Stamp of Uniformity

Although printing is usually associated with reading materials, the original impetus behind printing technology was the need to create identical copies of the same thing. Printing actually began with coining, when centralized states branded their coins with uniform numbers and symbols. In those days, written manuscripts were copied the old-fashioned way, letter by letter, by hand. Only the upper echelons of society were literate, books were costly, and the laborious and artistic method of copying matched the rarity of books.

The first major innovation in printing came with the Chinese invention of block printing by the eighth century AD. Block printing involved carving letters or images into a surface, inking that surface, and pressing it on to paper, parchment, or cloth. The method was used for a variety of purposes, from decorating clothes to copying religious scrolls. The blocks were usually made of wood, which posed a problem as the wood eventually decayed or cracked. Oftentimes entire pages of a manuscript, complete with illustrations, were carved into a single block that could be used again and again.

The Chinese also invented movable type, which would prove to be the prerequisite to efficient printing presses. Movable type is faster than block printing because individual characters are created by being cast into molds. Once this grab bag of individual characters is made, they can then be reused and rearranged in infinite combinations by changing the typeset. Movable type characters are also more uniform than the carved letters of block printing. Pi-Sheng invented this method in 1045 using clay molds. The method spread to Korea and Japan, and metal movable type was created in Korea by 1230.

# Supply and Demand

The Chinese didn't use movable type extensively because their language consists of thousands of characters, and movable type makes printing efficient only in a language with fewer letters. Meanwhile, Europeans used the imported concept of block printing to make popular objects like playing cards or illustrated children's books. During the Middle Ages, serious secular scholarship had all but disappeared in Europe, and the reproduction of new and classical texts was mostly confined to the Asian and Arab worlds. That is, until literacy began to spread among the middle classes, and lay people, especially in Germany, showed an interest in reading religious texts for themselves. Thus, German entrepreneur Johannes Gutenberg, the son of a coin minter, began to experiment with metal movable type pieces. It's believed Gutenberg was unfamiliar with the previously invented Chinese method, but at any rate, several other Europeans were experimenting with similar methods at the same time as Gutenberg.

By the 1440s, Gutenberg had set up a printing shop, and in 1450, he set out to produce a Bible. Gutenberg perfected several printing methods, such as right justification, and preferred alloys in the production of metal types. By 1455, Gutenberg's press had produced 200 copies of his Bible—quite the feat at the time, considering one Bible could take years to copy by hand. These Bibles were sold for less than hand-copied ones yet were still expensive enough for profit margins equivalent to modern-day millions.

Presses soon popped up all across Europe. By 1499, an estimated 15 million books had been produced by at least 1,000 printing presses, mostly in Germany and then throughout Italy. For the first time ever, ideas were not only dreamed up and written down—they were efficiently reproduced and spread over long distances. The proliferation of these first German printing presses is commonly credited with the end of the Middle Ages and the dawn of the Renaissance.

Art Happenings

# PICTURE PERFECT:
# MAKING WAX SCULPTURES

Making a wax likeness of a person may be a centuries-old art, but this sort of portraiture is still a complicated process.

## The First Stages

Ah, the wax sculpture—perhaps the most obvious sign that someone has made it as a cultural icon. The art of wax sculpting has been around since the 1700s, when the now well-known Madame Tussaud made her first figures. These days, before the statue slides its way into a museum, it has to make a long journey that begins with weeks of research.

Once a museum decides to commission a particular person's model, a team of artists begins to collect piles of photographs and measurements of the soon-to-be-immortalized person. But before they even think about building the separate parts and putting the pieces together, the museum must decide exactly how the end product should appear.

Curators consider every detail, ranging from the facial expression and posture to wardrobe and setting. They'll even go as far as interviewing barbers and dentists to get a better feel for the person's physical details. Once those decisions have been made and the data has been collected, it's time to start sculpting.

## Building the Face

Using a combination of photos and measurements and some-times even a real-life impression, the artists create a plaster mold of the head using regular clay. Next, they pour hot wax into this mold. Beeswax is often used along with manufactured petroleum-based waxes, mixed together with artificial coloring and chemicals to help the goo stay strong and resist heat. After everything is in place, it's time to let the magic happen.

## The Fine Details

Once the mold has cooled, the wax is removed and the assembly begins. Prosthetic eyes are selected to best match the person's gaze. Porcelain teeth, similar to dentures, are used to fill the kisser. And real human hair is brought in to be inserted, one strand at a time, into every spot where it's needed: the head, the eyebrows and eyelashes, and even the arms and chest. Specially trained workers use a tiny needle to painstakingly place every last hair perfectly. This process alone takes up to 60 hours. One can imagine that, in the case of hirsute comedian Robin Williams's model, it could take 60 days.

Next, painters use translucent paint to even out the skin tone and add in any blemishes or distinguishing features. The paint is put on in thin layers, allowing the wax to shine through and look more lifelike. The crew then puts all the pieces together and passes the final figure off to the next team.

## The Big Picture

Now that the model is done, the rest of the work begins. Seamstresses and costuming consultants come in to create the figure's wardrobe and fit it onto the body. Designers then assemble the full set, including backgrounds, props, and furnishings to match the moment frozen in time. At long last, the model is ready to be placed into the scene. After final touch-ups, engineers are hired to design lighting that will play up the sculpture's features. Finally, the journey is done, and the show is ready to open.

Altogether, the entire process usually takes a minimum of six months. Some cases have been more extreme: Royal London Wax Museum's model of former U.S. President

Art Happenings

Bill Clinton took eight months, and its sculpture of former Canadian Prime Minister Jean Chretien took just over a year. Museums say the creations can cost anywhere from $10,000 to $25,000, not including the various furnishings. Kind of makes the salon's $25 wax special seem a little more reasonable, doesn't it?

# Salvador Dalí and Harpo Marx: A Match Made in Surrealist Heaven

The great twentieth century surrealist artist Salvador Dalí knew how to put a brush to canvas, but after making fast friends with Harpo Marx of the Marx Brothers, Dalí was inspired to try his hand at writing comedy. Thus was born a surrealist comedy script that was deemed unmarketable— even by Hollywood standards.

## Dalí the Filmmaker

Salvador Dalí was never one to paint a dull picture. From melting watches to roses that float in the middle of the desert, Dalí painted the world as he imagined it, not as it was. And Dalí did not limit this dreamlike vision to painting—he designed clothing, furniture, and stage settings in Broadway productions. In effect, Dalí transferred his unique vision to whatever media would hold it. "Painting is an infinitely minute part of my personality," he said.

From a young age, Dalí had a particular interest in the surrealist potential of film. He grew up watching silent film comedic greats such as Charlie Chaplin and Buster Keaton. Slapstick comedic acts often had a distinct surrealist slant—after all, how many pie fights can a person encounter in a day? Dalí saw the potential inherent in cinema's ability to place one image right on top of another in time, thus allowing for the juxtaposition of bizarrely disconnected images, such as, say, a slashed human eye followed by a pink teddy bear. Dalí once described the epitome of film as "a succession of wonders."

At age 25, Dalí set to work making his imagined succession of wonders a surreality. He paired with friend and famed surrealist filmmaker Luis Bunuel to make a short film called *Un Chien Andalous* (1929), which is now considered a ground-breaking first in avant-garde cinema. His film career may have begun with this bang, but *Un Chien Andalous* and *L'Âge d'or* (1930) proved to be the only Dalí films to make it into production. In 1946, he collaborated with Walt Disney on a short six-minute animated film, *Destino*, that was abandoned as too strange and unmarketable. Eventually, *Destino* was released in 2003 after Dalí's death. He also made a short dream sequence for Hitchcock's *Spellbound*, but for the most part Dalí's film projects were nipped in the bud.

## Dalí the Comedian

The inspiration behind Dalí's wackiest unmade film script was his friendship with Harpo, the Marx brother who consistently hid crazy gags up his sleeve. Harpo's very persona was surreal: His character refused to speak, instead relying on the art of pantomime, whistles, and props to communicate. He wore outrageous outfits topped by his wild mat of curly clown hair and was a self-taught virtuoso harpist.

Dalí was enthralled with Harpo. After the two met in Paris in the summer of 1936, they strummed up an appropriately peculiar friendship. Dalí sent Harpo a gift: A gilded harp with barbed-wire strings and teaspoon tuning knobs. Delighted, Harpo returned the favor by sending Dalí a photograph of himself playing the harp with cut-up, bandaged fingers.

The following year, Dalí traveled to California to see Harpo. As he noted in a postcard, "I'm in Hollywood, where I've made contact with the three American Surrealists: Harpo Marx, Disney, and Cecil B. DeMille." According to the always-dramatic Dali, upon arrival, he found Harpo lying "naked, crowned with roses, and in the center of a veritable forest of harps." During their vacation, Dalí drew sketches of Harpo at his harp, grinning with a lobster on his head. The two also began collaboration on a surrealistic film called *Giraffes on Horseback Salad*. The film followed the misadventures of a Spanish businessman who comes to America and falls in love with a woman, to be played by Dalí's wife, Gala. The script also calls for burning giraffes wearing gas masks and Harpo catching Little People with a butterfly net. The film was never realized as MGM, the Marx Brothers' studio, refused to make it. The script does, however, still exist in a private collection—perhaps someday Dalí and Harpo's inimitable dream will come to fruition.

# I KNOW IT WHEN I SEE IT

What makes something "art"?

If you want to see a name-calling, hair-pulling intellectual fight (and who doesn't?), just yell this question in a crowded coffee shop. After centuries of debate and goatee-stroking, it's still a hot-button issue.

Before the fourteenth century, the Western world grouped painting, sculpture, and architecture with decorative crafts such as pottery, weaving, and the like. During the Renaissance, Michelangelo and the gang elevated the artist to the level of the poet—a genius who was touched by divine inspiration. Now, with God as a collaborator, art had to be beautiful, which meant that artists had to recreate reality in a way that transcended earthly experience.

In the nineteenth and twentieth centuries, artists rejected these standards of beauty; they claimed that art didn't need to fit a set of requirements. This idea is now widely accepted, though people still disagree over what is and isn't art.

A common modern view is that art is anything that is created for its own aesthetic value—beautiful or not—rather than to serve some other function. So, according to this theory, defining art comes down to the creator's intention. If you build a chair to have something to sit on, the chair isn't a piece of art. But if you build an identical chair to express yourself, that chair is a piece of art.

Marcel Duchamp demonstrated this in 1917, when he turned a urinal upside down and called it "Fountain." He was only interested in the object's aesthetic value. And just as simply as that: art.

This may seem arbitrary, but to the creator, there is a difference. If you build something for a specific purpose, you measure success by how well your creation serves that function. If you make pure art, your accomplishment is exclusively determined by how the creation makes you feel. Artists say that they follow their hearts, their muses, or God, depending on their beliefs. A craftsperson also follows a creative spirit, but his or her desire for artistic fulfillment is secondary to the obligation to make something that is functional.

Many objects involve both kinds of creativity. For example, a big-budget filmmaker follows his or her muse but generally acquiesces to studio demands to try to make the movie profitable. (For instance, the movie might be trimmed to ninety minutes.) Unless the director has full creative control, the primary function of the film is to get people to buy tickets. There's nothing wrong with making money from your art, but purists say that financial concerns should never influence the true artist.

By a purist's definition, a book illustration isn't art, since its function is to support the text and please the client—even if the text is a work of art. The counter view is that the illustration is art, since the illustrator follows his or her creative instincts to create it; the illustrator is as much an artistic collaborator as the writer.

Obviously, it gets pretty murky. But until someone invents a handheld art detector, the question of what makes something art will continue to spark spirited arguments in coffee shops the world over.

# THE MYSTERIOUS VOYNICH MANUSCRIPT

Dubbed the "World's Most Mysterious Book," the Voynich manuscript contains more than 200 vellum pages of vivid, colorful illustrations and handwritten prose. There's only one small problem: No one knows what any of it means. Or whether it means anything at all.

It was "discovered" in 1912 after being hidden from the world for almost 250 years. An American antique book dealer named Wilfried Voynich came across the medieval manuscript at an Italian Jesuit College. Approximately nine inches by six inches in size, the manuscript bore a light-brown vellum cover, which was unmarked, untitled, and gave no indication as to when it had been written or by whom. Bound inside were approximately 230 yellow parchment pages, most of which contained richly colored drawings of strange plants, celestial bodies, and other scientific matter. Many of the pages were adorned by naked nymphs bathing in odd-looking plumbing and personal-size washtubs. Handwritten text written in flowing script accompanied the illustrations.

Although Voynich was an expert antiquarian, he was baffled by the book's contents. And today—nearly a century later—the manuscript that came to bear his name remains a mystery.

## Weird Science

The mystery surrounding the Voynich manuscript begins with its content, which reads (so to speak) like a work of weird science presented in six identifiable "sections":

• a botanical section, containing drawings of plants that no botanist has ever been able to identify

• an astronomical section, with illustrations of the sun, moon, stars, and zodiac symbols surrounded by nymphs bathing in individual washtubs

• a "biological" section, showing perplexing anatomical drawings of chambers or organs connected by tubes— and which also features more nymphs swimming in their inner liquids

• a cosmological section, consisting mostly of unexplained circular drawings

• a pharmaceutical section, depicting drawings of plant parts (leaves, roots) placed next to containers

• a recipe section, featuring short paragraphs "bulleted" by stars in the margin

Weirder still are the ubiquitous nymphs—a nice touch perhaps, but how they relate to the subject is anyone's guess.

## Many Mysteries, Still No Answers

And then there's the manuscript's enigmatic text. The world's greatest cryptologists have failed to unravel its meaning. Even the American and British code breakers who cracked the Japanese and German codes in World War II were stumped. To this day, the Voynich manuscript has not been deciphered.

This, of course, has led to key unsolved questions, namely:

• Who wrote it? A letter found with the manuscript, dated 1666, credits Roger Bacon, a Franciscan friar who lived from 1214 to 1294. This has since been discredited because the manuscript's date of origin is generally considered to be between 1450 and 1500. There are as many theories about who wrote it as there are nymphs among its pages. In fact, some believe Voynich forged the whole thing.

• What is it? It was first thought to be a coded description of Bacon's early scientific discoveries. Since then, other theories ranging from an ancient prayer book written in a pidgin Germanic language to one big, elaborate hoax (aside from that supposedly perpetrated by Voynich) have been posited.

• Is it real writing? Is the script composed in a variation of a known language, a lost language, an encrypted language, an artificial language? Or is it just plain gibberish?

## What Do We Know?

Despite the aura of mystery surrounding the manuscript, it has been possible to trace its travels over the past 400 years. The earliest known owner was Holy Roman Emperor Rudolph II, who purchased it in 1586. By 1666, the manuscript had passed through a series of owners to Athanasius Kircher, a Jesuit scholar who hid it in the college where Voynich found it 250 years later.

After being passed down to various members of Voynich's estate, the manuscript was sold in 1961 to a rare-book collector who sought to resell it for a fortune. After failing to find a buyer, he donated it to Yale University, where it currently resides—still shrouded in mystery—in the Beinecke Rare Book and Manuscript Library.

## The Search for Meaning Continues

To this day, efforts to translate the Voynich manuscript continue. And still, the manuscript refuses to yield its secrets, leading experts to conclude that it's either an ingenious hoax or the ultimate unbreakable code. The hoax theory gained some ground in 2004 when Dr. Gordon Rugg, a computer science lecturer at Keele University, announced that he had replicated the Voynich manuscript using a low-tech device called a Cardan grille. According to Rugg, this proved that the manuscript was likely a fraud—a volume of gibberish created, perhaps, in an attempt to con money out of Emperor Rudolph II. Mystery solved? Well, it's not quite as simple as that. Many researchers remain unconvinced. Sure, Rugg may have proven that the manuscript might be a hoax. But the possibility that it is not a hoax remains. And thus, the search for meaning continues.

# A DISCOVERY OF BIBLICAL PROPORTIONS

While rounding up a stray animal near Qumran, Israel, in early 1947, Bedouin shepherd Mohammed el-Hamed stumbled across several pottery jars containing scrolls written in Hebrew. It turned out to be the find of a lifetime.

News of the exciting discovery of ancient artifacts spurred archaeologists to scour the area of the original find for additional material. Over a period of nine years, the remains of approximately 900 documents were recovered from 11 caves near the ruins of Qumran, a plateau community on the northwest shore of the Dead Sea. The documents have come to be known as the Dead Sea Scrolls.

Tests indicate that all but one of the documents were created between the second century BC and the first century AD. Nearly all were written in one of three Hebrew dialects. Most were written on animal hide. The scrolls represent the earliest surviving copies of Biblical documents. Approximately 30 percent of the material is from the Hebrew Bible. Every book of the Old Testament is represented with the exception of the Book of Esther and the Book of Nehemiah. Another 30 percent of the scrolls contain essays on subjects including blessings, war, community rule, and the membership requirements of a Jewish sect. About 25 percent of the material refers to Israelite religious texts not contained in the Hebrew Bible.

Since their discovery, debate about the meaning of the scrolls has been intense. One widely held theory subscribes to the belief that the scrolls were created at the village of Qumran and then hidden by the inhabitants. According to this theory, a Jewish sect known as the Essenes wrote the scrolls. Those subscribing to this theory have concluded that the Essenes hid the scrolls in nearby caves during the Jewish Revolt in AD 66, shortly before they were massacred by Roman troops.

A second major theory, put forward by Norman Golb, Professor of Jewish History at the University of Chicago, speculates that the scrolls were originally housed in various Jerusalem-area libraries and were spirited out of the city when the Romans besieged the capital in AD 68–70. Golb believes that the treasures documented on the so-called Copper Scroll could only have been held in Jerusalem. Golb also alleges that the variety of conflicting ideas found in the scrolls indicates that the documents are facsimiles of literary texts.

The documents were catalogued according to which cave they were found in and have been categorized into Biblical and non-Biblical works. Of the 11 caves, numbers 1 and 11 yielded the most intact documents, while number 4 held the most material—an astounding 15,000 fragments representing 40 percent of the total material found. Multiple copies of the Hebrew Bible have been identified, including 19 copies of the Book of Isaiah, 30 copies of Psalms, and 25 copies of Deuteronomy. Also found were previously unknown psalms attributed to King David, and even some stories about Abraham and Noah.

Most of the fragments appeared in print between 1950 and 1965, with the exception of the material from Cave 4. Publication of the manuscripts was entrusted to an international group led by Father Roland de Vaux of the Dominican Order in Jerusalem.

Access to the material was governed by a "secrecy rule"—only members of the international team were allowed to see them. In late 1971, 17 documents were published, followed by the release of a complete set of images of all the Cave 4 material. The secrecy rule was eventually lifted, and copies of all documents were in print by 1995.

Many of the documents are now housed in the Shrine of the Book, a wing of the Israel Museum located in Western Jerusalem. The scrolls on display are rotated every three to six months.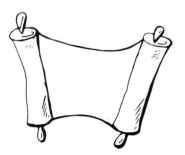

Art Happenings

# Chapter 5
# ODD ENCOUNTERS

## POPPING HIS TOP:
## THE SEAFORD POLTERGEIST

Poltergeists are the publicity hounds of the spirit world. While other ghosts are content to appear in the shadows and then vanish so that nobody's ever exactly sure what they saw, poltergeist activities are always very flashy and conspicuous. Need furniture rearranged or doors opened or slammed shut? How about knickknacks moved around or plates smashed? If so, just call your neighborhood poltergeist; they love to perform such mischief. Poltergeists don't care—they aren't part of the ghostly union. They just enjoy annoying (and scaring) the living.

### Pop! Pop! Pop!

The science of investigating poltergeist activity has come a long way since the days when people blamed it all on witchcraft. One of the cases that got folks thinking that there might be more to it was the story of the Seaford Poltergeist.

This entity first made itself known to the Herrmann family of Seaford, Long Island, in early February 1958. Mrs. Herrmann had just welcomed her children Lucille and Jimmy home from school when several bottles in various rooms of the house all popped their tops and spewed their contents all over. The family considered various explanations, such as excess humidity or pressure building up in the bottles, but the tops were all of the twist-off variety. Short of a miniature tornado yanking the tops off, there seemed to be no rational explanation.

After the same thing happened several more times, Mr. Herrmann began to suspect that his son Jimmy—who had an interest in science—was somehow pulling a fast one on the family. However, after carefully watching the child while the incident happened, Herrmann knew that unless his son was a future Einstein, there was no way that the boy could be responsible. With no "ghost busters" to consult, Mr. Herrmann did the next best thing he could in 1958: He called the police.

Dubious at first, they launched an investigation after witnessing some of the episodes firsthand. But answers were not forthcoming, and the incidents kept occurring. Even having a priest bless the house and sprinkle holy water in each of its rooms didn't help. An exorcism was considered but rejected because the incidents didn't resemble the work of a demon. Rather, they seemed to be the antics of a poltergeist (a noisy spirit).

## Explanation Unknown

Word of the events attracted the attention of the media as well as curiosity seekers. All explanations—from the scientifically sound (sonic booms, strong drafts, freakish magnetic waves) to the weird and wacky (Soviet satellite Sputnik)—were considered and dismissed. Although this was the Cold War era, it was unclear how tormenting a single American family fit into the Soviets' dastardly scheme of world domination.

What was far more worrisome was that the incidents seemed to be escalating in violence. Instead of just bottles popping open, objects such as a sugar bowl, a record player, and a heavy bookcase were tossed around. Fortunately, help soon arrived in the form of experts from Duke University's Parapsychology Laboratory. Their theory was that someone in the house was unwittingly moving objects via Recurrent Spontaneous Psychokinesis (RSPK). Children seemed to attract such activity, and the Duke team discovered that Jimmy had been at or near the scene of the incidents most of the time.

When one of the researchers spent time with the boy—playing cards, helping him with his homework, or just talking—the unusual activity declined. Two more incidents occurred in early March before the Seaford Poltergeist apparently packed its bags and moved on. After 67 recorded incidents in five weeks, the lives of the Herrmann family returned to normal. To this day, it is still unknown exactly what caused the strange events in the Herrmann household in early 1958.

# THE NAZCA LINES—PICTURES AIMED AT AN EYE IN THE SKY?

Ancient works of art etched into a desert floor in South America have inspired wild theories about who created them and why. Did space aliens leave them on long-ago visits? Decades of scientific research reject the popular notion, showing that the lines were the work of mere Earthlings.

Flying above the rocky plains northwest of Nazca, Peru, in 1927, aviator Toribio Mejía Xesspe was surprised to see gigantic eyes looking up at him. Then the pilot noticed that the orbs stared out of a bulbous head upon a cartoonish line drawing of a man, etched over hundreds of square feet of the landscape below.

The huge drawing—later called "owl man" for its staring eyes—turned out to be just one of scores of huge, 2,000-year-old images scratched into the earth over almost 200 square miles of the parched Peruvian landscape.

There is a 360-foot-long monkey with a whimsically spiraled tail, along with a 150-foot-long spider, and a 935-foot pelican. Other figures range from hummingbird to killer whale. Unless the viewer knows what to look for, they're almost invisible from ground level. There are also geometric shapes and straight lines that stretch for miles across the stony ground.

## The Theory of Ancient Astronauts

The drawings have been dated to a time between 200 BC and AD 600. Obviously, there were no airplanes from which to view them then. So why were they made? For whose benefit?

In his 1968 book *Chariots of the Gods?*, Swiss author Erich Von Däniken popularized the idea that the drawings and lines were landing signals and runways for starships that visited southern Peru long before our era. In his interpretation, the owl man is instead an astronaut in a helmet. Von Däniken's theory caught on among UFO enthusiasts. Many science fiction novels and films refer to this desert in Peru's Pampa Colorado region as a site with special significance to space travelers.

## Coming Down to Earth

Examined up close, the drawings consist of cleared paths—areas where someone removed reddish surface rocks to expose the soft soil beneath. In the stable desert climate—averaging less than an inch of rain per year—the paths have survived through many centuries largely intact.

Scientists believe the Nazca culture—a civilization that came before the Incas—drew the lines. The style of the artwork is similar to that featured on Nazca pottery. German-born researcher Maria Reiche (1903–1998) showed how the Nazca could have laid out the figures using simple surveying tools such as ropes and posts. In the 1980s, American researcher Joe Nickell duplicated one of the drawings, a condor, showing that the Nazca could have rendered parts of the figures "freehand"—that is, without special tools or even scale models. Nickell also demonstrated that despite their great size, the figures can be identified as drawings even from ground level. No alien technology would have been required to make them.

## Still Mysterious

As for why the Nazca doodled in the desert, no one is sure. Reiche noted that some of the lines have astronomical relevance. For example, one points to where the sun sets at the winter solstice. Some lines may also have pointed toward underground water sources.

Most scholars think that the marks were part of the Nazca religion. They may have been footpaths followed during ritual processions. And although it's extremely unlikely that they were intended for extraterrestrials, many experts think it likely that the lines were oriented toward Nazca gods—perhaps a monkey god, a spider god, and so on, who could be imagined gazing down from the heavens upon likenesses of themselves.

# IT'S A BIRD! IT'S A PLANE! IT'S ... AVROCAR?!?

Not all UFOs are alien spaceships. One top-secret program was contracted out by the U.S. military to an aircraft company in Canada.

Oh, the 1950s—a time of sock hops, drive-in movies, and the Cold War between America and the Soviet Union, when each superpower waged war against the other in the arenas of scientific technology, astronomy, and politics. It was also a time when discussion of life on other planets was rampant, fueled by the alleged crash of an alien spaceship near Roswell, New Mexico, in 1947.

## Watch the Skies

Speculation abounded about the unidentified flying objects (UFOs) spotted nearly every week by everyone from farmers to airplane pilots. As time passed, government authorities began to wonder if the flying saucers were, in fact, part of a secret Russian program to create a new type of air force. Fearful that such a craft would upset the existing balance of power, the U.S. Air Force decided to produce its own saucer-shape ship.

In 1953, the military contacted Avro Aircraft Limited of Canada, an aircraft manufacturing company that operated in Malton, Ontario, between 1945 and 1962. Project Silverbug was initially proposed simply because the government wanted to find out if UFOs could be manufactured by humans. But before long, both the military and the scientific community were speculating about its potential. Intrigued by the idea, designers at Avro—led by British aeronautical engineer John Frost—began working on the VZ-9-AV Avrocar. The round craft would have been right at home in a scene from the classic science fiction film *The Day the Earth Stood Still*. Security for the project was so tight that it probably generated rumors that America was actually testing a captured alien spacecraft—speculation that remains alive and well even today.

## Of This Earth

By 1958, the company had produced two prototypes, which were 18 feet in diameter and 3.5 feet tall. Constructed around a large triangle, the Avrocar was shaped like a disk, with a curved upper surface. It included an enclosed 124-blade turbo-rotor at the center of the triangle, which provided lifting power through an opening in the bottom of the craft. The turbo also powered the craft's controls. Although conceived as being able to carry two passengers, in reality a single pilot could barely fit inside the cramped space. The Avrocar was operated with a single control stick, which activated different panels around the ship. Airflow issued from a large center ring, which was controlled by the pilot to guide the craft either vertically or horizontally.

The military envisioned using the craft as "flying Jeeps" that would hover close to the ground and move at a maximum speed of 40 miles per hour. But that, apparently, was only going to be the beginning of the hovering age. Avro had its own grand plans, which included not just commercial Avrocars, but also a family-size Avrowagon, an Avrotruck for larger loads, Avroangel to rush people to the hospital, and a military Avropelican, which, like a pelican hunting for fish, would conduct surveillance for submarines.

## But Does It Fly?

The prototypes impressed the U.S. Army enough to award Avro a $2 million contract. Unfortunately, the Avrocar project was canceled when an economic downturn forced the company to temporarily close and restructure. When Avro Aircraft reopened, the original team of designers had dispersed. Further efforts to revive the project were unsuccessful, and repeated testing proved that the craft was inherently unstable.

It soon became apparent that whatever UFOs were spotted overhead, it was unlikely they came from this planet. Project Silverbug was abandoned when funding ran out in March 1961, but one of the two Avrocar prototypes is housed at the U.S. Army Transportation Museum in Fort Eustis, Virginia.

# Fireball in the Sky

While playing football on the afternoon of September 12, 1952, a group of boys in Flatwoods, West Virginia, saw a large fireball fly over their heads. The object seemed to stop near the hillside property of Bailey Fisher. Some thought the object was a UFO, but others said it was just a meteor. They decided to investigate.

Darkness was falling as the boys made their way toward the hill, so they stopped at the home of Kathleen May to borrow a flashlight. Seeing how excited the boys were, May, her two sons, and their friend, Eugene Lemon, decided to join them. The group set off to find out exactly what had landed on the hill.

## Walking into Darkness

As they neared the top of the hill, the group smelled a strange odor that reminded them of burning metal. Continuing on, some members of the group thought they saw an object that resembled a spaceship. Shining their flashlights in front of them, the group was startled when something not of this world moved out from behind a nearby tree.

## The Encounter

The description of what is now known as the Flatwoods Monster is almost beyond belief. It stood around 12 feet tall and had a round, reddish face from which two large holes were visible. Looming up from behind the creature's head was a large pointed hood. The creature, which appeared to be made of a dark metal, had no arms or legs and seemed to float through the air. Looking back, the witnesses believe what they saw was a protective suit or perhaps a robot rather than a monster.

**129**

When a flashlight beam hit the creature, its "eyes" lit up and it began floating toward the group while making a strange hissing noise. The horrible stench was now overpowering and some in the group immediately felt nauseous. Because she was at the head of the group, Kathleen May had the best view of the monster. She later stated that as the creature was moving toward her, it squirted or dripped a strange fluid on her that resembled oil but had an unusual odor to it.

Terrified beyond belief, the group fled down the hillside and back to the May house, where they telephoned Sheriff Robert Carr, who responded with his deputy, Burnell Long. After talking with the group, they gathered some men and went to the Fisher property to investigate. But they only found a gummy residue and what appeared to be skid marks on the ground. There was no monster and no spaceship. However, the group did report that the heavy stench of what smelled like burning metal was still in the air.

## The Aftermath

A. Lee Stewart, a member of the search party and also co-publisher of the *Braxton Democrat*, knew a good story when he saw one, so he sent the tale over the news wire, and almost immediately, people were asking Kathleen May for interviews. On September 19, 1952, May and Stewart discussed the Flatwoods Monster on national TV. For the show, an artist made a sketch of the creature based on May's description, but he took some liberties, and the resulting sketch was so outrageous that people started saying the whole thing was a hoax.

Slowly, though, others came forward to admit that they too had seen a strange craft flying through the sky near Flatwoods on September 12. One witness described it as roughly the size of a single-car garage. He said that he lost sight of the craft when it appeared to land on a nearby hill.

Since that night in 1952, the Flatwoods Monster has never been seen again, leaving many people to wonder what exactly those people encountered. A monster? An alien from another world? Or perhaps nothing more than a giant owl? There were far too many witnesses to deny that they stumbled upon something strange that night.

# UNIDENTIFIED SUBMERGED OBJECTS

Much like their flying brethren, unidentified submerged objects captivate and mystify. But instead of vanishing into the skies, USOs, such as the following, plunge underwater.

## Sighting at Puerto Rico Trench

In 1963, while conducting exercises off the coast of Puerto Rico, U.S. Navy submarines encountered something extraordinary. The incident began when a sonar operator aboard an accompanying destroyer reported a strange occurrence. According to the seaman, one of the subs traveling with the armada broke free from the pack to chase a USO. This quarry would be unlike anything the submariners had ever pursued.

Underwater technology in the early 1960s was advancing rapidly. Still, vessels had their limitations. The U.S.S. *Nautilus*, though faster than any submarine that preceded it, was still limited to about 20 knots (23 miles per hour). The bathyscaphe *Trieste*, a deep-sea submersible, could exceed 30,000 feet in depth, but the descent took as long as five hours. Once there, the vessel could not be maneuvered side to side.

Knowing this, the submariners were stunned by what they witnessed. The USO was moving at 150 knots (170 miles per hour) and hitting depths greater than 20,000 feet!

No underwater vehicles on Earth were capable of such fantastic numbers. Even today, modern nuclear subs have top speeds of about 25 knots (29 miles per hour) and can operate at around 800-plus feet below the surface.

Thirteen separate crafts witnessed the USO as it criss-crossed the Atlantic Ocean over a four-day period. At its deepest, the mystery vehicle reached 27,000 feet. To this day, there's been no earthly explanation offered for the occurrence.

## USO with a Bus Pass

In 1964, London bus driver Bob Fall witnessed one of the strangest USO sightings. While transporting a full contingent of passengers, the driver and his fares reported seeing a silver, cigar-shape object dive into the nearby waters of the River Lea. The police attributed the phenomenon to a flight of ducks, despite the obvious incongruence. Severed telephone lines and a large gouge on the river's embankment suggested something far different.

## Shag Harbour Incident

The fishing village of Shag Harbour lies on Canada's East Coast. This unassuming hamlet is to USOs what Roswell, New Mexico, is to UFOs. Simply put, it played host to the most famous occurrence of a USO ever recorded.

On the evening of October 4, 1967, the Royal Canadian Mounted Police (RCMP) were barraged by reports of a UFO that had crashed into the bay at Shag Harbour. Laurie Wickens and four friends witnessed a large object (approximately 60 feet in diameter) falling into the water just after 11:00 p.m. Floating approximately 1,000 feet off the coast they could clearly detect a yellow light on top of the object.

The RCMP promptly contacted the Rescue Coordination Center in Halifax to ask if any aircraft were missing.

None were. Shortly thereafter, the object sank into the depths of the water and disappeared from view.

When local fishing boats went to the USO crash site, they encountered yellow foam on the water's surface and detected an odd sulfuric smell. No survivors or bodies were ever found. The Royal Canadian Air Force officially labeled the occurrence a UFO, but because the object was last seen under water, such events are now described as USOs.

## Pascagoula Incident

On November 6, 1973, at approximately 8:00 p.m., a USO was sighted by at least nine fishermen anchored off the coast of Pascagoula, Mississippi. The fishermen witnessed an underwater object an estimated five feet in diameter that emitted a strange amber light.

First to spot the USO was Rayme Ryan. He repeatedly poked at the light-emitting object with an oar. Each time he contacted the strange object, its light would dim and it would move a few feet away, then brighten once again.

Fascinated by the ethereal quality of this submerged question mark, Ryan summoned the others. For the next half hour, the cat-and-mouse game played out in front of the fishermen until Ryan struck the object with a particularly forceful blow. With this action, the USO disappeared from view.

The anglers moved about a half mile away and continued fishing. After about 30 minutes, they returned to their earlier location and were astounded to find that the USO had returned. At this point, they decided to alert the Coast Guard.

After interviewing the witnesses, investigators from the Naval Ship Research and Development Laboratory in Panama City, Florida, submitted their findings: At least nine persons had witnessed an undetermined light source whose characteristics

Odd Encounters

and actions were inconsistent with those of known marine organisms or with an uncontrolled human-made object. Their final report was inconclusive, stating that the object could not be positively identified.

## THE CHAMPION OF AMERICAN LAKE MONSTERS

In 1609, French explorer Samuel de Champlain was astonished to see a thick, eight- to 10-foot-tall creature in the waters between present-day Vermont and New York. His subsequent report set in motion the legend of Champ, the "monster" in Lake Champlain.

### Eerie Encounters

Even before Champlain's visit, Champ was known to Native Americans as Chaousarou. Over time, Champ has become one of North America's most famous lake monsters. News stories of its existence were frequent enough that in 1873, showman P. T. Barnum offered $50,000 for the creature, dead or alive. That same year, Champ almost sank a steamboat, and in the 1880s, a number of people, including a sober sheriff, were treated to glimpses of it splashing playfully off shore. It is generally described as dark in color (olive green, gray, or brown) with a serpentlike body.

Sightings have continued into modern times, and witnesses have compiled some film evidence that is difficult to ignore. In 1977, a woman named Sandra Mansi photographed a long-necked creature poking its head out of the water near

St. Albans, Vermont, close to the Canadian border. She estimated the animal was 10 to 15 feet long and told an investigator that its skin looked "slimy" and similar to that of an eel. Mansi presented her photo and story at a 1981 conference held at Lake Champlain. Although she had misplaced the negative by then, subsequent analyses of the photo have generally failed to find any evidence that it was manipulated.

In September 2002, a researcher named Dennis Hall, who headed a lake monster investigation group known as Champ Quest, videotaped what looked like three creatures undulating through the water near Ferrisburgh, Vermont. Hall claimed that he saw unidentifiable animals in Lake Champlain on 19 separate occasions.

In 2006, two fishermen captured digital video footage of what appeared to be parts of a very large animal swimming in the lake. The images were thoroughly examined under the direction of ABC News technicians, and though the creature on the video could not be proved to be Champ, the team could find nothing to disprove it, either.

## Champ or Chump?

As the sixth-largest freshwater lake in the United States (and stretching about six miles into Quebec, Canada), Lake Champlain provides ample habitat and nourishment for a good-size water cryptid, or unknown animal. The lake plunges as deep as 400 feet in spots and covers 490 square miles.

Skeptics offer the usual explanations for Champ sightings: large sturgeons, floating logs or water plants, otters, or an optical illusion caused by sunlight and shadow. Others think Champ could be a remnant of a species of primitive whale called a zeuglodon or an ancient marine reptile known as a plesiosaur, both believed by biologists to be long extinct. But until uncontestable images of the creature's entire body are produced, this argument will undoubtedly continue.

Champ does claim one rare, official nod to the probability of its existence: Legislation by both the states of New York and Vermont proclaim that Champ is a protected—though unknown—species and make it illegal to harm the creature in any way.

# THE KECKSBURG INCIDENT

Did visitors from outer space once land in a western Pennsylvania thicket?

## Dropping in for a Visit

On December 9, 1965, an unidentified flying object streaked through the late-afternoon sky and landed in Kecksburg—a rural Pennsylvania community about 40 miles southeast of Pittsburgh. This much is not disputed. However, specific accounts vary widely from person to person. Even after closely examining the facts, many people remain undecided about exactly what happened. "Roswell"-type incidents—ultra-mysterious in nature and reeking of a governmental cover-up—have an uncanny way of causing confusion.

## Trajectory-Interruptus

A meteor on a collision course with Earth will generally "bounce" as it enters the atmosphere. This occurs due to friction, which forcefully slows the average space rock from 6 to 45 miles per second to a few hundred miles per hour, the speed at which it strikes Earth and officially becomes a meteorite. According to the official explanation offered by the U.S. Air Force, it was a meteorite that landed in Kecksburg. However, witnesses reported that the object completed back and forth maneuvers before landing at a very low speed—moves that an unpowered chunk of earthbound rock simply cannot perform. Strike one against the meteor theory.

## An Acorn-Shape Meteorite?

When a meteor manages to pierce Earth's atmosphere, it has the physical properties of exactly what it is: a space rock. That is to say, it will generally be unevenly shaped, rough, and darkish in color, much like rocks found on Earth. But at Kecksburg, eyewitnesses reported seeing something far, far different. The unusual object they described was bronze to golden in color, acorn-shape, and as large as a Volkswagen Beetle automobile. Unless the universe has started to produce uniformly shaped and colored meteorites, the official explanation seems highly unlikely. Strike two for the meteor theory.

## Markedly Different

Then there's the baffling issue of markings. A meteorite can be chock-full of holes, cracks, and other such surface imperfections. It can also vary somewhat in color. But it should never, ever have markings that seem intelligently designed. Witnesses at Kecksburg describe intricate writings similar to Egyptian hieroglyphics located near the base of the object. A cursory examination of space rocks at any natural history museum reveals that such a thing doesn't occur naturally. Strike three for the meteor theory. Logically following such a trail, could an unnatural force have been responsible for the item witnessed at Kecksburg? At least one man thought so.

## Rigor Mortis

Just after the Kecksburg UFO landed, reporter John Murphy arrived at the scene. Like any seasoned pro, the newsman immediately snapped photos and gathered eyewitness accounts of the event. Strangely, FBI agents arrived, cordoned off the area, and confiscated all but one roll of his film. Undaunted, Murphy assembled a radio documentary entitled *Object in the Woods* to describe his experience. Just before the special was to air, the reporter received an unexpected visit by two men. According to a fellow employee, a dark-suited pair identified themselves as government agents and subsequently confiscated a portion of Murphy's audiotapes. A week later, a clearly perturbed Murphy aired a watered-down version of his documentary. In it, he claimed that certain interviewees requested their accounts be removed for fear of retribution at the hands of police, military, and government officials. In 1969, John Murphy was struck dead by an unidentified car while crossing the street.

## Resurrected by Robert Stack

In all likelihood the Kecksburg incident would have remained dormant and under-explored had it not been for the television show *Unsolved Mysteries*. In a 1990 segment, narrator Robert Stack took an in-depth look at what occurred in Kecksburg, feeding a firestorm of interest that eventually brought forth two new witnesses. The first, a U.S. Air Force officer stationed at Lockbourne AFB (near Columbus, Ohio), claimed to have seen a flatbed truck carrying a mysterious object as it arrived on base on December 10, 1965. The military man told of a tarpaulin-covered conical object that he couldn't identify and a "shoot to kill" order given to him for anyone who ventured too close. He was told that the truck was bound for Wright–Patterson AFB in Dayton, Ohio, an installation that's alleged to contain downed flying saucers. The other witness was a building contractor who claimed to have delivered 6,500 special bricks to a hanger inside Wright–Patterson AFB on December 12, 1965. Curious, he peeked inside the hanger and saw a "bell-shaped" device, 12-feet high, surrounded by several men wearing anti-radiation style suits. Upon leaving, he was told that he had just witnessed an object that would become "common knowledge" in the next 20 years.

## Will We Ever Know the Truth?

Like Roswell before it, we will probably never know what occurred in western Pennsylvania back in 1965. The more that's learned about the case, the more confusing it becomes. For instance, the official 1965 meteorite explanation contains more holes than Bonnie and Clyde's death car, and other explanations, such as orbiting space debris (from past U.S. and Russian missions) reentering Earth's atmosphere, seem equally preposterous. In 2005, as the result of a new investigation launched by the Sci-Fi Television Network, NASA asserted that the object was a Russian satellite. According to a NASA spokesperson, documents of this investigation were somehow misplaced in the 1990s. Mysteriously, this finding directly contradicts the official Air Force version that nothing at all was found at the Kecksburg site. It also runs counter to a 2003 report made by NASA's own Nicholas L. Johnson, Chief Scientist for Orbital Debris. That document shows no missing satellites at the time of the incident. This includes a missing Russian Venus probe (since accounted for)—the very item that was once considered a prime crash candidate.

## Brave New World

These days, visitors to Kecksburg will be hard-pressed to find any trace of the encounter—perhaps that's how it should be. Since speculation comes to an abrupt halt whenever a concrete answer is provided, Kecksburg's reputation as "Roswell of the East" looks secure, at least for the foreseeable future. But if one longs for proof that something mysterious occurred there, they need look no further than the backyard of the Kecksburg Volunteer Fire Department. There, in all of its acorn-shape glory, stands a full-scale mock-up of the spacecraft reportedly found in this peaceful town on December 9, 1965. There too rests the mystery, intrigue, and romance that have accompanied this alleged space traveler for more than 40 years.

# Alleged Celebrity UFO Sightings

It's not just moonshine-swilling farmers in rural areas who claim to have seen UFOs hovering in the night sky. Plenty of celebrities have also reportedly witnessed unidentified flying objects and have been happy to talk about their experiences afterward.

## Jimmy Carter

Not even presidents are immune from UFO sightings. During Jimmy Carter's presidential campaign of 1976, he told reporters that in 1969, before he was governor of Georgia, he saw what could have been a UFO. "It was the darndest thing I've ever seen," he said of the incident. He claimed that the object that he and a group of others had watched for ten minutes was as bright as the moon. Carter was often referred to as "the UFO president" after being elected because he filed a report on the matter.

## David Duchovny

In 1982, long before he starred as a believer in the supernatural on the hit sci-fi series *The X-Files*, David Duchovny thought he saw a UFO. Although, by his own admission, he's reluctant to say with any certainty that it wasn't something he simply imagined as a result of stress and overwork. "There was something in the air and it was gone," he later told reporters. "I thought: 'You've got to get some rest, David.'"

## Ronald Reagan

Former actor and U.S. president Ronald Reagan witnessed UFOs on two occasions. Once during his term as California governor (1967–1975), Reagan and his wife Nancy arrived late to a party hosted by actor William Holden. Guests including Steve Allen and Lucille Ball reported that the couple excitedly described how they had just witnessed a UFO while driving along the Pacific Coast Highway. They had stopped to watch the event, which made them late to the party.

Reagan also confessed to a *Wall Street Journal* reporter that in 1974, when the gubernatorial jet was preparing to land in Bakersfield, California, he noticed a strange bright light in the sky. The pilot followed the light for a short time before it suddenly shot up vertically at a high rate of speed and disappeared from sight. Reagan stopped short of labeling the light a UFO, of course. As actress Lucille Ball said in reference to Reagan's first alleged UFO sighting, "After he was elected president, I kept thinking about that event and wondered if he still would have won if he told everyone that he saw a flying saucer."

## William Shatner

For decades, the man who played Captain Kirk in the original *Star Trek* series claimed that an alien saved his life. When the actor and a group of friends were riding their motorbikes through the desert in the late 1960s, Shatner was inadvertently left behind when his bike wouldn't restart after driving into a giant pothole. Shatner said that he spotted an alien in a silver suit standing on a ridge and that it led him to a gas station and safety. Shatner later stated in his autobiography, *Up Till Now*, that he made up the part about the alien during a television interview.

# Ohio's Mysterious Hangar 18

An otherworldly legend makes its way from New Mexico to Ohio when the wreckage from Roswell ends up in the Midwest.

Even those who aren't UFO buffs have overheard a little about the infamous Roswell Incident. But what most people don't know is that according to legend, the mysterious aircraft was recovered (along with some alien bodies), secreted out of the area, and came to rest just outside of Dayton, Ohio.

## Something Crashed in the Desert

While the exact date is unclear, sometime during the first week of July 1947, Mac Brazel decided to go out and check his property for fallen trees and other damage after a night of heavy storms and lightning. Brazel came across an area of his property littered with strange debris unlike anything he had ever seen before—some of the debris even had strange writing on it.

Brazel showed some of the debris to a few neighbors and then took it to the office of Roswell sheriff George Wilcox, who called authorities at Roswell Army Air Field. After speaking with Wilcox, intelligence officer Major Jesse Marcel drove out to the Brazel ranch and collected as much debris as he could. He then returned to the airfield and showed the debris to his commanding officer, Colonel William Blanchard, commander of the 509th Bomb Group that was stationed at the Roswell Air Field. Upon seeing the debris, Blanchard dispatched military vehicles and personnel back out to the Brazel ranch to see if they could recover anything else.

## "Flying Saucer Captured!"

On July 8, 1947, Colonel Blanchard issued a press release stating that the wreckage of a "crashed disk" had been recovered. The bold headline of the July 8 edition of the *Roswell Daily Record* read: "RAAF Captures Flying Saucer on Ranch in Roswell Region." Newspapers around the world ran similar headlines. But then, within hours of the Blanchard release, General Roger M. Ramey, commander of the Eighth Air Force in Fort Worth, Texas, retracted Blanchard's release for him and issued another statement saying there was no UFO. Blanchard's men had simply recovered a fallen weather balloon.

Before long, the headlines that had earlier touted the capture of a UFO read: "It's a Weather Balloon" and " 'Flying Disc' Turns Up as Just Hot Air." Later editions even ran a staged photograph of Major Jesse Marcel, who was first sent to investigate the incident, kneeling in front of weather balloon debris. Most of the general public seemed content with the explanation, but there were skeptics.

## Whisked Away to Hangar 18?

Those who believe that aliens crash-landed near Roswell claim that, under cover of darkness, large portions of the alien spacecraft were brought out to the Roswell Air Field and loaded onto B-29 and C-54 aircrafts. Those planes were then supposedly flown to Wright-Patterson Air Force Base, just outside of Dayton. Once the planes landed, they were taxied over to Hangar 18 and unloaded. According to legend, it's all still there.

There are some problems with the story, though. For one, none of the hangars on Wright-Patterson Air Force Base are officially known as "Hangar 18." There are no buildings designated with the number 18 either. Rather, the hangars are labeled 1A, 1B, 1C, and so on. And there's also the fact that none of the hangars seem large enough to house and conceal an alien spacecraft. But just because there's nothing listed as Hangar 18 on a Wright-Patterson map doesn't mean it's not there. Conspiracy theorists believe that hangars 4A, 4B, and 4C might be the infamous Hangar 18. As for the overall size of the hangars, it's believed that most of the wreckage has been stored down in giant underground

Odd Encounters

tunnels and chambers deep under the hangar, both to protect the debris and to keep it safe from prying eyes. It is said that Wright-Patterson is currently conducting experiments on the wreckage to see if scientists can reverse-engineer the technology.

## What's the Deal?

The story of Hangar 18 only got stranger as the years went on, starting with the government's Project Blue Book, a program designed to investigate reported UFO sightings across the United States. Between 1947 and 1969, Project Blue Book investigated more than 12,000 UFO sightings before being disbanded. And where was Project Blue Book headquartered? Wright-Patterson Air Force Base.

Then in the early 1960s, Arizona senator Barry Goldwater, himself a retired major general in the U.S. Army Air Corps (and a friend of Colonel Blanchard), became interested in what, if anything, had crashed in Roswell. When Goldwater discovered Hangar 18, he first wrote directly to Wright-Patterson and asked for permission to tour the facility but was quickly denied. He then approached another friend, General Curtis LeMay, and asked if he could see the "Green Room" where the UFO secret was being held. Goldwater claimed that LeMay gave him "holy hell" and screamed at Goldwater, "Not only can't you get into it, but don't you ever mention it to me again."

Most recently, in 1982, retired pilot Oliver "Pappy" Henderson attended a reunion and announced that he was one of the men who had flown alien bodies out of Roswell in a C-54 cargo plane. His destination? Hangar 18 at Wright-Patterson. Although no one is closer to a definitive answer, it seems that the legend of Hangar 18 will never die.

# THE "MOON ILLUSION"

The moon looks bigger when it's near the horizon, a phenomenon that has flummoxed brilliant minds for thousands of years. Aristotle attempted an explanation around 350 BC, and today's scientists still don't know for sure what's going on.

## Here's What We Do Know

We may not know exactly why the moon looks bigger when it's near the horizon—something that's known as the "moon illusion"—but great thinkers have at least ruled out several possible explanations. Hey, that's progress.

First, the moon is not closer to Earth when it's at the horizon. In fact, it's closer when it's directly overhead.

Second, your eye does not physically detect that the moon is bigger when it's near the horizon. The moon creates a .15-millimeter image on the retina, no matter where it is. You can test this yourself: Next time you see a big moon looming low behind the trees, hold a pencil at arm's length and note the relative size of the moon and the eraser. Then wait a few hours and try it again when the moon is higher in the sky. You'll see that the moon is exactly the same size relative to the eraser. The .15-millimeter phenomenon rules out atmospheric distortion as an explanation for the moon's apparent change in size.

Third, a moon on the horizon doesn't look larger just because we're comparing it to trees, buildings, and the like. Airline pilots experience the same big-moon illusion when none of these visual cues are present. Also, consider the fact that when the moon is higher in the sky and we look at it through the same trees or with the same buildings in the foreground, it doesn't look as large as it does when it's on the horizon.

Odd Encounters

## A Matter of Perception

What's going on? Scientists quibble over the details, but the common opinion is that the "moon illusion" must be the result of the brain automatically interpreting visual information based on its own unconscious expectations. We instinctively take distance information into account when deciding how large something is. When you see faraway building, for example, you interpret it as big because you factor in the visual effect of distance.

But this phenomenon confuses us when we attempt to visually compute the size of the moon. According to the most popular theory, this is because we naturally perceive the sky as a flattened dome when, in reality, it's a spherical hemisphere. This perception might be based on our understanding that the ground is relatively flat. As a result, we compute distance differently, depending on whether something is at the horizon or directly overhead.

According to this flattened-dome theory, when the moon is near the horizon, we have a fairly accurate sense of its distance and size. But when the moon is overhead, we unconsciously make an inaccurate estimate of its distance. As a result of this error, we automatically estimate its size incorrectly.

In other words, based on a faulty understanding of the shape of the sky, the brain perceives reality incorrectly and interprets the moon as being smaller when it's overhead than when it's on the horizon. That's right—your brain is tricking you. So what are you going to believe—science or your lying eyes?

# THE GREAT TEXAS AIRSHIP MYSTERY

Roswell, New Mexico, may be the most famous potential UFO crash site, but did Texas experience a similar event in the nineteenth century?

One sunny April morning in 1897, a UFO crashed in Aurora, Texas.

Six years before the Wright Brothers' first flight and 50 years before Roswell, a huge, cigar-shape UFO was seen in the skies. It was first noted on November 17, 1896, about a thousand feet above rooftops in Sacramento, California. From there, the spaceship traveled to San Francisco, where it was seen by hundreds of people.

## A National Tour

Next, the craft crossed the United States, where it was observed by thousands. Near Omaha, Nebraska, a farmer reported the ship on the ground, making repairs. When it returned to the skies, it headed toward Chicago, where it was photographed on April 11, 1897, the first UFO photo on record. On April 15, near Kalamazoo, Michigan, residents reported loud noises "like that of heavy ordnance" coming from the spaceship.

Two days later, the UFO attempted a landing in Aurora, Texas, which should have been a good place. The town was almost deserted, and its broad, empty fields could have been an ideal landing strip.

## No Smooth Sailing

However, at about 6 a.m. on April 17, the huge, cigar-shape airship "sailed over the public square and, when it reached the north part of town, collided with the tower of Judge Proctor's windmill and went to pieces with a terrific explosion,

Odd Encounters

scattering debris over several acres of ground, wrecking the windmill and water tank and destroying the judge's flower garden."

That's how Aurora resident and cotton buyer S. E. Haydon described the events for *The Dallas Morning News*. The remains of the ship seemed to be strips and shards of a silver-colored metal. Just one body was recovered. The newspaper reported, "while his remains are badly disfigured, enough of the original has been picked up to show that he was not an inhabitant of this world."

On April 18, reportedly, that body was given a good, Christian burial in the Aurora cemetery, where it may remain to this day. A 1973 effort to exhume the body and examine it was successfully blocked by the Aurora Cemetery Association.

## A Firsthand Account

Although many people have claimed the Aurora incident was a hoax, an elderly woman was interviewed in 1973 and clearly recalled the crash from her childhood. She said that her parents wouldn't let her near the debris from the spacecraft, in case it contained something dangerous. However, she described the alien as "a small man."

Aurora continues to attract people interested in UFOs. They wonder why modern Aurora appears to be laid out like a military base. Nearby, Fort Worth seems to be home to the U.S. government's experts in alien technology. Immediately after the Roswell UFO crash in 1947, debris from that spaceship was sent to Fort Worth for analysis.

## Is There Any Trace Left?

*The Aurora Encounter*, a 1986 movie, documents the events that began when people saw the spacecraft attempt a landing at Judge Proctor's farm. Today, the Oates gas station marks the area where the UFO crashed.

Metal debris was collected from the site in the 1970s and studied by North Texas State University. That study called one fragment "most intriguing": It appeared to be iron but wasn't magnetic; it was shiny and malleable rather than brittle, as iron should be.

As recently as 2008, UFOs have appeared in the north central Texas skies. In Stephenville, a freight company owner and pilot described a low-flying object in the sky, "a mile long and half a mile wide." Others who saw the ship several times during January 2008 said that its lights changed configuration, so it wasn't an airplane. The government declined to comment.

Today, a plaque at the Aurora cemetery mentions the spaceship, but the alien's tombstone—which, if it actually existed, is said to have featured a carved image of a spaceship—was stolen many years ago.

## STRANGE LIGHTS IN MARFA

If anyone is near Marfa at night, they should watch for odd, vivid lights over nearby Mitchell Flat. Many people believe that the lights from UFOs or even alien entities can be seen. The famous Marfa Lights are about the size of basketballs and are usually white, orange, red, or yellow. These unexplained lights only appear at night and usually hover above the ground at about shoulder height. Some of the lights—alone or in pairs—drift and fly around the landscape.

From cowboys to truck drivers, people traveling in Texas near the intersection of U.S. Route 90 and U.S. Route 67 in southwest Texas have reported the lights. And these baffling lights don't just appear on the ground. Pilots and airline passengers claim to have seen the Marfa Lights from the skies. So far, no one has proved a natural explanation for the floating orbs.

## Eyewitness Information

Two 1988 reports were especially graphic. Pilot R. Weidig was about 8,000 feet above Marfa when he saw the lights and estimated them rising several hundred feet above the ground. Passenger E. Halsell described the lights as larger than the plane and noted that they were pulsating. In 2002, pilot B. Eubanks provided a similar report.

In addition to what can be seen, the Marfa Lights may also trigger low-frequency electromagnetic waves—which can be heard on special receivers—similar to the "whistlers" caused by lightning. However, unlike waves from power lines and electrical storms, the Marfa whistlers are extremely loud. They can be heard as the orbs appear, and then they fade when the lights do.

## A Little Bit about Marfa

Marfa is about 60 miles north of the Mexican border and about 190 miles southeast of El Paso. This small, friendly Texas town is 4,800 feet above sea level and covers 1.6 square miles.

In 1883, Marfa was a railroad water stop. It received its name from the wife of the president of the Texas and New Orleans Railroad, who chose the name from a Russian novel that she was reading. A strong argument can be made that this was Dostoyevsky's *The Brothers Karamazov*. The town grew slowly, reaching its peak during World War II when the U.S. government located a prisoner of war camp, the Marfa Army Airfield, and a chemical warfare brigade nearby. (Some skeptics suggest that discarded chemicals may be causing the Marfa Lights, but searchers have found no evidence of such.)

Today, Marfa is home to about 2,500 people. The small town is an emerging arts center with more than a dozen artists' studios and art galleries. However, Marfa remains most famous for its light display. The annual Marfa Lights Festival is one of the town's biggest events, but the mysterious lights attract visitors year-round. The Marfa Lights are seen almost every clear night, but they never manifest during the daytime. The lights appear between Marfa and nearby Paisano Pass, with the Chinati Mountains as a backdrop.

## Widespread Sightings

The first documented sighting was by 16-year-old cowhand Robert Reed Ellison during an 1883 cattle drive. Seeing an odd light in the area, Ellison thought he'd seen an Apache campfire. When he told his story in town, however, settlers told him that they'd seen lights in the area, too, and they'd never found evidence of campfires.

Two years later, 38-year-old Joe Humphreys and his wife, Sally, also reported lights at Marfa. In 1919, cowboys on a cattle drive paused to search the area for the origin of the lights. Like the others, they found no explanation for what they had seen.

In 1943, the Marfa Lights came to national attention when Fritz Kahl, an airman at the Marfa Army Base, reported that airmen were seeing lights that they couldn't explain. Four years later, he attempted to fly after them in a plane but came up empty again.

## Explanations?

Some skeptics claim that the lights are headlights from U.S. 67, dismissing the many reports from before cars were in the Marfa area. Others insist that the lights are swamp gas, ball lightning, reflections off mica deposits, or a nightly mirage.

At the other extreme, a contingent of people believe that the floating orbs are friendly observers of life on Earth. For example, Mrs. W. T. Giddings described her father's early twentieth century encounter with the Marfa Lights. He'd become lost during a blizzard, and according to his daughter, the lights "spoke" to him and led him to a cave where he found shelter.

Most studies of the phenomenon, however, conclude that the lights are indeed real but cannot be explained. The 1989 TV show *Unsolved Mysteries* set up equipment to find an explanation. Scientists on the scene could only comment that the lights were not made by people.

## Share the Wealth

Marfa is the most famous location for "ghost lights" and "mystery lights," but it's not the only place to see them. Here are just a few of the legendary unexplained lights that attract visitors to dark roads in Texas on murky nights.

• In southeast Texas, a single orb appears regularly near Saratoga on Bragg Road.

• The Anson Light appears near Mt. Hope Cemetery in Anson, by U.S. Highway 180.

• Since 1850, "Brit Bailey's Light" glows five miles west of Angleton near Highway 35 in Brazoria County.

• In January 2008, Stephenville attracted international attention when unexplained lights—and perhaps a metallic spaceship—flew fast and low over the town.

The Marfa Lights appear over Mitchell Flat, which is entirely private property. However, the curious can view the lights from a Texas Highway Department roadside parking area about nine miles east of Marfa on U.S. Highway 90. Seekers should arrive before dusk for the best location, especially during bluebonnet season (mid-April through late May), because this is a popular tourist stop.

The Marfa Lights Festival takes place during Labor Day weekend each year. This annual celebration of Marfa's mystery includes a parade, arts and crafts booths, great food, and a street dance.

# E. T. Phone Canada?

Do extraterrestrials prefer Canada? The nation ranks first in UFO sightings per capita, with a record high of 1,004 reported in 2008 and about 10 percent of Canadians claiming to have encountered one.

## What's That?

Though recorded instances of UFO sightings on Canadian soil date back to the 1950s, extraterrestrial encounters emerged most prominently on the global radar in 1967 with two startling occurrences. The first happened when a quartz prospector near a mine at Falcon Lake in Manitoba was allegedly burned by a UFO.

The second followed in October of that year at Shag Harbour, Nova Scotia, when several witnesses—including residents, the Royal Canadian Mounted Police, and an Air Canada pilot—reported strange lights hovering above the water and then submerging. A search of the site revealed only odd yellow foam, suggesting something had indeed gone underwater, but whether it was a UFO remains a mystery.

Odd Encounters

## A Growing Phenomenon

Since then, the number of sightings in Canada has increased nearly every year. Most take place in sparsely populated regions—the rationale being that "urban glow" obscures the lights of spaceships and that country folk spend more time outdoors and thus have better opportunities to glimpse UFOs. It may also be that rural areas are simply more conducive to extraterrestrial activity.

Most sightings reported are of the "strange light" and "weird flying vessel" variety, and indeed most have rather banal explanations (stars, airplanes, towers). Still, each year between 1 and 10 percent of sightings remain a mystery.

# TO THE MOON!

Television and film star Jackie Gleason was fascinated with the paranormal and UFOs. But he had no idea that an innocent game with an influential friend would lead him face-to-face with his obsession.

Jackie Gleason was a star of the highest order. The rotund actor kept television audiences in stitches with his portrayal of hardheaded but ultimately lovable family man Ralph Kramden in the 1955 sitcom *The Honeymooners*. He made history with his regularly aimed, but never delivered, threats to TV wife Alice, played by Audrey Meadows: "One of these days Alice, one of these days, pow, right in the kisser," and "Bang, zoom! To the moon, Alice!"

But many fans didn't know that Gleason was obsessed with the supernatural, and he owned a massive collection of memorabilia on the subject. It was so large and impressive that the University of Miami, Florida, put it on permanent exhibit after his death in 1987. He even had a house built in the

shape of a UFO, which he christened, "The Mothership."
The obsession was legendary, and it climaxed in an unimaginable way.

## A High Stakes Game

An avid golfer, Gleason also kept a home close to Inverrary Golf and Country Club in Lauderhill, Florida. A famous golfing buddy lived nearby—U.S. President Richard M. Nixon, who had a compound on nearby Biscayne Bay. The Hollywood star and the controversial politician shared a love of the links, politics, and much more.

The odyssey began when Gleason and Nixon met for a golf tournament at Inverrary in February 1973. Late in the day their conversation turned to a topic close to Gleason's heart—UFOs. To the funnyman's surprise, the president revealed his own fascination with the subject, touting a large collection of books that rivaled Gleason's. They talked shop through the rest of the game, but Gleason noticed reservation in Nixon's tone, as if the aides and security within earshot kept the president from speaking his mind. He would soon learn why.

Later that evening around midnight, an unexpected guest visited the Gleason home. It was Nixon, alone. The customary secret service detail assigned to him was nowhere to be seen. Confused, Gleason asked Nixon the reason for such a late call. He replied only that he had to show Gleason something. They climbed into Nixon's private car and sped off. The drive brought them to Homestead Air Force Base in South Miami-Dade County. Nixon took them to a large, heavily guarded building. Guards parted as the pair headed inside the structure, Gleason following Nixon past labs before arriving at a series of large cases. The cases held wreckage from a downed UFO, Nixon told his friend. Seeing all of this, Gleason had his doubts and imagined himself the target of an elaborately constructed hoax.

Odd Encounters

Leaving the wreckage, the pair entered a chamber holding six (some reports say eight) freezers topped with thick glass. Peering into the hulls, Gleason later said he saw dead bodies—but not of the human variety. The remains were small, almost childlike in stature, but withered in appearance and possessing only three or four digits per hand. They were also severely mangled, as if they had been in a devastating accident.

Returning home, Gleason was giddy. His obsession had come full circle. The enthusiasm changed in the weeks that followed, however, shifting to intense fear and worry. A patriotic American, Gleason couldn't reconcile his government's secrecy about the UFO wreckage. Traumatized, he began drinking heavily and suffered from severe insomnia.

## The "Truth" Comes Out

Gleason kept details of his wild night with Nixon under wraps. Unfortunately, his soon-to-be-ex-wife didn't follow his lead. Beverly Gleason spilled the beans in *Esquire* magazine and again in an unpublished memoir on her marriage to Gleason. Supermarket tabloids ate the story up.

Gleason only opened up about his night with Nixon in the last weeks of his life. Speaking to Larry Warren, a former Air Force pilot with his own UFO close encounter, a slightly boozy Gleason let his secret loose with a phrase reminiscent of his *Honeymooners* days: "We've got 'em— Aliens!"

# Chapter 6

# IDENTITY QUESTIONS

## MOLLY PITCHER: REBEL MILITIAWOMAN

Historians disagree about Molly; not over whether she lived, but over her true identity. Did a cannon cocker's wife truly step up and serve a gun under fire in the American Revolution?

**Was Molly Pitcher real?** A couple of Revolutionary women's stories sound a lot like Molly's. Because women have "pitched in" during battle in just about every war, that's neither surprising nor a revelation. It wasn't rare in that era for wives to accompany their husbands on military duty, to say nothing of those daring few women who masqueraded as men. So who was Molly? Many historians say she was an Irish immigrant named Mary Hays (later McCauly). Some believe that Molly was Margaret Corbin, a Pennsylvania native. The most likely case is that both were real women who did pretty much as history credits them and that the legend of Molly Pitcher commingles the two.

**What did Mary Hays do?** The story, likely accurate, credits her first with bringing water (the "pitcher" part explained) to the artillery gunners at the Battle of Monmouth (1778). It wasn't just drinking water; a soldier had to wet-sponge a cannon after a shot in order to douse any residual embers. If he or she didn't, the person pushing in the next powder charge would suffer the consequences. Accounts describe Mary as a woman who was always ready with a choice profanity and was as brave as any man, and she is widely credited with evacuating wounded men. After her husband fell wounded, she stepped forward to help crew his gun. Mary died around 1832.

**And Margaret Corbin?** Her tale enters focus at the Battle of Fort Washington (1776) and has her first helping her husband crew a cannon, then firing it unassisted after his death in action. (That would be possible, but very slow.) Taken out of action by grapeshot—a cannon firing musket balls as a super shotgun—she was evacuated and given a military pension by the Continental government. Considering said government's notorious poverty and lousy credit, there's doubt whether poor Margaret ever collected any money in time to help her. She died in 1789, a partly disabled veteran.

**How did the stories get so muddled together?** One must consider the times. No one videotaped Mary or Margaret; eyewitnesses spoke or wrote of their deeds. Others retold the tales, perhaps inflating or deemphasizing them. As the war lingered on, people who had heard both stories probably assumed they were variants of the same story, and they retold it in their own words. Regardless, dozens of American women besides Mary and Margaret fought for independence; many thousands more helped the cause with all their strength. Molly Pitcher is an emblem, a Rosie the Riveter of her era.

# IDENTITIES LOST: THE DRUIDS AND THE PICTS

What do you know about the Druids? How about the Picts? Chances are, what you know (or think you know) is wrong. These two "lost" peoples are saddled with serious cases of mistaken identity.

Most contemporary perceptions of the Druids and Picts tend to be derived from legend and lore. As such, our conceptions of these peoples range from erroneous and unlikely to just plain foolish.

Let's start with the Druids. They are often credited with the building of Stonehenge, the great stone megalith believed to be their sacred temple, as well as their arena for savage human sacrifice rituals. True or False?

False. First off, Stonehenge was built around 2000 BC—about 1,400 years before the Druids emerged. Second, though we know admittedly little of Druidic practice, it seemed to be traditional and conservative. The Druids did have specific divinity-related beliefs, but it is not known whether they actually carried out human sacrifices.

What about the Picts? Although often reduced to a mythical race of magical fairies, the Picts actually ruled Scotland before the Scots.

So who were the Druids and the Picts?

## The Druids—The Priestly Class

As the priestly class of Celtic society, the Druids served as the Celts' spiritual leaders—repositories of knowledge about the world and the universe, as well as authorities on Celtic history, law, religion, and culture. In short, they were the pre-servers of the Celtic way of life.

The Druids provided the Celts with a connection to their gods, the universe, and the natural order. They preached of the power and authority of the deities and taught the im-mortality of the soul and reincarnation. They were experts in astronomy and the natural world. They also had an in-nate connection to all things living: They preferred holding great rituals among natural shrines provided by the forests, springs, and groves.

To become a Druid, one had to survive extensive training. Druid wannabes and Druid-trained minstrels and bards had to endure as many as 20 years of oral education and memorization.

## More Powerful than Celtic Chieftains

In terms of power, the Druids took a backseat to no one. Even the Celtic chieftains, well-versed in power politics, recognized the overarching authority of the Druids. Celtic society had well-defined power and social structures and territories and property rights. The Druids were deemed the ultimate arbiters in all matters relating to such. If there was a legal or financial dispute between two parties, it was unequivocally settled in special Druid-presided courts. Armed conflicts were immediately ended by Druid rulings. Their word was final.

In the end, however, there were two forces to which even the Druids had to succumb—the Romans and Christianity. With the Roman invasion of Britain in AD 43, Emperor Claudius mandated that the practice of Druidism throughout the Roman Empire was to be outlawed. The Romans destroyed the last vestiges of official Druidism in Britain with the annihilation of the Druid stronghold of Anglesey in AD 61. Surviving Druids fled to unconquered Ireland and Scotland, only to become completely marginalized by the influence of Christianity within a few centuries.

Stripped of power and status, the Druids of ancient Celtic society disappeared. They morphed into wandering poets and storytellers with no connection to their once illustrious past.

## The Picts—The Painted People

The Picts were, in simplest terms, the people who inhabited ancient Scotland before the Scots. Their origins are unknown, but some scholars believe that the Picts were descendants of the Caledonians or other Iron Age tribes who invaded Britain.

No one knows what the Picts called themselves; the origin of their name comes from other sources and probably derives from the Pictish custom of tattooing or painting their bodies. The Irish called them Cruithni, meaning "the people of the designs." The Romans called them Picti, which is Latin for "painted people"; however, the Romans probably used the term as a general moniker for all the untamed peoples living north of Hadrian's Wall.

## A Second-Hand History

The Picts themselves left no written records. All descriptions of their history and culture come from second-hand accounts. The earliest of these is a Roman account from AD 297 stating that the Picti and the Hiberni (Irish) were already well-established enemies of the Britons to the south.

The Picts were also well-established enemies of each other. Before the arrival of the Romans, the Picts spent most of their time fighting amongst themselves. The threat posed by the Roman conquest of Britain forced the squabbling Pict kingdoms to come together and eventually evolve into the nation-state of Pictland. The united Picts were strong enough not only to resist conquest by the Romans, but also to launch periodic raids on Roman-occupied Britain.

Having defied the Romans, the Picts later succumbed to a more peaceful invasion launched by Irish missionaries. Arriving in Pictland in the late sixth century, they succeeded in converting the polytheistic Pict elite within two decades. Much of the known history of the Picts comes from the Irish Christian annals. If not for the writings of the Romans and the Irish missionaries, we might not have knowledge of the Picts today.

Despite the existence of an established Pict state, Pictland disappeared with the changing of its name to the Kingdom of Alba in AD 843, a move signifying the rise of the Gaels as the dominant people in Scotland. By the eleventh century, virtually all vestiges of them had vanished.

# ARE YOU RELATED TO GENGHIS KHAN?

Your DNA may carry the stuff you need to conquer the world.

## From Riches To Rags To Riches

Genghis Khan was one of the first self-made men in history. He was born to a tribal chief in 1162, probably at Dadal Sum, in the Hentii region of what is now Mongolia. At age 9, Genghis was sent packing after a rival tribe poisoned his father. For three years, Genghis and the remainder of his family wandered the land living from hand to mouth.

Genghis was down, but not out. After convincing some of his tribesmen to follow him, he eventually became one of the most successful political and military leaders in history, uniting the nomadic Mongol tribes into a vast sphere of influence. The Mongol Empire lasted from 1206 to 1368 and was the largest contiguous dominion in world history, stretching from the Caspian Sea to the Sea of Japan. At the empire's peak, it encompassed more than 700 tribes and cities.

## A Uniter, Not a Divider

Genghis gave his people more than just land. He introduced a writing system, wrote the first laws to govern all Mongols, regulated hunting, and created a judicial system for fair trials. His determination to create unity swept old rivalries aside and made everyone feel like a single Mongol people.

Today, Genghis Khan is seen as a founding father of Mongolia. However, he is not so fondly remembered in the Middle East and Europe, where he is regarded as a ruthless and bloodthirsty conqueror.

## Who's Your Daddy?

It seems that Genghis was father of more than the Mongol nation. Recently, an international team of geneticists determined that one in every 200 men now living is a relative of the great Mongol ruler. More than 16 million men in central Asia have been identified as carrying the same Y chromosome as Genghis Khan.

A key reason is this: Genghis's sons and other male descendants had many children by many women; one son, Tushi, may have had 40 sons of his own, and one of Genghis's grandsons, Chinese dynastic ruler Kublai Khan, fathered 22 sons with recognized wives and an unknown number with the scores of women he kept as concubines.

Genetically speaking, Genghis continues to "live on" because the male chromosome is passed directly from father to son, with no change other than random mutations (which are typically insignificant). When geneticists identify those mutations, called "markers," they can chart the course of male descendants through centuries. Is the world large enough for 16 million personal empires? Time—and genetics—will reveal the answer.

# HEY, IT'S THE FREEMASONS!

For many, talk of "Freemasonry" conjures up images of intricate handshakes, strange rituals, and harsh punishment for revealing secrets about either. In actuality, the roots of the order are brotherhood and generosity. Throughout the ages,

Masons have been known to fiercely protect their members and the unique features of their society.

The fantastically named Most Ancient and Honorable Society of Free and Accepted Masons began like other guilds; it was a collection of artisans brought together by their common trade, in this case, stone cutting and crafting. (There are many speculations as to when the society first began. Some believe it dates back to when King Solomon's temple was built. Others believe the guild first formed in Scotland in the sixteenth century.) The Freemasons made the welfare of their members a priority. Group elders devised strict work regulations for masons, whose skills were always in demand and were sometimes taken advantage of.

Organized Freemasonry emerged in Great Britain in the mid-seventeenth century with the firm establishment of Grand Lodges and smaller, local Lodges. (No one overarching body governs Freemasonry as a whole, though lodges worldwide are usually linked either to England or France.) In 1730, transplanted Englishmen established the first American Lodge in Virginia, followed in 1733 by the continent's first chartered and opened Grand Lodge in Massachusetts. Boasting early American members including George Washington, Benjamin Franklin, and John Hancock, Freemasonry played a part in the growth of the young nation in ways that gradually attracted curiosity, speculation, and concern.

The source of the organization's mysterious reputation lay partly in its secrecy: Masons were prohibited from revealing secrets (some believed Masons would be violently punished if they revealed secrets, though the Masons deny such rumors). The Masonic bond also emphasized a commitment to one another. Outsiders feared the exclusivity smacked of conspiracy and compromised the motives of Masons appointed to juries or elected to public office. And nonmembers wondered about the meanings of the Freemasons' peculiar traditions (such as code words and other secretive forms of recognition between members) and symbolism (often geometric shapes or tools, such as the square and compass). Design elements of the one-dollar bill, including the Great Seal and the "all-seeing eye," have been credited to founding fathers such as Charles Thomson and other Masons.

Freemasonry in the United States suffered a serious blow in September 1826 when New York Masons abducted a former "brother" named William Morgan. Morgan was about to publish a book of Masonic secrets, but before he could, he was instead ushered north to the Canadian border and, in all likelihood, thrown into the Niagara River.

His disappearance led to the arrest and conviction of three men on kidnapping charges (Morgan's body was never found)—scant penalties, locals said, for crimes that surely included murder.

The affair increased suspicion of the brotherhood, spawning an American Anti-Mason movement and even a political party dedicated to keeping Freemasons out of national office.

In the decades following the Civil War, men were again drawn to brotherhood and fellowship as they searched for answers in a turbulent age, and Freemasonry slowly regained popularity. Today, Freemasonry remains an order solidly devoted to its own members, charitable causes, and the betterment of society. It has a worldwide membership of at least five million. Its members are traditionally male, though certain associations now permit women.

Despite the name, most members are not stonemasons. They are, however, required to have faith in a supreme being, but not necessarily the Christian god (Mohammed, Buddha, and so forth are all acceptable).

# THE CATCHER WAS A SPY

When it comes to character assessments, you gotta listen to Casey Stengel. And the Ol' Professor claimed Moe Berg was "the strangest man ever to put on a baseball uniform." But Berg wasn't just strange in a baseball uniform, he was strange and mysterious in many ways—some of them deliberate.

Moe Berg lived a life shrouded in mystery and marked by contradictions. He played alongside Babe Ruth, Lefty Grove, Jimmie Foxx, and Ted Williams; he moved in the company of Norman Rockefeller, Albert Einstein, and international diplomats; and yet he was often described as a loner. He was well-liked by teammates but preferred to travel by himself. He never married, and he made few close friends.

## "The Brainiest Guy in Baseball"

Moe was a bright kid from the beginning, with a special fondness for baseball. As the starting shortstop for Princeton University, where he majored in modern languages, Moe was a star. He was fond of communicating with his second baseman in Latin, leaving opposing base runners scratching their heads.

He broke into the majors in 1923 as a shortstop with the Brooklyn Robins (later the Dodgers). He converted to catcher and spent time with the White Sox, Senators, Indians, and Red Sox throughout his career. A slow runner and a poor fielder, Berg nevertheless eked out a 15-season big-league career. Pitchers loved him behind the plate. They praised his intelligence and loved his strong, accurate arm. And while he once went 117 games without an error, he rarely nudged his batting average much past .250. His weak bat often kept him on the bench and led journalists to note, "Moe Berg can speak 12 languages flawlessly and can hit in none." He was, however, a favorite of sportswriters, many of whom considered him "the brainiest guy in baseball."

He earned his law degree from Columbia University, attending classes in the off-seasons and even during spring training and partial seasons with the White Sox. When Berg was signed by the Washington Senators in 1932, his life took a sudden change. In Washington, Berg became a society darling, delighting the glitterati with his knowledge and wit. Certainly it was during his Washington years that he made the contacts that would serve him in his espionage career.

## Time in Tokyo and on TV

Berg first raised eyebrows in the intelligence community at the start of World War II when he shared home movies of Tokyo's shipyards, factories, and military sites, which he had secretly filmed while on a baseball trip in 1934. While barnstorming through Japan along with Ruth, Lou Gehrig, and Foxx, Berg delighted Japanese audiences with his fluency in their language and familiarity with their culture. He even addressed the Japanese parliament.

But one day he skipped the team's scheduled game and went to visit a Tokyo hospital, the highest building in the city. He sneaked up to the roof and took motion picture films of the Tokyo harbor. Some say those photos were used by the U.S. military as they planned their attack on Tokyo eight years later. Berg maintained that he had not been sent to Tokyo on a formal assignment, that he had acted on his own initiative to take the film and offer it to the U.S. government upon his return. Whether or not that was the case, Berg's undercover career had begun.

On February 21, 1939, Berg made the first of several appearances on the radio quiz show *Information, Please!* He was an immense hit, correctly answering nearly every question he was asked. Commissioner Kenesaw Mountain Landis was so proud of how intelligent and well-read the second-string catcher was that he told him, "Berg, in just 30 minutes you did more for baseball than I've done the entire time I've been commissioner." But Berg's baseball time was beginning to wind down; 1939 was his last season.

## Secret Agent Man

Berg's intellect and elusive lifestyle were ideal for a post-baseball career as a spy. He was recruited by the Office of Strategic Services (predecessor to the CIA) in 1943 and served in several capacities. He toured 20 countries in Latin America early in WWII, allegedly on a propaganda mission to bolster the morale of soldiers there. But what he was really doing was trying to determine how much the Latin countries could help the U.S. war effort.

His most important mission for the OSS was to gather information on Germany's progress in developing an atomic bomb. He worked undercover in Italy and Switzerland and reported information to the States throughout 1944. One of his more daring assignments was a visit to Zurich, Switzerland, in December 1944, where he attended a lecture by German nuclear physicist Werner Heisenberg. If Heisenberg indicated the Germans were close to developing nukes, Berg had been directed to assassinate the scientist. Luckily for Heisenberg, Berg determined that German nuclear capability was not yet within the danger range.

## Life After the War

On October 10, 1945, Berg was awarded the Medal of Freedom (now the Presidential Medal of Freedom) but turned it down without explanation. (After his death, his sister accepted it on his behalf.)

After the war he was recruited by the CIA. It is said that his is the only baseball card to be found in CIA headquarters.

After his CIA career ended, Berg never worked again.
He was often approached to write his memoirs. When he
agreed, in 1960 or so, the publisher hired a writer to aid.
Berg quit the project in fury when the writer indicated he
thought Berg was Moe Howard, founder of the *Three Stooges*. But his unusual career turns were later immortalized in
the Nicholas Dawidoff book *The Catcher Was a Spy*. At age
70, Berg fell, injuring himself. He died in the hospital. His last
words were to ask a nurse, "What did the Mets do today?"

# HITLER'S DEATH, A HOAX?

Rumors of Hitler's survival persisted for years. The charred
corpse was a double; he had offspring; he was living in
South America, keeping that old Nazi spirit alive. Some of
the wilder tales were fueled by Soviet propaganda.

They were false. In 1993 the Russian government opened
the old Soviet files. We now know beyond any reasonable
doubt what happened. The NKVD (Russian intelligence)
investigation began the moment Soviet troops overran
the Führerbunker. They exhumed the Hitler and Goebbels
bodies, bringing in close acquaintances for positive identification; for example, Eva and Adolf 's former dentist and his
assistant both recognized their own professional handiwork.
The original announcement had been correct: Adolf Hitler
had died April 30, 1945. After sending Hitler's jaw back to
Moscow for safekeeping, the NKVD secretly reburied the
other remains at a military base near Magdeburg, German
Democratic Republic (East Germany).

In 1970, the Soviet military prepared to hand over the Magdeburg base to the East Germans. The KGB (successor to the
NKVD) dared not leave the Nazi remains. On April 4, 1970,
the KGB exhumed the fragmentary remains of Adolf and Eva

Hitler and the Goebbels family. Hitler's skull was identified, and the bullet-holed portion was sent to Moscow. The next day, the KGB incinerated the rest of the remains, crushed them to dust and dumped what was left in a nearby river.

Therefore, of Eva Braun and the Goebbels family nothing at all remains. Of Hitler, today only his jaw and a skull fragment exist in Russian custody.

# VALACHI SPEAKS

On June 22, 1962, in the federal penitentiary in Atlanta, Georgia, a man serving a sentence of 15 to 20 years for heroin trafficking picked up a steel pipe and murdered another convict. The killer was Joseph "Joe Cargo" Valachi; the intended victim was Joseph DiPalermo—but Valachi got the wrong man and killed another inmate, Joe Saupp. This mistake touched off  one of the greatest criminal revelations in history.

Joe Valachi, a 59-year-old Mafia "soldier," was the first member of the Mafia to publicly acknowledge the reality of that criminal organization—making La Cosa Nostra (which means "this thing of ours") a household name. He opened the doors to expose an all-pervasive, wide-ranging conglomerate of crime families, the existence of which was repeatedly denied by J. Edgar Hoover and the FBI. By testifying against his own organization, Valachi violated the code of silence.

## The Boss's Orders

Vito Genovese was the boss of New York's mighty Genovese crime family. Valachi had worked for the family most of his life—mostly as a driver, but also as a hit man, enforcer, numbers runner, and drug pusher. When Valachi went to prison after having been found guilty of some of these activities, Genovese believed the small-time operator had betrayed him to obtain a lighter sentence for himself. So Genovese put a $100,000 bounty on Valachi's head. He and Valachi were actually serving sentences in the same prison when Valachi killed Joe Saupp—mistaking him for Joseph DiPalermo, whom he thought had been assigned by Genovese to murder him. Whether or not Valachi had broken the code of silence and betrayed Genovese before the bounty was placed on his head, he certainly did it with a vengeance afterward.

But why did Valachi turn informer? The answer to that question isn't entirely clear. Most speculate that Valachi was afraid of a death sentence for killing Saupp and agreed to talk to the Feds in exchange for a lighter sentence.

## The Cat Is Out of the Bag

Valachi was a barely literate, street-level miscreant whose knowledge of the workings of the organization was limited. However, when he was brought before John L. McClellan's Senate Permanent Investigations Subcommittee in October 1963, he began talking beyond his personal experience, relaying urban legends as truth, and painting a picture of the Mafia that was both fascinating and chilling.

All in all, Joe Valachi helped identify 317 members of the Mafia. His assistance gave Attorney General Robert Kennedy "a significant addition to the broad picture of organized crime." Unlike Hoover, Bobby Kennedy had no problem acknowledging the Mafia. (One theory about Hoover's denials is that they were a result of long-term Mafia blackmail regarding his homosexuality.)

Valachi's revelations ran the gamut from minor accuracies to babbling exaggerations, as well as from true to false, but the cat was out of the bag. Americans became fascinated with crime families, codes of honor, gang wars, hit killings, and how widely the Mafia calamari had stretched its tentacles. Very private criminals suddenly found their names splashed across headlines and blaring from televisions. During the next three years in the New York-New Jersey-Connecticut metropolitan area, more organized criminals were arrested and jailed than in the previous 30 years. Whatever safe conduct pass the Mafia may have held had expired.

## On the Screen and in Print

When journalist Peter Maas interviewed Valachi and came out with *The Valachi Papers*, the U.S. Department of Justice first encouraged but then tried to block its publication. Regardless, the book was released in 1968. This work soon became the basis of a movie that starred Charles Bronson as Joe Valachi. The novel *The Godfather* was published in 1969, and in the film *The Godfather: Part II*, the characters of Willie Cicci and Frank Pentangeli were reportedly inspired by Valachi.

The $100,000 bounty on the life of Joseph Valachi was never claimed. In 1966, Valachi unsuccessfully attempted to hang himself in his prison cell using an electrical cord. Five years later, he died of a heart attack at La Tuna Federal Correctional Institution in Texas. He had outlived his chief nemesis, Genovese, by two years.

# WALT DISNEY: FBI MAN OR MOUSE?

As the creator of the most famous cartoon mouse in the world, Walt Disney carefully protected and shielded the rodent and his friends from anything that could put their world in a bad light. But it seems that Disney, whose entertainment empire was as pure as Snow White, may have protected and shielded other facets of his life from public view—ones that might have darkened his squeaky-clean image.

## Young Walter

Walt Disney was born in Chicago on December 5, 1901, to parents Elias and Flora. His father was a farmer and carpenter, running the household with an overly firm hand. Walt and his siblings, working the Disney land near Kansas City, often found themselves on the receiving end of a strap as their dad doled out the discipline. As a young boy, Walt took advantage of his infrequent free time by drawing, improvising his supplies by using a piece of coal on toilet paper. When the Disneys moved back to Chicago in 1917, Walt attended art classes at the Chicago Academy of Fine Arts.

Armed with forged birth records, Walt joined the American Red Cross Ambulance Corps and entered World War I in 1918, just before it ended. He returned to Kansas City, where two of his brothers continued to run the Disney farm. Although he was rejected as a cartoonist for the Kansas City Star, Walt soon began to create animated film ads for movie theaters, working with a young Ub Iwerks, who eventually became an important member of Disney Studios.

In 1922, Disney started Laugh-O-Gram Films, producing short cartoons based on fairy tales. But the business closed within a year, and Walt headed to Hollywood, intent on directing feature films. Finding no work as a director, he revisited the world of film animation. With emotional and financial support from his brother Roy, Walt slowly began to make a name for Disney Brothers Studios on the West Coast. The company introduced "Oswald the Lucky Rabbit" in 1927 but lost the popular character the next year to a different company. Disney was left in the position of having to create another cute and clever cartoon animal.

## The Tale of the Mouse

According to Disney, the Kansas City office of Laugh-O-Gram Films was rampant with mice. One mouse was a particular favorite of Walt. This rodent became the inspiration for

Disney's next cartoon character. Working with Iwerks, and borrowing copiously from their former meal ticket Oswald, Disney Studios produced *Steamboat Willie* in November 1928. With a voice provided by Disney himself, Mickey Mouse quickly became a hit in movie theaters. The animated star introduced additional Disney icons, including girlfriend Minnie Mouse, the always-exasperated Donald Duck, faithful hound Pluto, and dim-but-devoted pal Goofy. Disney's cartoons won every Animated Short Subject Academy Award during the 1930s.

## A Dark Side of Disney

As Disney Studios moved into animated feature films (which everyone said would never work), Walt began to wield the power he'd gained as one of Hollywood's most prominent producers. What's more, his strict upbringing and harsh bouts of discipline had left him with a suspicious, ultraconservative mindset. Bad language by employees in the presence of women resulted in immediate discharge—no matter the inconvenience. Disney was prone to creating a double standard between himself and his employees. For example, although Walt kept his dashing mustache for most of his life, all other Disney workers were prohibited from wearing any facial hair. While he considered his artists and animators "family," he treated them in the same way Elias Disney had treated his family—unfairly. Promised bonuses turned into layoffs. Higher-paid artists resorted to giving their assistants raises out of their own pockets. By 1941, Disney's animators went on strike, supported by the Screen Cartoonists Guild. Walt was convinced, and stated publicly, that the strike was the result of Communist agitators infiltrating Hollywood. Settled after five weeks, the Guild won on all counts, and the "Disney family" became cynically known as the "Mouse Factory."

## An Even Darker Side

Disney was suspected of being a Nazi sympathizer; he often attended American Nazi Party meetings before the beginning of World War II. When prominent German filmmaker Leni Riefenstahl tried to screen her films for Hollywood studios, only Disney agreed to meet her. Yet, when World War II began, Disney projected a strictly all-American image and became closely allied with J. Edgar Hoover and the FBI.

According to more than 500 pages of FBI files, Disney was recruited by Hoover in late 1940 to be an informant, flagging potential Communist sympathizers among Hollywood stars and executives. In September 1947, Disney was called by the House Un-American Activities Committee to testify on Communist influence in the motion picture industry. He fingered several of his former artists as Reds, again blaming much of the 1941 labor strike on their efforts. He also identified the League of Women Voters as a Communist-fronted organization. Later that evening, his wife pointed out that he meant the League of Women Shoppers, a consumer group that had supported the Guild strike. Disney's testimony contributed to the "Hollywood Blacklist," which included anyone in the industry even remotely suspected of Communist affiliation. The list resulted in many damaged or lost careers, as well as a number of suicides in the cinematic community. Included in the turmoil was Charlie Chaplin, whom Disney referred to as "the little Commie."

The FBI rewarded Walt Disney for his efforts by naming him "SAC–Special Agent in Charge" in 1954, just as he was about to open his first magical amusement park, Disneyland. Disney and Hoover continued to be pen pals into the 1960s; the FBI made script "suggestions" for *Moon Pilot*, a Disney comedy that initially spoofed the abilities of the Bureau. The bumbling FBI agents in the screenplay became generic government agents before the film's release.

After a lifetime of chain-smoking, Disney developed lung cancer and died in December 1966. His plans for Disney World in Florida had just begun—the park didn't open until 1971.

Upon his passing, many remembered the man as kindly "Uncle Walt," while others saw him as the perfect father for a mouse—since he had always seemed to be a bit of a rat.

# CONTROVERSIAL QUEEN

In establishing the identity of the Egyptian queen Nefertiti, scholars find themselves up to their necks in conflicting information.

Like Cleopatra, Nefertiti is one of the most famous queens of ancient Egypt. She's also often referred to as "The Most Beautiful Woman in the World," largely due to the 1912 discovery of a painted limestone bust of Nefertiti depicting her stunning features: smooth skin, full lips, and a graceful swanlike neck—quite the looker! Now housed in Berlin's Altes Museum, the likeness has become a widely recognized symbol of ancient Egypt and one of the most important artistic works of the pre-modern world. But the bust, like almost everything about the famous queen, is steeped in controversy.

## Conflicting Accounts

It wasn't until the bust surfaced in the early twentieth century that scholars began sorting out information about Nefertiti's life. Her name means "the beautiful one is come," and some think she was a foreign princess, not of Egyptian blood. Others believe she was born into Egyptian royalty, that she was the niece or daughter of a high government official named Ay, who later became pharaoh. But basically, no one knows her origins for sure.

When the beautiful one was age 15, she married Amenhotep IV, who later became king of Egypt. Nefertiti was thus promoted to queen. No one really knows when this happened—other than that it was in the 18th Dynasty—but it's safe to say that it was a really long time ago (as in, the 1340s BC). Nefertiti appears in many reliefs of the period, often accompanying her husband in various ceremonies—a testament to her political power.

An indisputable fact about both Nefertiti and Amenhotep IV is that they were responsible for bringing monotheism to ancient Egypt. Rather than worship the vast pantheon of Egyptian gods—including the supreme god, Amen-Ra—the couple devoted themselves to exclusively worshipping the sun god Aten. In fact, as a sign of this commitment, Amenhotep IV changed his named to Akhenaten. Similarly, Nefertiti changed her name to Neferneferuaten-Nefertiti, meaning, "The Aten is radiant of radiance [because] the beautiful one is come." (But we're guessing everyone just called her "Nef.") Again, it's unclear as to why the powerful couple decided to turn from polytheism. Maybe there were political reasons. Or perhaps the two simply liked the idea of one universal god.

## Disappearance/Death?

In studying Egyptian history, scholars discovered that around 14 years into Akhenaten's reign, Nefertiti seems to disappear. There are no more images of her, no historical records. Perhaps there was a conflict in the royal family, and she was banished from the kingdom. Maybe she died in the plague that killed half of Egypt. A more interesting speculation is that she disguised herself as a man, changed her named to Smenkhkare, and went on to rule Egypt alongside her husband. But—all together now—*no one knows for sure*!

During a June 2003 expedition in Egypt's Valley of the Kings, an English archeologist named Joann Fletcher unearthed a mummy that she suspected to be Nefertiti. But despite the fact that the mummy probably is a member of the royal family from the 18th Dynasty, it was not proven to be female. Many Egyptologists think there is not sufficient evidence to prove that Fletcher's mummy is Nefertiti. So, that theory was something of a bust.

In 2009, Swiss art historian Henri Sierlin published a book suggesting that the bust is a copy. He claimed that the sculpture was made by an artist named Gerard Marks on the request of Ludwig Borchardt, the German archeologist responsible for discovering the bust in 1912. Despite the mysteries surrounding Nefertiti, there's no question that she was revered in her time. At the temples of Karnak are inscribed the words: "Heiress, Great of Favours, Possessed of Charm, Exuding Happiness . . . Great King's Wife, Whom He Loves, Lady of Two Lands, Nefertiti."

# CROCKEFELLER

What began as a search to find a missing girl uncovered 30 years of fraud, fake identities, and possible foul play. Before Christian Karl Gerhartstreiter was a convict, he was a con artist.

It started as a case of parental kidnapping not uncommon in custody battles: In July 2008, Clark Rockefeller, a descendant of the moneyed oil family, absconded with his seven-year-old daughter during a court-supervised visitation in Boston.

But oddly, FBI databases showed no record of a Clark Rockefeller, and the Rockefeller family denied any connection. His ex-wife, millionaire consultant Sandra Boss, confessed he had no identification, no social security number, and no driver's license. *So who was this guy?* The FBI released his picture, hoping for information. And that's when the stories—and aliases—began pouring in.

## Fake Foreign Exchange

His real identity is Christian Karl Gerhartstreiter, a German national who came to the United States in 1978 at age 17, claiming to be a foreign exchange student. In truth, he showed up unannounced on the doorstep of a Connecticut family he'd met on a train in Europe, who'd suggested he look them up if he ever visited the States.

After living with them briefly, he posted an ad describing himself as an exchange student in search of a host and was taken in by the Stavio family. They threw him out after it became clear he expected to be treated like royalty. During this time, Gerhartstreiter allegedly became enamored with the *Gilligan's Island* character Thurston Howell III, the ascot-wearing millionaire, and even adopted Howell's snobbish accent.

## Bogus Brit

In 1980, "Chris Gerhart" enrolled at the University of Wisconsin-Milwaukee as a film major and persuaded another student to marry him so that he could get his green card. Shortly after the wedding, he left school and headed to Los Angeles to pursue a film career—this time posing as the dapper British blue-blood Christopher Chichester (a name he borrowed from his former high school teacher).

He settled in the swanky town of San Marino, living in a building with newlyweds John and Linda Sohus. The couple went missing in 1985, around the same time Chichester moved away; allegedly, he went back to England following a death in the family.

Chichester resurfaced in Greenwich, Connecticut, as former Hollywood producer and business tycoon Christopher Crowe. It was under this name that, in 1988, he tried to sell a truck that had belonged to the Sohuses. Police investigators traced the Sohus's missing truck to Connecticut, and they soon realized that Crowe and Chichester were the same person. But by then, he'd already vanished.

## Mock Rock

Now he was Manhattan's Clark Rockefeller, the new darling of the elite. It was here that he met and married the Ivy League-educated business whiz Sandra Boss. For most of their 12-year marriage, Sandra believed his elaborate stories. She even believed he'd filed the paperwork for their marriage to be legal (it appears he hadn't).

Eventually, however, Sandra grew suspicious. She filed for divorce and won full custody of their seven-year-old daughter, Reigh, and the two moved to London. Clark was limited to three court-supervised visits per year. It was on the first of these visits that he kidnapped her.

## Conclusion

In August 2008, the con man was arrested in Baltimore, and Reigh was returned to her mother. In June 2009, a judge sentenced him to four to five years in prison.

Gerhartstreiter says he has no recollection of his life before the 1990s. And he insists on being called Mr. Rockefeller because that's his name, thank you very much.

# CANADA'S CRYPTIC CASTAWAY

This mute amputee has a foothold in Nova Scotian folklore—nearly a century after his death.

# Who Is This Man?

On September 8, 1863, two fishermen in Sandy Cove, Nova Scotia, discovered an unusual treasure washed ashore: a lone man in his twenties with newly amputated legs, left with just a loaf of bread and jug of water. There were a few clues, such as his manner of dress, that led the townspeople to speculate on whether the fellow was a gentleman or an aristocrat. But there was no point in asking him—he didn't speak. In fact, he was said to have uttered only three words after being found: "Jerome" (which the villagers came to call him), "Columbo" (perhaps the name of his ship), and "Trieste," an Italian village.

Based on these three words, the villagers theorized he was Italian and concocted various romantic stories about his fate: that he was an Italian nobleman captured and mutilated by pirates (or perhaps a pirate himself ), a seaman punished for threatening mutiny, or maybe he was an heir to a fortune who had been crippled and cast away by a jealous rival.

## Charity Case

Jerome was taken to the home of Jean and Juliette Nicholas, a French family who lived across the bay in Meteghan. There was still a chance Jerome could be French and Jean was fluent in five languages. (Although none of which proved successful in communicating with Jerome.)

In 1870, the Nicholases moved away. The town, enthralled with their mysterious nobleman, rallied together and paid the Comeau family $140 a year to take him in. On Sundays after mass, locals would stop by and pay a few cents for a look at the maimed mute. Jerome lived with the Comeaus for the next 52 years until his death on April 19, 1912.

Records suggest Jerome was no cool-headed castaway. Though he never spoke intelligibly, hearing some words (specifically "pirate") would put him in a rage. It's also been said that he was particularly anxious about the cold, spending winters with his leg stumps shoved under the stove for warmth. Though in his younger days he enjoyed sitting in the sun, he allegedly spent the last 20 years of his life as a shut-in, huddled by the stove.

## Mystery Revealed

Jerome's panic about the cold makes sense—if the latest hypotheses about him are true. Modern historians have posited a couple of different theories, both of which trace Jerome to New Brunswick.

One group of scholars uncovered a story in New Brunswick about a man who was behaving erratically and couldn't (or wouldn't) speak. To rid themselves of him, members of his community put him on a boat to New England—but not without first chopping off his legs. The man never made it to New England but instead wound up on the beach at Sandy Cove.

Another theory links Jerome to a man—probably European—who was found in 1861, pinned under a fallen tree in Chipman, New Brunswick, with frozen legs. Without a doctor nearby, the man was sent down the St. John River to Gagetown and then shipped back to Chipman, where he was supported for two years by the parish and nicknamed "Gamby" (which means "legs" in Italian). At that point, the parish got tired of taking care of him and paid a captain to drop him across the bay in Nova Scotia. Another account suggests that after the surgery, the man wasn't returned to Gagetown but put right on a boat.

Regardless of which theory is more accurate, all suggest that the reason for Jerome's arrival in Nova Scotia is that an entire town disowned him.

But New Brunswick's loss has been Nova Scotia's gain. There, Jerome is a local legend. He has been the subject of a movie (1994's *Le secret de Jérôme*), and a home for the handicapped bears his name. Tourists can even stop by his grave for a quick snapshot of the headstone, which reads, quite simply, "Jerome."

# The Real "Man Who Never Was"

When a drowned corpse washed ashore in Spain holding a briefcase of plans to invade Sardinia and Greece, the Nazis thought they'd made an astounding catch. They couldn't have been more wrong.

The rough tides rolled up against the southern Spanish coast in the spring of 1943, carrying the disheveled corpse of a British major who appeared to have drowned after his plane crashed somewhere off shore. The body, one of thousands of military men who had met their end in the Mediterranean waters, floated atop a rubber life jacket as the current pulled it slowly toward Huelva, Spain. With a war raging in Tunisia just across the sea, a drifting military corpse was not such an unusual event.

But this body was different, and it drew the immediate attention of Spanish authorities sympathetic to German and Italian Fascists. Chained to the corpse was a briefcase filled with dispatches from London to Allied Headquarters in North Africa concerning the upcoming Allied invasions of Sardinia and western Greece. The information was passed on to the Nazis, who accepted their apparent stroke of good luck, and now anticipated an Allied strike on the "soft underbelly of Europe."

Unfortunately for them, the whole affair was a risky, carefully contrived hoax.

Identity Questions

# Rigging the "Trojan Horse"

Operation Mincemeat was conceived by British intelligence agents as a deception to convince the Italians and Germans that the target of the next Allied landings would be somewhere other than Sicily, the true target. To throw the Fascists off the trail, British planners decided to find a suitable corpse—a middle-aged white male—put the corpse in the uniform of a military courier, and float the corpse and documents off the coast of Huelva, Spain, where a local Nazi agent was known to be on good terms with local police.

The idea of planting forged documents on a dead body was not new to the Allies. In August 1942, British agents planted a corpse clutching a fake map of minefields in a blown-up scout car. The map was picked up by German troops and made its way to Rommel's headquarters. He obligingly routed his panzers away from the "minefield" and into a region of soft sand, where they quickly bogged down.

This deception, however, would be much grander. If the planted documents made their way up the intelligence chain, Hitler and Mussolini would be expecting an invasion far from the Sicilian coast that Generals Eisenhower, Patton, and Montgomery had targeted for invasion in July 1943.

# The Making of a Major

Operation Mincemeat, spearheaded by Lieutenant Commander Ewen Montagu, a British naval intelligence officer, and Charles Cholmondeley of Britain's MI5 intelligence service, found its "host" in early 1943 when a single Welshman living in London committed suicide by taking rat poison. The substance produced a chemical pneumonia that could be mistaken for drowning.

The two operatives gave the deceased man a new, documented identity: "Major William Martin" of the Royal Marines.

They literally kept the "major" on ice while arrangements for his new mission were made. To keep Spanish authorities from conducting an autopsy—which would give away the body's protracted post-mortem condition—the agents decided to make "Major Martin" a Roman Catholic, giving him a silver cross and a St. Christopher medallion.

They dressed the body, complete with Royal Marine uniform and trench coat, and gave him identity documents and personal letters (including a swimsuit photo of his "fiancée," an intelligence bureau secretary). With a chain used by bank couriers, they fixed the briefcase to his body.

Martin's documents were carefully prepared to show Allied invasions being planned for Sardinia and Greece (the latter bearing the code name Operation Husky). They also indicated that an Allied deception plan would try to convince Hitler that the invasion would take place in Sicily (the site of the real Operation Husky). With everything in order, the agents carefully placed the corpse into a sealed container—dry ice kept the body "fresh" for the ride out to sea.

The submarine HMS *Seraph* carried "Major Martin" on his final journey. On April 28, the *Seraph* left for the Andalusian coast, and two days later the body of a Royal Marine officer washed ashore. Within days, photographs of the major's documents were on their way to Abwehr intelligence agents in Berlin.

## Taking the Bait

Abwehr, Hitler, and the German High Command swallowed the story. After the war, British intelligence determined that Martin's documents had been opened and resealed before being returned by the Spanish. The German General Staff, believing the papers to be genuine, had alerted units in the Mediterranean to be ready for an invasion of Sardinia and Greece. They moved one panzer division and air and naval assets off the Peloponnese, and disputed Italian fears of an impending invasion of Sicily.

The Allies captured Sicily in July and August 1943, and after the war, Commander Montagu wrote a bestselling account of Operation Mincemeat titled, *The Man Who Never Was*. The book was made into a film thriller a few years later.

Who was Major William Martin? The original body appears to have been a 34-year-old depressed Welsh alcoholic named Glyndwr Michael, and "Major Martin's" tombstone in Spain bears Michael's name. Historians have debated the identity of "Major Martin," however, theorizing that a "fresher" corpse from a sunken aircraft carrier was substituted closer to the launch date.

Whoever the real "Major Martin" may have been, one thing is certain: He saved thousands of lives, and became a war hero and action movie star in the process—quite an accomplishment for a dead man!

## GONE WITHOUT A TRACE

While we all watch in amazement as magicians make everything from small coins to giant buildings disappear, in our hearts, we all know it's a trick. Things don't just disappear, especially not people. Or do they?

### Louis Le Prince

The name Louis Aimé Augustin Le Prince doesn't mean much to most people, but some believe he was the first person to record moving images on film, a good seven years before Thomas Edison. Whether or not he did so is open to debate, as is what happened to him on September 16, 1890. On that day, Le Prince's brother accompanied him to the train station in Dijon, France, where he was scheduled to take the express train to Paris. When the train reached Paris, however, Le Prince and his luggage were nowhere to be found. The train was searched, as were the tracks between Dijon and Paris, but no sign of Le Prince or his luggage was ever found. Theories about his disappearance range from his being murdered for trying to fight Edison over the patent of the first motion picture to his family forcing him to go into hiding to keep him safe from people who wanted his patents for themselves. Others believe that Le Prince took his own life because he was nearly bankrupt.

## Dorothy Arnold

After spending most of December 12, 1910, shopping in Manhattan, American socialite Dorothy Arnold told a friend she was planning to walk home through Central Park. She never made it. Fearing that their daughter had eloped with her one-time boyfriend George Griscom Jr., the Arnolds immediately hired the Pinkerton Detective Agency, although they did not report her missing to police until almost a month later. Once the press heard the news, theories spread like wildfire, most of them pointing the finger at Griscom. Some believed he had murdered Arnold, but others thought she had died as the result of a botched abortion. Still others felt her family had banished her to Switzerland and then used her disappearance as a cover-up. No evidence was ever found to formally charge Griscom, and Arnold's disappearance remains unsolved.

## Frederick Valentich

To vanish without a trace is rather unusual. But to vanish in an airplane while chasing a UFO—now that's unique. Yet that's exactly what happened to 20-year-old pilot Frederick Valentich on the night of October 21, 1978. Shortly after 7:00 p.m., while flying a Cessna 182L to King Island, Australia, Valentich radioed that an "unidentified craft" was hovering over his plane. For the next several minutes,

Identity Questions

he attempted to describe the object, which had blinking lights and was "not an aircraft." At approximately 7:12 p.m., Valentich stated that he was having engine trouble. Immediately after that, the flight tower picked up 17 seconds of "metallic, scraping sounds." Then all was silent. A search began immediately, but no trace of Valentich or his plane was ever found. Strangely enough, the evening Valentich disappeared, there were numerous reports of UFOs seen all over the skies of Australia.

## Frank Morris, John Anglin, and Clarence Anglin

Officially, records show that there was never a successful escape from Alcatraz Prison while it was in operation. Of course, those records leave out the part that three men might have made it, but they disappeared in the process.

After spending two years planning their escape, inmates Frank Morris and brothers Clarence and John Anglin placed homemade dummies in their bunks, crawled through hand-dug tunnels, and made their way to the prison roof. Then they apparently climbed down, hopped aboard homemade rafts, and made their way out into San Francisco Bay.

The next day, one of the largest manhunts in history began. Pieces of a raft and a life preserver were found floating in the bay, as well as a bag containing personal items from the escapees, but that was all. The official report stated that in all likelihood, the men drowned. However, a 2003 episode of *Mythbusters* determined that the men may have survived.

# THE DEATH OF JOHN DILLINGER . . . OR SOMEONE WHO LOOKED LIKE HIM

On July 22, 1934, outside the Biograph Theater on Chicago's north side, John Dillinger, America's first Public Enemy

Number One, passed from this world into the next in a hail of bullets. Or did he? Conspiracy theorists believe that FBI agents shot and killed the wrong man and covered it all up when they realized their mistake. So what really happened that night? Let's first take a look at the main players in this gangland soap opera.

## Hoover Wants His Man

Born on June 22, 1903, John Dillinger was in his early thirties when he first caught the FBI's eye. They thought they were through with him in January 1934, when he was arrested after shooting a police officer during a bank robbery in East Chicago, Indiana. However, Dillinger managed to stage a daring escape from his Indiana jail cell using a wooden gun painted with black shoe polish.

Once Dillinger left Indiana in a stolen vehicle and crossed into Illinois, he was officially a federal fugitive. J. Edgar Hoover, then director of the FBI, promised a quick apprehension, but Dillinger had other plans. He seemed to enjoy the fact that the FBI was tracking him—rather than go into hiding, he continued robbing banks. Annoyed, Hoover assigned FBI Agent Melvin Purvis to ambush Dillinger. Purvis's plan backfired, though, and Dillinger escaped, shooting and killing two innocent men in the process. After the botched trap, the public was in an uproar and the FBI was under close scrutiny. To everyone at the FBI, the message was clear: Hoover wanted Dillinger, and he wanted him ASAP.

## The Woman in Red

The FBI's big break came in July 1934 with a phone call from a woman named Anna Sage. Sage was a Romanian immigrant who ran a Chicago-area brothel. Fearing that she might be deported, Sage wanted to strike a bargain with the feds. Her proposal was simple: In exchange for not being deported, Sage was willing to give the FBI John Dillinger. According to Sage, Dillinger was dating Polly Hamilton, one of her former employees. Melvin Purvis personally met with Sage and told her he couldn't make any promises but he would do what he could about her pending deportation.

Several days later, on July 22, Sage called the FBI office in Chicago and said that she was going to the movies that night with Dillinger and Hamilton. Sage quickly hung up but not before saying she would wear something bright so that agents could pick out the threesome in a crowd. Not knowing which movie theater they were planning to go to, Purvis dispatched several agents to the Marbro Theater, while he and another group of agents went to the Biograph. At approximately 8:30 p.m., Purvis believed he saw Dillinger, Sage, and Hamilton enter the Biograph. As she had promised, Sage indeed wore something bright—an orange blouse. However, under the marquee lights, the blouse's color appeared to be red, which is why Sage was forever dubbed "The Woman in Red."

Purvis tried to apprehend Dillinger right after he purchased tickets, but he slipped past Purvis and into the darkened theater. Purvis went into the theater but was unable to locate Dillinger in the dark. At that point, Purvis left the theater, gathered his men, and made the decision to apprehend Dillinger as he was exiting the theater. Purvis positioned himself in the theater's vestibule, instructed his men to hide outside, and told them that he would signal them by lighting a cigar when he spotted Dillinger. That was their cue to move in and arrest Dillinger.

## "Stick 'em up, Johnny!"

At approximately 10:30 p.m., the doors to the Biograph opened and people started to exit. All of the agents' eyes were on Purvis. When a man wearing a straw hat, accompanied by two women, walked past Purvis, the agent quickly placed a cigar in his mouth and lit a match. Perhaps sensing something was wrong, the man turned and looked at Purvis, at which point Purvis drew his pistol and said, "Stick 'em up, Johnny!" In response, the man turned as if he was going to run away, while at the same time reaching for what appeared to be a gun. Seeing the movement, the other agents opened fire. As the man ran away, attempting to flee down the alleyway alongside the theater, he was shot four times on his left side and once in the back of the neck before crumpling on the pavement. When Purvis reached him and checked for vitals, there were none. Minutes later, after being driven to a local hospital, John Dillinger was pronounced DOA. But as soon as it was announced that Dillinger was dead, the controversy began.

## Dillinger Disputed

Much of the basis for the conspiracy stems from the fact that Hoover, both publicly and privately, made it clear that no matter what, he wanted Dillinger caught. On top of that, Agent Purvis was under a lot of pressure to capture Dillinger, especially since he'd failed with a previous attempt. Keeping that in mind, it would be easy to conclude that Purvis, in his haste to capture Dillinger, might have overlooked a few things.

First, it was Purvis alone who pointed out the man he thought to be Dillinger to the waiting agents. Conspiracy theorists contend that Purvis fingered the wrong man that night, and an innocent man ended up getting killed as a result. As evidence, they point to Purvis's own statement: While they were standing at close range, the man tried to pull a gun, which is why the agents had to open fire. But even though agents stated they recovered a .38-caliber Colt automatic from the victim's body (and even had it on display for many years), author Jay Robert Nash discovered that

that particular model was not even available until a good five months after Dillinger's alleged death! Theorists believe that when agents realized they had not only shot the wrong man, but an unarmed one at that, they planted the gun as part of a cover-up.

Another interesting fact that could have resulted in Purvis's misidentification was that Dillinger had recently undergone plastic surgery in an attempt to disguise himself. In addition to work on his face, Dillinger had attempted to obliterate his fingerprints by dipping his fingers into an acid solution. On top of that, the man who Purvis claimed was Dillinger was wearing a straw hat the entire time Purvis saw him. It is certainly possible that Purvis did not actually recognize Dillinger but instead picked out someone who merely looked like him. If you remember, the only tip Purvis had was Sage telling him that she was going to the movies with Dillinger and his girlfriend.

Did Purvis see Sage leaving the theater in her orange blouse and finger the wrong man simply because he was standing next to Sage and resembled Dillinger? Or was the whole thing a setup orchestrated by Sage and Dillinger to trick the FBI into executing an innocent man?

## So Who Was It?

If the man shot and killed outside the theater wasn't John Dillinger, who was it? There are several conflicting accounts, but one speculation is that it was a man named Jimmy Lawrence, who was dating Polly Hamilton.

If you believe in the conspiracy, Lawrence was simply in the wrong place at the wrong time. Or possibly, Dillinger purposely sent Lawrence to the theater hoping FBI agents would shoot him, allowing Dillinger to fade into obscurity.

Of course, those who don't believe in the conspiracy say the reason Lawrence looked so much like Dillinger is because he was Dillinger using an alias. Further, Dillinger's sister, Audrey Hancock, identified his body. Finally, they say it all boils down to the FBI losing or misplacing the gun Dillinger had the night he was killed and inadvertently replacing it with the wrong one. Case closed.

Not really, though. It seems that whenever someone comes up with a piece of evidence to fuel the conspiracy theory, someone else has something to refute it. Some have asked that Dillinger's body be exhumed and DNA tests be performed, but nothing has come of it yet. Until that happens, we'll probably never know for sure what really happened on that hot July night back in 1934. But that's okay, because real or imagined, everyone loves a good mystery.

# "FIFTEEN WOMEN ON A DEAD WOMAN'S CHEST..."

If Calico Jack had heard the famous pirate song sung this way, would he have declared it blasphemous? Don't bet your booty.

## Women of the Sea

Throughout history, women have received more than their share of omissions, and this certainly was the case during the Golden Age of Piracy. Although it's true that men were the predominant players in this high-seas melodrama, women had important roles. Most people have heard of Captain Kidd, Blackbeard, and Calico Jack, but those same people might scratch their heads while trying to recall Anne Bonny, Lady Mary Killigrew, and Mary Read.

Despite their relative anonymity, female swashbucklers were as much a part of the pirate experience as garish costumes and hand-held telescopes. In fact, the story of female pirates is at least as captivating as buried treasures or mutinous uprisings.

Female pirates date back at least as far as the fifth century, but the most notable figures appeared long after that. Mary Killigrew, a lady under Queen Elizabeth I, operated in the late sixteenth century. In her most celebrated outing, Killigrew and her shipmates boarded a German vessel off of Falmouth, Cornwall. Once on deck, they killed the crew and stole their cargo. When later brought to trial for the murders, Killigrew was sentenced to death. With some well-placed bribes and a queen sympathetic to her plight, however, she was eventually acquitted. Her bold tale is said to have inspired female pirates yet to come.

## The Story of Mary and Anne

The exploits of pirates Mary Read and Anne Bonny rank among those of their male counterparts. Read was born in London in the late seventeenth century and spent her entire childhood disguised as a boy. The reasons for her unusual dress are lost to time, but Read's thirst for adventure has never been in question.

Working as a "footboy" for a wealthy French woman, "Mark" Read eventually grew tired of such drudgery and signed on for sea duty aboard a man-o'-war. From there, the cross-dressed woman joined the Flemish army, where she served two stints. Eventually, Read booked passage on a ship bound for the West Indies. While on this fateful journey, her vessel was attacked and captured by none other than Captain (Calico) Jack Rackham.

A dashing figure in her male persona, Read drew the amorous gaze of Bonny, who was Calico Jack's mistress and a pirate in her own right. Upon the discovery of Read's gender, the two became friends, and they struck a deal to continue the ruse. The game wouldn't last long. A jealous Calico Jack confronted the pair, and he too learned the truth. Finding appeal in the prospect of having two female pirates on his crew, the captain let things stand.

Adventure-loving Read took well to her life of piracy and soon fell in love with a young sailor. This upset a veteran crewmate, who challenged the would-be Lothario to a duel. Fearful that her man would be killed by the strapping seaman, Read demanded her own showdown. She was granted her wish. After the combatants discharged their pistols, both stood unscathed. When they reached for their swords, Read cunningly ripped her shirt open and exposed her breasts. The stunned seaman hesitated, and Read, in classic pirate fashion, swung her cutlass. It found its mark.

## Courageous Buccaneers

Read's victory would be short lived. Charged with piracy after their ship was seized by Jamaican authorities in 1720, Read, Bonny, and Calico Jack were tried and sentenced to hang. When asked in court why a woman might wish to become a pirate and face such a sentence, Read cockily replied, "As to hanging, it is no great hardship, for were it not for that, every cowardly fellow would turn pirate and so unfit the seas, that men of courage must starve." Read could easily have added "women of courage" to her answer. She and other female pirates had pillaged at least that much.

# Chapter 7
# HISTORICAL ODDITIES

## WHO BETRAYED ANNE FRANK?

Anne Frank and her family thwarted Nazis for two years, hiding in Amsterdam. They might have remained hidden and waited out the war, but someone blew their cover.

Annelies Marie Frank was born in Frankfurt am Main, Germany, on June 12, 1929. Perhaps the most well-known victim of the Holocaust, she was one of approximately 1.5 million Jewish children killed by the Nazis. Her diary chronicling her experience in Amsterdam was discovered in the Franks' secret hiding place by friends of the family and first published in 1947. Translated into more than 60 languages, *Anne Frank: The Diary of a Young Girl* has sold 30 million copies and is one of the most read books in the world.

The diary was given to Anne on her 13th birthday, just weeks before she went into hiding. Her father, Otto Frank, moved his family and four friends into a secret annex of rooms above his office at 263 Prinsengracht, near a canal in central Amsterdam, on July 6, 1942. They relied on trustworthy business associates, employees, and friends, who risked their own lives to help them. Anne poignantly wrote her thoughts, yearnings, and descriptions of life in the secret annex in her diary, revealing a vibrant, intelligent young woman struggling to retain her ideals in the direst of circumstances.

On August 4, 1944, four or five Dutch Nazi collaborators under the command of an Austrian Nazi police investigator entered the building and arrested the Franks and their friends. The family was deported to Auschwitz, where they were separated and sent to different camps. Anne and her sister, Margot, were sent to Bergen-Belsen, where they both died of typhus a few weeks before liberation. Anne was 15 years old. Otto Frank was the only member of the group to survive the war.

Dutch police, Nazi hunters, and historians have attempted to identify the person who betrayed the Franks. Searching for clues, the Netherlands Institute for War Documentation (NIWD) has examined records on Dutch collaboration with the Nazis, the letters of Otto Frank, and police transcripts dating from the 1940s. The arresting Nazi officer was also questioned after the war by Nazi hunter Simon Wiesenthal, but he could not identify who informed on the Franks. For decades suspicion centered on Willem Van Maaren, who worked in the warehouse attached to the Franks' hiding place, but two police investigations found no evidence against him.

Two recent theories have been offered about who betrayed the Franks. British author Carol Anne Lee believes it was Anton Ahlers, a business associate of Otto's who was a petty thief and member of the Dutch Nazi movement. Lee argues that Ahlers informed the Nazis to collect the bounty paid to Dutch civilians who exposed Jews. She suggests he may have split the reward with Maarten Kuiper, a friend of Ahlers who was one of the Dutch Nazi collaborators who raided the secret annex. Ahlers was jailed for collaboration with the Nazis after the war, and members of his own family, including his son, have said they believe he was guilty of informing on the Franks.

Austrian writer Melissa Müller believes that a cleaning lady, Lena Hartog, who also worked in the warehouse, reported the Franks because she feared that if they were discovered, her husband, an employee of Otto Frank, would be deported for aiding Jews.

The NIWD has studied the arguments of both writers and examined the evidence supporting their theories. Noting that all the principals involved in the case are no longer living, it concluded that neither theory could be proved.

## MILLIONS OF MUMMIES

It sounds like the premise of a horror movie—millions of excess mummies just piling up. But for the Egyptians, this was simply an excuse to get a little creative.

The ancient Egyptians took death seriously. Their culture believed that the afterlife was a dark and tumultuous place where departed souls needed protection throughout eternity. By preserving their bodies as mummies, Egyptians provided their souls with a resting place—without which they would wander the afterlife forever.

Starting roughly around 3000 BC, Egyptian morticians began making a healthy business on the mummy trade. On receiving a corpse, they would first remove the brain and internal organs and store them in canopic jars. Next, they would stuff the body with straw to maintain its shape, cover it in salt and oils to preserve it from rotting, and then wrap it in linens—a process that could take up to 70 days. Finally, the finished mummies would be sealed into a decorated sarcophagus, now ready to face eternity.

Mummies have always been a source of great mystery and fascination. The tales of mummy curses were wildly popular in their time, and people still flock to horror movies involving vengeful mummies. Museum displays, especially King Tut or Ramses II, remain a sure-fire draw, allowing patrons the chance for a remarkably preserved glimpse of ancient Egypt.

At first, mummification was so costly it remained the exclusive domain of the wealthy, usually royalty. However, when the middle class began adopting the procedure, the mummy population exploded.

Soon people were mummifying everything–even crocodiles. The practice of mummifying the family cat was also common; the owners saw it as an offering to the cat goddess Bast.

Even those who could not afford to properly mummify their loved ones unknowingly contributed to the growing number of mummies. These folks buried their deceased in the Egyptian desert, where the hot, arid conditions dried out the bodies, creating natural mummies. When you consider that this burial art was in use for more than 3,000 years, it's not surprising that over time the bodies began piling up–literally.

So, with millions of mummies lying around, local entrepreneurs began looking for ways to cash in on these buried treasures. To them, mummies were a natural resource, not unlike oil, which could be extracted from the ground and sold at a heavy profit to eager buyers around the world.

## Mummy Medicine

In medieval times, Egyptians began touting mummies for their secret medicinal qualities. European doctors began importing mummies, boiling off their oils and prescribing it to patients. The oil was used to treat a variety of disorders, including sore throats, coughs, epilepsy, poisoning, and skin disorders. Contemporary apothecaries also got into the act, marketing pulverized mummies to noblemen as a cure for nausea.

The medical establishment wasn't completely sold on the beneficial aspects of mummy medicine, however. Several doctors voiced their opinions against the practice, one writing that: "It ought to be rejected as loathsome and offensive," and another claiming: "This wicked kind of drugge doth nothing to help the diseased." A cholera epidemic, which broke out in Europe, was blamed on mummy bandages, and the use of mummy medicine was soon abandoned.

## Mummy Merchants

Grave robbers, a common feature of nineteenth century Egypt, made a huge profit from mummies. Arab traders would raid ancient tombs, sometimes making off with hundreds of bodies. These would be sold to visiting English merchants who, on returning to England, could resell them to the wealthy. Victorian socialites would buy mummies and hold fashionable parties, inviting friends over to view the unwrapping of their Egyptian prize.

## Mummies in Museums

By the mid-nineteenth century, museums were becoming common in Europe, and mummies were prized exhibits. Curators, hoping to make a name for their museums, would travel to Egypt and purchase a mummy to display back home. This provided a steady stream of revenue for the unscrupulous mummy merchants. In the 1850s, the Egyptian government finally stopped the looting of their priceless heritage. Laws were passed allowing only certified archaeologists access to mummy tombs, effectively putting the grave robbers out of business.

## Mummy Myths

There are so many stories regarding the uses of mummies that it's often hard to separate fact from fiction. Some historians suggest the linens that comprised mummy wrappings were used by nineteenth century American and Canadian industrialists to manufacture paper. At the time, there was a huge demand for paper, and suppliers often ran short of cotton rags—a key ingredient in the paper-making process. Although there's no concrete proof, some historians claim that when manufacturers ran out of rags, they imported mummies to use in their place.

Another curious claim comes courtesy of Mark Twain. In his popular 1869 travelogue *The Innocents Abroad*, Twain wrote: "The fuel [Egyptian train operators] use for the locomotive is composed of mummies three thousand years old, purchased by the ton or by the graveyard for that purpose." This item, almost assuredly meant as satire, was taken as fact by readers and survives to this day. However, there is no historical record of Egyptian trains running on burnt mummies. Besides, the mischievous Twain was never one to let a few facts get in the way of a good story. Perhaps those who believe the humorist's outlandish claim might off set it with another of his famous quotes: "A lie can travel halfway around the world while the truth is putting on its shoes."

## SANDSTONE GATEWAY TO HEAVEN

For hundreds of years, rumors of the lost city of Angkor spread among Cambodian peasants. On a stifling day in 1860, Henri Mahout and his porters discovered that the ancient city was more than mere legend.

French botanist and explorer Henri Mahout wiped his spectacles as he pushed into the Cambodian jungle clearing. Gasping for breath in the rain forest's mists, he gazed down weed-ridden avenues at massive towers and stone temples wreathed with carvings of gods, kings, and battles. The ruins before him were none other than the temples of Angkor Wat.

Although often credited with the discovery of Angkor Wat, Mahout was not the first Westerner to encounter the site. He did, however, bring the "lost" city to the attention of the European public when his travel journals were published in 1868. He wrote: "One of these temples—a rival to that of Solomon, and erected by some ancient Michelangelo—might take an honorable place beside our most beautiful buildings."

Mahout's descriptions of this "new," massive, unexplored Hindu temple sent a jolt of lightning through Western academic circles. Explorers from Europe combed the jungles of northern Cambodia in an attempt to explain the meaning and origin of the mysterious lost shrine.

## The Rise of the Khmer

Scholars first theorized that Angkor Wat and other ancient temples in present-day Cambodia were about 2,000 years old. However, as they began to decipher the Sanskrit inscriptions, they found that the temples had been erected during the ninth through twelfth centuries. While Europe languished in the Dark Ages, the Khmer Empire of Indochina was reaching its zenith.

The earliest records of the Khmer people date back to the middle of the sixth century. They migrated from southern China and Tibet and settled in what is now Cambodia. The early Khmer retained many Indian influences from the West— they were Hindus, and their architecture evolved from Indian methods of building.

In the early ninth century, King Jayavarman II laid claim to an independent kingdom called Kambuja. He established his capital in the Angkor area some 190 miles north of the modern Cambodian capital of Phnom Penh. Jayavarman II also introduced the cult of devaraja,

which claimed that the Khmer king was a representative of Shiva, the Hindu god of chaos, destruction, and rebirth. As such, in addition to the temples built to honor the Hindu gods, temples were also constructed to serve as tombs when kings died.

The Khmer Empire built more than 100 stone temples spread out over about 40 miles. The temples were built from laterite (a material similar to clay that forms in tropical climates) and sandstone. The sandstone provided an open canvas for the statues and reliefs celebrating the Hindu pantheon that decorates the temples.

## Home of the Gods

During the first half of the twelfth century, Kambuja's King Suryavarman II decided to raise an enormous temple dedicated to the Hindu god Vishnu, a religious monument that would subdue the surrounding jungle and dramatically illustrate the power of the Khmer king. His masterpiece—the largest temple complex in the world—would be known to history by its Sanskrit name, "Angkor Wat," or "City of Temple."

Pilgrims visiting Angkor Wat in the twelfth century would enter the temple complex by crossing a square, 600-foot-wide moat that ran some four miles in perimeter around the temple grounds. Approaching from the west, visitors would tread the moat's causeway to the main gateway. From there, they would follow a spiritual journey representing the path from the outside world through the Hindu universe and into Mount Meru, the home of the gods. They would pass a giant statue of an eight-armed Vishnu as they entered the western gopura, or gatehouse, known as the "Entrance of the Elephants." They would then follow a stone walkway decorated with nagas (mythical serpents) past sunken pools and column-studded buildings once believed to house sacred temple documents.

At the end of the stone walkway, a pilgrim would step up to a rectangular platform surrounded with galleries featuring six-foot-high bas-reliefs of gods and kings. One depicts the Churning of the Ocean of Milk, a Hindu story in which gods and demons churn a serpent in an ocean of milk to extract the elixir of life. Another illustrates the epic battle of monkey warriors against demons whose sovereign had kidnapped Sita, Rama's beautiful wife. Others depict the gruesome fates awaiting the wicked in the afterlife.

A visitor to King Suryavarman's kingdom would next ascend the dangerously steep steps to the temple's second level, an enclosed area boasting a courtyard decorated with hundreds of dancing apsaras, female images ornamented with jewelry and elaborately dressed hair.

For kings and high priests, the journey would continue with a climb up more steep steps to a 126-foot-high central temple, the pinnacle of Khmer society. Spreading out some 145 feet on each side, the square temple includes a courtyard cornered by four high conical towers shaped to look like lotus buds. The center of the temple is dominated by a fifth conical tower soaring 180 feet above the main causeway; inside it holds a golden statue of the Khmer patron, Vishnu, riding a half-man, half-bird creature in the image of King Suryavarman.

## Disuse and Destruction

With the decline of the Khmer Empire and the resurgence of Buddhism, Angkor Wat was occupied by Buddhist monks, who claimed it as their own for many years. A cruciform gallery leading to the temple's second level was decorated with 1,000 Buddhas; the Vishnu statue in the central tower was replaced by an image of Buddha. The temple fell into various states of disrepair over the centuries and is now the focus of international restoration efforts.

# THE MYSTERY OF
# THE 700-YEAR-OLD PIPER

It's an intriguing story about a mysterious piper and more than 100 missing children. Made famous by the eponymous Brothers Grimm, this popular fairy tale has captivated generations of boys and girls. But is it actually more fact than fiction?

The legend of The Pied Piper of Hameln documents the story of a mysterious musician who rid a town of rats by enchanting the rodents with music from his flute. The musician led the mesmerized rats to a nearby river, where they drowned. When the townsfolk refused to settle their debt, the rat catcher returned several weeks later, charmed a group of 130 children with the same flute, and led them out of town. They disappeared—never to be seen again.

It's a story that dates back to approximately AD 1300 and has its roots in a small German town called Hameln. Several accounts written between the fourteenth and seventeenth centuries tell of a stained-glass window in the town's main church. The window pictured the Pied Piper with hands clasped, standing over a group of youngsters. Encircling the window was the following verse (this is a rough translation): "In the year 1284, on John's and Paul's day was the 26th of June. By a piper, dressed in all kinds of colors, 130 children born in Hameln were seduced and lost at the calvarie near the koppen."

The verse is quite specific: precise month and year, exact number of children involved in the incident, and detailed place names. Because of this, some scholars believe this window, which was removed in 1660 and either accidentally destroyed or lost, was created in memory of an actual event. Yet, the verse makes no mention of the circumstances regarding the departure of the children or their specific fate. What exactly happened in Hameln, Germany, in 1284? The truth is, no one actually knows—at least not for certain.

## Theories Abound

Gernot Hüsam, the current chairman of the Coppenbrügge Castle Museum, believes the word "koppen" in the inscription may reference a rocky outcrop on a hill in nearby Coppenbrügge, a small town previously known as Koppanberg. Hüsam also believes the use of the word "calvarie" is in reference to either the medieval connotation of the gates of hell—or since the Crusades—a place of execution.

One theory put forward is that Coppenbrügge resident Nikolaus von Spiegelberg recruited Hameln youth to emigrate to areas in Pomerania near the Baltic Sea. This theory suggests the youngsters were either murdered, because they took part in summertime pagan rituals, or drowned in a tragic accident while in transit to the new colonies.

But this is not the only theory. In fact, theories concerning the fate of the children abound. Here are some ideas about what really happened:

• They suffered from the Black Plague or a similar disease and were led from the town to spare the rest of the population.

• They were part of a crusade to the Holy Land.

• They were lost in the 1260 Battle of Sedemünder.

• They died in a bridge collapse over the Weser River or a landslide on Ith Mountain.

• They emigrated to settle in other parts of Europe, including Maehren, Oelmutz, Transylvania, or Uckermark.

- They were actually young adults who were led away and murdered for performing pagan rituals on a local mountain.

Historians believe that emigration, bridge collapse/natural disaster, disease, or murder are the most plausible explanations.

## Tracing the Piper's Path

Regardless of what actually happened in Hameln hundreds of years ago, the legend of the Pied Piper has endured. First accounts of the Piper had roots to the actual incident, but as time passed, the story took on a life of its own.

Early accounts of the legend date back to 1384, at which time a Hameln church leader was said to be in possession of a chorus book with a Latin verse related to the legend written on the front cover by his grandmother. The book was misplaced in the late seventeenth century and has never been found.

The oldest surviving account—according to amateur Pied Piper historian Jonas Kuhn—appears as an addition to a fourteenth century manuscript from Luneburg. Written in Latin, the note is almost identical to the verse on the stained-glass window and translates roughly to:

"In the year of 1284, on the day of Saints John and Paul on the 26th of June 130 children born in Hamelin were seduced By a piper, dressed in all kinds of colors, and lost at the place of execution near the koppen."

Physician and philosopher Jobus Fincelius believed the Pied Piper was the devil. In his 1556 book *Concerning the Wonders of His Times*, Fincelius wrote: "It came about in Hameln in Saxony on the River Weser . . . the Devil visibly in human form walked the lanes of Hameln and by playing a pipe lured after him many children to a mountain. Once there, he with the children . . . could no longer be found."

In 1557, Count Froben Christoph von Zimmern wrote a chronicle detailing his family's lineage. Sprinkled throughout the book were folklore tales including one that referenced the Pied Piper. For some unknown reason, the count introduced rats into his version of the story: "He passed through the streets of the town with his small pipe . . . immediately all the rats . . . collected outside the houses and followed his footsteps." This first insertion of rodents into the legend led other writers to follow suit.

In 1802, Johan Wolfgang Goethe wrote "Der Rattenfanger," a poem based loosely on the legend. The monologue was told in the first person through the eyes of the rat catcher. Goethe's poem made no direct reference to the town of Hameln, and in Goethe's version the Piper played a stringed instrument instead of a pipe. The Piper also made an appearance in Goethe's literary work *Faust*.

Jacob and Wilhelm Grimm began collecting European folktales in the early 1800s. Best known for a series of books that documented 211 fairy tales, the brothers also published two volumes between 1816 and 1818 detailing almost 600 German folklore legends. One of the volumes contained the story of Der Rattenfanger von Hameln.

The Grimm brothers' research for The Pied Piper drew on 11 different sources, from which they deduced two children were left behind (a blind child and a mute child); the piper led the children through a cave to Transylvania; and a street in Hameln was named after the event.

## No End in Sight

While the details of the historical event surrounding the legend of The Pied Piper have been lost to time, the mystique of the story endures. Different versions of the legend have even appeared in literature outside of Germany: A rat catcher from Vienna helped rid the nearby town of

Korneuburg of rats. When he wasn't paid, he stole off with the town's children and sold them as slaves in Constantinople. A vagabond rid the English town of Newton on the Isle of Wight of their rats, and when he wasn't paid, led the town's children into an ancient oak forest where they were never seen again. A Chinese version had a Hangchow district official use magic to convince the rats to leave his city.

The legend's plot has been adapted over time to fit whichever media is currently popular and has been used as a story line in children's books, ballet, theatre, and even a radio drama. The intriguing mystery of the piper will continue to interest us as long as there is mystery surrounding the original event.

# THE LIBRARY OF THE MUSES

By far the most famous library in history, the Library of Alexandria held an untold number of ancient works. Its fiery destruction meant the irrecoverable loss of a substantial part of the world's intellectual history.

## The Library's Beginnings

The cities of ancient Mesopotamia (e.g., Uruk, Nineveh, Babylon) and Egypt (e.g., Thebes, Memphis) had cultivated archives and libraries since the Bronze Age, but the idea for a library as grand as Alexandria did not occur in Greek culture until the Hellenistic Age, when Alexander the Great's conquests brought both Greece and these former civilizations under Macedonian rule. Previous Greek libraries were owned by individuals; the largest belonged to Aristotle (384–322 BC), whose work and school (the Lyceum) in Athens were supported by Alexander.

When Alexander died suddenly in 323 BC, his generals carved his empire into regional dynasties. The Hellenistic dynasties competed with each other for three centuries (until each was in turn conquered by either Rome or Parthia). Each dynasty desired cultural dominance, so they invited famous artists, authors, and intellectuals to live and work in their capital cities. Alexander's general Ptolemy, who controlled Egypt, decided to develop a collection of the world's learning (the Library) and a research center, the Mouseion (the Museum, or "Temple of the Muses"), where scholars on subsidy could study and add their research to the collection.

This idea may well have come from Demetrius of Phaleron (350–280 BC), Ptolemy's advisor and the former governor of Athens, who had been a pupil at the Lyceum, but the grand project became one of the hallmarks of the Ptolemaic dynasty. Under the first three Ptolemies, the Museum, a royal library, and a smaller "daughter" library at the Temple of Serapis (the Serapeum) were built and grew as Alexandria became the intellectual, as well as commercial, capital of the Hellenistic world.

Egypt and Alexandria offered the Ptolemies distinct advantages for accomplishing their goals. Egypt was not only immensely rich, which gave it the wealth to purchase materials and to bring scholars to Alexandria, but it was the major producer of papyrus, a marsh reed that was beaten into a flat surface and made into scrolls for writing and copying. Alexandria was also the commercial hub of the Mediterranean, and goods and information from all over the world passed through its port.

## Bibliomania: So Many Scrolls, So Little Time

Acquiring materials for the libraries and Museum became somewhat of an obsession for the Ptolemies. Although primarily focused on Greek and Egyptian works, their interests included translating other traditions into Greek. Among the most important of these efforts was the production of the Septuagint, a Greek version of the Jewish scriptures.

Besides employing agents to scour major book markets and to search out copies of works not yet in the library, boats coming into Alexandria were required to declare any scrolls on board. If they were of interest, the scrolls were confiscated and copied, and the owners were given the copies and some compensation. Ptolemy III (285–222 BC) may have acquired Athens' official state collection of the plays of Aeschylus, Sophocles, and Euripides in a similar way—putting up 15 talents of silver as a guarantee while he had the plays copied, then foregoing the treasure in favor of keeping the originals. Whether or not this is true, it speaks to the value he placed on getting important works and the resources he had at his disposal to do so.

Alexandria's efforts were fueled by a competition with the Hellenistic kingdom of Pergamum (modern Bergamo, Turkey), which created its own library. Each library sought to claim new finds and to produce new editions, leading at times to the acquisition of forgeries and occasional embarrassment. Alexandria tried to undercut its rival by cutting off papyrus exports, but Pergamum perfected a method for making writing material out of animal skins (now called "parchment" from the Latin pergamina). Eventually, however, Alexandria got the upper hand when the Roman general Marcus Antonius (Mark Antony) conquered Pergamum and made a present of its library to his lover, the Ptolemaic Queen Cleopatra.

Estimates as to the number of volumes in the Alexandrian library ranged wildly even in antiquity, generally between 200,000 and 700,000. Estimates are complicated by the fact that it isn't clear whether the numbers originate from works or scrolls: Some scrolls contained one work, some multiple works, and long works like the Iliad took multiple scrolls. Over time, a complex cataloguing system evolved, which culminated in a bibliographic survey of the library's holdings called the Pinakes. The survey was put together by the great Hellenistic scholar and poet Callimachus of Cyrene (305–240 BC). Unfortunately, this important work only exists in fragments today.

## Burning Down the House

The Royal Library and its holdings were accidentally set aflame in 48 BC when Caesar (who had taken Cleopatra's side in her claim to the throne against her brother) tried to burn his way out of being trapped in the port by opposing forces. Further losses probably occurred in AD 271 when Emperor Aurelian destroyed part of the Museum while recapturing Alexandria from Queen Zenobia's forces. The "daughter" library of the Serapeum was finally destroyed by Christians under Emperor Theodosius. But by then, much of the contents (like the contents of other great civic libraries of antiquity) had decayed or found their way into other hands, leaving the classical heritage scattered and fragmented for centuries. Much later, Christians dramatically blamed the burning of the library holdings on Muslim conquerors. Although this made for a good story, the legendary contents of the library were already long gone.

# THE MOUND BUILDERS: MYTHMAKING IN EARLY AMERICA

The search for an improbable past, or, how to make a mountain out of a molehill.

In the early 1840s, the fledgling United States was gripped by a controversy that spilled from the parlors of the educated men in Boston and Philadelphia—the core of the nation's intellectual elite—onto the pages of the newspapers printed for mass edification. In the tiny farming village of Grave Creek, Virginia (now West Virginia), on the banks of the Ohio River stood one of the largest earthen mounds discovered during white man's progress westward. The existence of these mounds, spread liberally throughout the Mississippi Valley, Ohio River Valley, and much of the southeast, was commonly known and had caused a great deal of speculative excitement since Europeans had first arrived on the continent. Hernando de Soto, for one, had mentioned the mounds of the Southeast during his wandering in that region.

## Money Well Spent

The colonists who settled the East Coast noticed that the mounds, which came in a variety of sizes and shapes, were typically placed near excellent sites for villages and farms.

The Grave Creek mound was among the first of the major earthworks discovered by white men in their westward expansion. By 1838, the property was owned and farmed by the Tomlinson family. Abelard B. Tomlinson took an interest in the mound on his family's land and decided to open a vertical shaft from its summit, 70 feet high, to the center. He discovered skeletal remains at various levels and a timbered vault at the base containing the remains of two individuals. More importantly, he discovered a sandstone tablet inscribed with three lines of characters of unknown origin.

## Who Were the Mound Builders?

Owing to the general belief that the aborigines were lazy and incapable of such large, earthmoving operations and the fact that none of the tribes who dwelt near the mounds claimed any knowledge of who had built them, many nineteenth century Americans believed that the mound builders could not have been the ancestors of the Native American tribes they encountered.

Wild and fantastic stories arose, and by the early nineteenth century, the average American assumed that the mound builders had been a pre-Columbian expedition from the Old

World–Vikings, Israelites, refugees from Atlantis–all these and more had their champions. Most agreed, however, that the New World had once hosted and given rise to a civilization as advanced as that of the Aztecs and Incas who had then fallen into disarray or been conquered by the savage barbarians that now inhabited the land. Speculation on the history of the mound builders led many, including Thomas Jefferson, to visit mounds and conduct their own studies.

## Mormons and the Mounds

Meanwhile, the Grave Creek tablet fanned the flames of a controversy that was roaring over the newly established, and widely despised, Church of Jesus Christ of Latter Day Saints, founded by Joseph Smith.

The Mormon religion is based upon the belief that the American continent was once inhabited by lost tribes of Israel who divided into warring factions and fought each other to near extinction. The last surviving prophet of these people, Mormon, inscribed his people's history upon gold tablets, which were interred in a mound near present-day Palmyra, New York, until they were revealed to 15-year-old Joseph Smith in 1823. Though many Americans were ready to believe that the mounds represented the remains of a non-aboriginal culture, they were less ready to believe in Smith's new religion.

Smith and his adherents were persecuted horribly, and Smith was killed by an angry mob while leading his followers west. Critics of the Saints (as the Mormons prefer to be called) point to the early nineteenth century publication of several popular books purporting that the earthen mounds of North America were the remains of the lost tribes of Israel. These texts claimed that evidence would eventually be discovered to support their author's assertions. That the young Smith should have his revelation so soon after these fanciful studies were published struck many observers as entirely too coincidental. Thus, Abelard Tomlinson's excavation of the sandstone tablet with its strange figures ignited the passions of both Smith's followers and his detractors.

## Enter the Scholar

Into this theological, and ultimately anthropological, maelstrom strode Henry Rowe Schoolcraft, a mineralogist whose keen interest in Native American history had led to his appointment as head of Indian affairs. While working in Sault Ste. Marie, Schoolcraft married a native woman and mastered the Ojibwa language. Schoolcraft traveled to Grave Creek to examine Tomlinson's tablet and concluded that the figures were indeed a language but deferred to more learned scholars to determine just which language they represented.

The opinions were many and varied—from Celtic runes to early Greek; experts the world over weighed in with their opinions. Nevertheless, Schoolcraft was more concerned with physical evidence and close study of the mounds themselves, and he remained convinced that the mounds and the artifacts they carried were the products of ancestors of the Native Americans.

Schoolcraft's theory flew in the face of both those who sought to defend and those who sought to debunk the Mormon belief, and it would be more than three decades until serious scholarship and the emergence of true archeological techniques began to shift opinion on the subject.

## Answers Proposed, but Questions Still Abound

History has vindicated Schoolcraft's careful and thoughtful study of the mounds. Today, we know that the mound builders were not descendants of Israel, nor were they the offspring of Vikings. They were simply the ancient and more numerous predecessors of the Native Americans, who constructed the mounds for protection from floods and as burial sites, temples, and defense strongholds. As for the Grave Creek tablet: Many scholars have concluded that the figures are not a written language but simply a fanciful design whose meaning, if ever there was one, has been lost to the ages. Still others believe the figures represent a language we have yet to positively identify. Though the Smithsonian Institute has several etchings of the tablet in its collection, the whereabouts of the actual tablet have been lost to the ages.

## Sorry, Mates, but Aussies Didn't Invent the Boomerang

Contrary to popular myth, lore, and Australian drinking songs, boomerangs, or "The Throwing Wood," as proponents prefer to call them, did not originate down under.

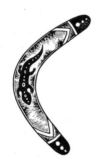

The colonists, adventurers, prisoners, and explorers who ventured into the heart of the Australian wilderness may be excused for believing that the local aborigines created these little aerodynamic marvels, considering the proficiency with which they used the wooden devices to bring down wild game and wilder colonials. The gyroscopic precision with which boomerangs were (and still are) crafted by primitive peoples continues to intrigue and astonish those who come in contact with the lightweight, spinning missiles, which—if thrown correctly—actually will return to their throwers.

### Many Returns

As a weapon of war and especially as a tool for hunting small game, the boomerang has been around for nearly 10,000 years. In fact, evidence of boomerangs has been discovered in almost every nook and cranny in the world. Pictures of boomerangs can be found in Neolithic-era cave drawings in France, Spain, and Poland. The "lagobolon," or "hare club," as it was called, was commonly used by nobles in Crete around 2000 BC. And King Tut, ruler of Egypt around 1350 BC, had a large collection of boomerangs—several of which were found when his tomb was discovered in the 1920s.

The Greek mythological hero Hercules is depicted tossing about a curved "clava" or "throwing stick" on pottery made during the Homeric era. Carthaginian invaders in the second century BC were bombarded by Gallic warriors who rained "catela" or "throwing clubs." The Roman historian Horace describes a flexible wooden "caia" used by German tribes, saying "if thrown by a master, it returns to the one who threw it." Roman Emperor Caesar Augustus's favorite contemporary author, Virgil, also describes a similar curved missile weapon in use by natives of the province of Hispania.

However, Europeans can no more claim the invention of the boomerang than their Australian cousins can. Archaeologists have found evidence of boomerang use throughout Neolithicera Africa, from Sudan to Niger, and from Cameroon to Morocco. Tribes in southern India, the American southwest, Mexico, and Java all used the boomerang, or something very similar, and for the same purposes.

Australians, however, can be credited with bringing the boomerang to the fresh attention of the modern world. They helped popularize it both as a child's toy and as an item for sport. A World Cup is held every other year, and enthusiasts and scientists still compete to design, construct, and throw the perfect boomerang.

Though the tool, weapon, or toy known today as a boomerang did not originate in Australia—or at least did not originate exclusively in Australia—the word itself is Australian. *Boomerang* is a blending of the words, woomerang and bumarin, terms used by different groups of Australian aborigines to describe their little wooden wonders.

# Shroud of Turin: Real or Fake?

Measuring roughly 14 feet long by 3 feet wide, the Shroud of Turin features the front and back image of a man who was 5 feet, 9 inches tall. The man was bearded and had shoulder-length hair parted down the middle. Dark stains on the Shroud are consistent with blood from a crucifixion.

First publicly displayed in 1357, the Shroud of Turin has apparent ties to the Knights of Templar. At the time of its first showing, the Shroud was in the hands of the family of Geoffrey de Charney, a Templar who had been burned at the stake in 1314 along with Jacques de Molay. Some accounts say it was the Knights who removed the cloth from Constantinople, where it was kept in the thirteenth century.

Some believe the Shroud of Turin is the cloth that Jesus was wrapped in after his death. All four gospels mention that the body of Jesus was covered in a linen cloth prior to the resurrection. Others assert that the cloth shrouded Jacques de Molay after he was tortured by being nailed to a door.

Still others contend that the Shroud was the early photographic experiments of Leonardo da Vinci. He mentioned working with "optics" in some of his diaries and wrote his notes in a sort of mirrored handwriting style, some say, to keep his experiments secret from the church.

Is the Shroud of Turin authentic? In 1988, scientists using carbon-dating concluded that the material in the Shroud was from around 1260 to 1390, which seems to exclude the possibility that the Shroud bears the image of Jesus.

# THE DAY KING TUT'S TOMB WAS OPENED

There was a time when archaeology was commissioned privately by wealthy individuals. Some of these benefactors desired to advance historical knowledge, while others simply hoped to enhance their personal collections of antiquities. The much-heralded opening of the tomb of the Pharaoh Tutankhamun, better known today as "King Tut," represented one of the last hurrahs for these old days of archaeology.

## Who Was King Tut, Anyway?

King Tut was an ancient Egyptian ruler, or pharaoh. His full name, Tutankhamun, meant to say that he was the living image of the sun god, Amun. Tut ruled Egypt from 1333–1324 BC, during what is referred to as the New Kingdom period. Sometimes called "The Boy King," he became pharaoh when he was 9 years old and died at age 19. Researchers believe Tut died from an infection caused by a broken leg.

## How Was His Tomb Located?

Finding the tomb required scholarship, persistence, patience, and lots of digging. A wealthy Englishman, Lord Carnarvon, sponsored one of the day's brightest archaeologists, Howard Carter. With Carnarvon's backing, Carter poked around in Egypt between 1917 and 1922 with little luck. Then, in November 1922, just as Lord Carnarvon was ready to give up, Carter uncovered steps leading down to a tomb marked with Tut's royal seals. Carter dashed off a communiqué to Carnarvon, telling him to get to Egypt, and fast.

## What Happened Next?

Carnarvon wasted no time, and once the sponsor reached the scene, Carter was ready to cut his way into the tomb. Workers soon exposed a sealed doorway bearing Tut's name. Those present would witness the unveiling of history as Carter peered into the tomb. However, thanks to the meticulous nature of archaeology, work on Tut's tomb could only happen at a slow pace. The entire process stretched across ten years.

## What Was in There?

The contents of the tomb were incredible. It was clear that ancient plunderers had twice raided the tomb for some smaller items. Although they did leave the place a mess, many amazing treasures remained. Carter and company catalogued piles of priceless artifacts, including gold statues and everything from sandals to chariots. Tut's mummified body had been placed in an ornate coffin, and canopic jars held his internal organs. In addition, two mummified premature babies, thought to be Tut's children, were found. Tut was also buried with everything he would need to be stylish in the afterlife, including ornate bows and gloves fit for a pharaoh. Scholars would spend years preserving and studying the artifacts in the tomb.

King Tut's tomb was the archaeological find of that decade—perhaps even the find of the twentieth century.

# CIVIL WAR MYTHS

There's a certain romance to the tales that have circulated in the almost 150 years since the Civil War. Many are true, but many others are laced with falsehoods.

## Myth: The Civil War was America's first disagreement over slavery.

The founders of the United States had been concerned with the ownership of slaves, particularly as it played out in the issue of states' rights, since the Articles of Confederation were ratified in 1781. A confederation, by definition, is a loose alignment of states, each with the power to self-regulate. The Southern states favored slavery, and every time the issue of states' rights emerged on the national front, the South would threaten to secede.

Other landmark Congressional acts and court judgments that influenced slavery in America before the Civil War include the Three-Fifths Compromise in the Constitution, the Missouri Compromise of 1820, the Compromise of 1850, the Kansas-Nebraska Act, and the Dred Scott Decision.

## Myth: The Emancipation Proclamation freed all the slaves in America.

Lincoln wrote the edict in September 1862, and it went into effect on January 1, 1863. The language of the document was clear: Any slave that was still held in the states that had seceded from the Union was "forever free" as of January 1, 1863.

Significantly, this edict did not include border states in which slaves were still held, such as Kentucky or Missouri, because Lincoln didn't want to stoke rebellion there. As one might expect, the Southern states paid hardly any attention to the announcement by the Union president. They'd already turned their backs on him and his nation, and as far as they were concerned, the Union president held no power over them.

## Myth: The Union soldiers firmly believed in the cause of freeing the slaves.

For the most part, soldiers had little, if any, opinion on slavery. At first, many men enlisted in the Union army as a romantic adventure. Early opinion estimated that the war would end within a few months, and many decided they could afford that much time away from their work, school, or home life.

**Myth: The South's secession was the first time in American history a state tried to leave the Union.**

During the War of 1812, New England almost seceded in order to protect its trade with Great Britain. In the 1850s, President James Buchanan, who held office immediately before Abraham Lincoln, stated the federal government would not resort to force in order to prevent secession. In 1869, four years after the end of the war, the Supreme Court declared the act of state secession to be unconstitutional.

**Myth: The Confederate attack on Fort Sumter was the first act of Southern aggression against Northern targets.**

The attack on Fort Sumter was preceded by attacks on other forts and military installations in Confederate territory. On January 9, 1861, Mississippi followed South Carolina to become the second state to secede from the Union. Within a week, Mississippi's governor ordered an armed battery placed on the bluff above the wharf at Vicksburg. His declared intention was to force Union vessels to stop to be searched—after all, it was rumored that a cannon had been sent to a Baton Rouge arsenal. Intentions aside, the fact is the battery actually fired on a number of vessels in order to make them come about, including the *Gladiator,* the *Imperial*, and the *A.O. Tyler.*

Prior to this incident, the Confederate Congress had approved the creation of a volunteer army of 100,000 soldiers—far larger than any military force that was intended strictly for keeping the peace would presumably need to be.

**Myth: Abraham Lincoln wrote his Gettysburg Address on the back of an envelope while riding the train on his way to make the speech.**

Lincoln would never have waited until the last minute to write such an important oration, which was part of the consecration of the Gettysburg Cemetery in November 1863. But even if he had, the train ride itself would have prevented legible writing. The 1860s-period train cars bounced, swayed, and made horseback riding seem smooth by comparison. Several drafts of the Gettysburg Address (including what is referred to as the "reading draft") have been archived at the Library of Congress and other academic institutions. They are written—very legibly—on lined paper and Executive Mansion stationery.

**Myth: The "Taps" bugle call was first used by Union Captain Robert Ellicombe after Ellicombe discovered his son dead on the battlefield wearing a Confederate uniform. The son had been a music student, and the music for "Taps" was found in the boy's pocket. Captain Ellicombe had it played as tribute during his son's funeral.**

There is no proof that Captain Robert Ellicombe even existed at all, and certainly there is no record of any captain by that name in the Union army during the Civil War. "Taps" actually came from Union General Daniel Butterfield, although it is not certain whether Butterfield composed the tune or adapted it from an earlier piece of music. Not happy with the existing bugle call for lights out, which the general thought was too formal, he presented his bugler, Oliver Norton, with the replacement during the summer of 1862. Although it was soon used by both Union and Confederate armies as a funeral call, it did not become an official bugle call until after the war.

## SACAJAWEA'S STORY

There aren't many tour guides as famous as Sacajawea, but in truth, she wasn't a guide at all—she had no idea where she was going, and she didn't even speak English!

## Hooking Up with Lewis and Clark

Meriwether Lewis (a soldier) and William Clark (a naturalist) were recruited by President Thomas Jefferson to explore the upper reaches of the Missouri River. Their job was to find the most direct route to the Pacific Ocean—the legendary Northwest Passage. Setting out in 1803, they worked their way up the Missouri River and then stopped for the winter to build a fort near a trading post in present-day North Dakota. This is where they met the pregnant Shoshone teenager known as Sacajawea.

Actually, they met her through her husband, Toussaint Charbonneau. He was a French fur trader who lived with the Shoshone (he is said to have purchased Sacajawea from members of another group who had captured her, so it may be inaccurate to call her his "wife"). Although Sacajawea is credited with guiding Lewis and Clark's expedition to the Pacific, the only reason she (and her newborn baby) went along at all was that her husband had been hired as a translator.

## Pop Culture Icon

The myth of Sacajawea as the Native American princess who pointed the way to the Pacific was created and perpetuated by the many books and movies that romanticized her story. For example, the 1955 movie *The Far Horizons*, which starred Donna Reed in "yellow-face" makeup, introduced the fictional plotline of a romance between Sacajawea and William Clark. Over time, she has evolved to serve as a symbol of friendly relations between the U.S. government and Native Americans. In 2000, she was given the U.S. Mint's ultimate honor when it released the Sacajawea Golden Dollar. At the same time, though, the Mint's website incorrectly states that she "guided the adventurers from the Northern Great Plains to the Pacific Ocean and back."

## The Real Sacajawea

The only facts known about Sacajawea come from the journals of Lewis and Clark's expedition team. According to these, we know that she did not translate for the group—with the exception of a few occasions when they encountered other Shoshone. But because she did not speak English, she served as more of a go-between for her husband, the explorers, and members of other tribes they encountered in their travels. Concerning her knowledge of a route to the Pacific, Lewis and Clark knew far more about the land than she did. Only when they reached the area occupied by her own people was she able to point out a few landmarks, but they were not of any great help.

This isn't to say that she did not make important contributions to the journey's success. Journals note that Sacajawea was a great help to the team when she took it upon herself to rescue essential medicines and supplies that had been washed into a river. Her knowledge of edible roots and plants was invaluable when game and other sources of food were hard to come by. Most important, Sacajawea served as a sort of human peace symbol. Her presence reassured the various Native American groups who encountered Lewis and Clark that the explorers' intentions were peaceful. No Native American woman, especially one with a baby on her back, would have been part of a war party.

There are two very different accounts of Sacajawea's death. Although some historical documents say she died in South Dakota in 1812, Shoshone oral tradition claims she lived until 1884 and died in Wyoming. Regardless of differing interpretations of her life and death, Sacajawea will always be a heroine of American history.

# Chapter 8
# ENTERTAINMENT ENIGMAS

## Philo T. Farnsworth—The Teenager Who Invented Television

Responsible for what may have been the most influential invention of the twentieth century, this farm boy never received the recognition he was due.

Philo T. Farnsworth's brilliance was obvious from an early age. In 1919, when he was only 12, he amazed his parents and older siblings by fixing a balky electrical generator on their Idaho farm. By age 14, he had built an electrical laboratory in the family attic and was setting his alarm early so he could get up and read science journals for an hour before doing the chores.

Farnsworth hated the drudgery of farming. He often daydreamed solutions to scientific problems as he worked. During the summer of 1921, he was particularly preoccupied with the possibility of transmitting moving pictures through the air.

Around the same time, big corporations like RCA were spending millions of research dollars trying to find a practical way to do just that. As it turned out, most of their work was focused on a theoretical dead-end. Back in 1884, German scientist Paul Nipkow had patented a device called the Nipkow disc. By rotating the disc rapidly while passing light through tiny holes, an illusion of movement could be created. In essence, the Nipkow disc was a primitive way to scan images. Farnsworth doubted that this mechanical method of scanning could ever work fast enough to send images worth watching. He was determined to find a better way.

His "Eureka!" moment came as he plowed a field with a horse team. Swinging the horses around to start another row, Farnsworth glanced back at the furrows behind him. Suddenly, he realized that the scanning could be done electronically, line-by-line. Light could be converted into streams of electrons and then back again with such rapidity that the eye would be fooled. He immediately set about designing what would one day be called the cathode ray tube. Seven years would pass, however, before he was able to display a working model of his mental breakthrough.

Upon graduating from high school, Farnsworth enrolled at the University of Utah but dropped out after a year because he could no longer afford the tuition. Almost immediately, though, he found financial backers and moved to San Francisco to continue his research. The cathode ray tube he developed there became the basis for all television. In 1930, a researcher from RCA named Vladimir Zworykin visited Farnsworth's California laboratory and copied his invention. When Farnsworth refused to sell his patent to RCA for $100,000, the company sued him. The legal wrangling continued for many years and, though Farnsworth eventually earned royalties from his invention, he never did get wealthy from it.

By the time Farnsworth died in 1971, there were more homes on Earth with televisions than with indoor plumbing. Ironically, the man most responsible for television appeared on the small screen only once. It was a 1957 appearance on the game show *I've Got a Secret*. Farnsworth's secret was that "I invented electric television at the age of 15." When none of the panelists guessed Farnsworth's secret, he left the studio with his winnings—$80 and a carton of Winston cigarettes.

# BASED ON A TRUE FAKE

When movies try to depict fact, it's almost inevitable that a little bit (or a lot) of fiction will get in the way.

The problem with movies that claim to be based on a true story is not the definition of true—it's the definition of based on. Movies tend to take some parts of a particular event or story and focus on them—thereby exaggerating their importance and relevance—while ignoring other circumstances completely. Here are a few examples.

## A Beautiful Mind

John Nash is a mathematician whose work in game theory earned him a 1994 Nobel Prize in Economics. He attended Princeton University and worked on his equilibrium theory. After earning a doctorate in 1950, he continued to work on his thesis, part of which became the Nash Equilibrium. In 1951, he was hired as a member of the MIT mathematics faculty. In 1957, he married Alicia Lopez-Harrison de Lardé, and shortly after that, he was admitted to a mental hospital for schizophrenia. The couple had a son in 1959 but divorced in 1963. They became friendly again in 1970, renewed their romantic relationship in 1994, and remarried in 2001.

But in the movie A Beautiful Mind, Nash is plagued by schizophrenia throughout his education at Princeton. He struggles to maintain relationships with his classmates but flourishes as he discovers various mathematical theories. He is also asked by the government to decode covert Soviet messages. He gets married and has a son but is slowly eaten up by his schizophrenia until he's hospitalized. Through the love of his wife and his own strength of will, however, he becomes an award-winning recluse who is happily accepted within the hallowed halls of higher education.

One catch is that Nash's true-life delusions were auditory, not visual. Also, while the movie portrayed John and Alicia's marriage as a tense one, it also portrayed it as continuous. There are at least two more important changes the movie made to Nash's life: The pen ceremony at Princeton never really happened, and Nash never gave a rousing yet humble speech when he received his Nobel Prize.

## Catch Me If You Can

Frank Abagnale was a con artist who passed bad checks during five years in the 1960s. He impersonated a pilot, a physician, an attorney, and a teacher. Once captured, Abagnale had the dubious distinction of having 26 countries with extradition orders against him. After serving in prison for his crimes, he founded Abagnale & Associates, a legitimate company that advises businesses on fraud.

In the movie, a lonely only child deals with his wacky dad and nervous mom, but in no time, he's on his way to New York, alone and fending for himself. This is where the story takes off into fraud and impersonations, with an FBI agent chasing Abagnale around the globe. In reality, no FBI agent chased Abagnale down. *Catch Me If You Can* follows Abagnale's life, which already seems pretty exaggerated, and exaggerates it even more. In the movie, Abagnale writes $10 million in bad checks; in reality the total was only $2.5 million. And Abagnale was never on the FBI's Ten Most Wanted list.

## Finding Neverland

Scottish novelist and dramatist J. M. Barrie created Peter Pan. Barrie's traumatic childhood included the death of his brother and the withdrawal of his mother, crushed by her son's death. As an adult, Barrie moved to London, where he became a journalist, then a novelist, then a playwright. He became friends with the Llewelyn Davies family, who provided the inspiration for his fictional work. Eventually, after the deaths of the boys' parents, Barrie ended up providing support for the sons of the family. Barrie died of pneumonia on June 19, 1937.

In the movie *Finding Neverland*, we're treated to the moment when Barrie meets and befriends the Llewelyn Davies children and their mother. The movie then weaves the lives of Barrie and the family together. It's a sweet story but it's only a sliver of the real events.

The real Barrie had many literary friends, famous ones at that, and a prolific outpouring of books and plays. When the real Barrie initially met and befriended the Llewelyn Davies children, their father was alive; in the movie, he's already dead. In the film, there are four children; in reality, there were five. Most importantly, Barrie suffered from psychogenic dwarfism—he was four feet tall. In the film, Barrie is played by Johnny Depp, who is significantly taller than that.

## THE GREAT PIANO CON

Lauded late in life as a great piano virtuoso, British pianist Joyce Hatto produced the largest collection of recorded piano pieces in the history of music production. But were they hers?

Joyce Hatto was known as an extraordinary pianist. Her recorded repertoire available in the UK grew to more than 100 CDs and included some of the most difficult piano pieces around. What was truly amazing is that she somehow managed to record this music while suffering the effects of cancer and dealing with the usual wear and tear of an aging body. How did she do it? Perhaps her penchant for plagiarism helped. As it turned out, the majority of her works were stolen from other artists' recordings and then reproduced as her own!

Having enjoyed a full, albeit rather insignificant, career as a concert pianist, Hatto abandoned her stage show in 1976 to focus on her advancing disease. On the cusp of 50, she had only a few recorded numbers under her belt. However, that soon changed, as she spent her remaining years prolifically, but as it turned out, falsely, adding to that collection.

## The CD Deluge Begins

That Hatto's husband, William Barrington-Coupe, ran the Concert Artists Recordings label under which her recordings were released undoubtedly helped to assist in the harmonious heist. His music business acumen provided both the technological savvy to engineer the pieces that had been previously released by other pianists and the means to unleash the forged works on an unsuspecting public.

Of course, the scam couldn't last forever. Internet rumors began surfacing in 2005, but *Gramophone*, a monthly music magazine in London, wasn't able to definitively break the news of the deception until February 2007, about eight months after Hatto's death. In fact, her death at age 77 may have actually been an impetus for the discovery.

After Hatto's passing, her celebrity fire burned hotter than ever. Beloved by a small fan base during her life, Hatto-mania came out in full force upon her death. Some even deemed her one of the great pianists of modern times. But with that superstar status came a renewed flurry of suspicions surrounding the likelihood of a woman of her age and ailing health being able to produce such a copious collection. *Gramophone* issued a summons for anyone who knew of any fraudulence. Months passed with no evidence, until a reader finally contacted the magazine to reveal his strange findings. As it turned out, this man's computer actually discovered the deceit.

## The Con Revealed

Popping in a purported CD of Hatto hits, the reader's computer identified that a particular ditty was not a work of Hatto but one by little-known pianist Lazlo Simon. The reader immediately contacted *Gramophone* with his discovery. Based on his report, *Gramophone* sent the recordings to a sound engineer, who put music science to the test, comparing sound waves from Hatto's ostensible recording of Liszt's *Transcendental Studies* to Simon's version. An identical match was uncovered! After that, more and more tested pieces attributed to Hatto were found to belong to other musicians.

Hatto and husband were able to manage the ruse by utilizing music technology to recycle others' recordings and reproduce them as Hatto's own; by that same technology, the deceptive duo was discovered. So, how could the pair not foresee that music science would reveal them, even as they used its wizardry themselves? Barrington-Coupe has not, as of yet, produced a viable answer.

Although he denied any wrongdoing at first, Barrington-Coupe eventually confessed to the fraud, defending his actions by insisting that Hatto knew nothing of the scheme and he had made very little money on it. He further claimed that the whole plot was inspired by nothing more than his love for his ailing wife and his attempt to make her feel appreciated by the music community during her final years. An assertion such as this can neither be proved nor disproved, but *Gramophone* pointed out that Barrington-Coupe continued to sell the false CDs after she had died.

# Clarifications on Kong

The most famous inhabitant of Skull Island, he has elicited both screams and sympathy from moviegoers. But contrary to rumor, King Kong was never played by a man in an ape suit.

We've all heard the term "800-pound gorilla" in reference to something considered big and bad, and in Hollywood, they don't get any bigger or badder. Standing a whopping 50 feet tall and weighing in excess of 800 pounds, Kong has captured the imaginations of millions since his premiere in 1933.

Much has been written and said about how Kong was brought to life, and for decades many believed that in some of his scenes, Kong was simply a man in a monkey suit. But such claims are patently false. With the exception of a few scenes that featured a life-size bust or a giant mechanical hand, Kong was made real through a meticulous and time-consuming process known as stop-motion animation. Despite his towering onscreen presence, the mighty Kong was nothing more than an 18-inch articulated metal skeleton (referred to as an armature) covered with rubber and rabbit fur.

## Birth of a King

When King Kong first hit theaters, moviegoers were awestruck. They watched in amazement as vicious dinosaurs came to life and a huge gorilla ravaged the streets of New York City until biplanes blasted him off the top of the Empire State Building. It was unlike anything they had seen before, and the movie raked in several times the $650,000 it cost to produce.

The myth that King Kong was a man in an ape suit was started by an inaccurate article in an issue of *Modern Mechanix and Inventions*, which featured illustrations showing how a stuntman was used for the scenes in which Kong scaled the Empire State Building.

## The Mighty Myth Grows

Thirty years later, a poorly researched Associated Press wire story added to the myth by reporting that King Kong had been portrayed by Hollywood stuntman Carmen Nigro. In the article, Nigro made a number of outrageous claims, including the "fact" that Fay Wray was an animated doll and that Nigro had worn "fur-covered ballet slippers with suction pads" to help him stay on the skyscraper. Nigro also claimed to have starred in *Mighty Joe Young* (1949) as another supersize cinematic simian created through the artistry of stop-motion animation. Both apes were animated by the gifted Willis O'Brien, who won an Academy Award for his special effects work on *Mighty Joe Young*.

Although the original King Kong was only a model, he has been portrayed by a man in a suit in other movies over the years. The Japanese monster smash *King Kong vs. Godzilla*

(1962), for example, featured an embarrassingly bad gorilla suit and a storyline that had the famous ape duking it out with Japan's favorite super-lizard. The movie is notable for having two endings: In the version shown in Japan, Godzilla wins. In the version seen by people in the United States, Kong is the victor.

## SOUND SECRETS

Take a Hollywood movie scene: A leather-jacketed hero scuffles with a bad guy and then walks through the snow before driving into the night. Sounds good, right? But what you really heard was a Foley artist punching a roasted chicken with a rubber kitchen glove and squeezing two balloons together while walking in a sandbox filled with cornstarch.

# Things Are Not What They Seem

Whether you notice it or not, the sound of a movie can be as entertaining as the visual experience. But unbeknownst to many viewers, many of the sounds are not captured at the time of filming. Instead, they're either recorded in the studio by Foley artists or pulled from a library of sound bites that are not used until the sound is mixed for the movie.

The term "Foley artist" was used as early as 1927 when Al Jolson's movie *The Jazz Singer* became the first movie recorded with sound. In those days, recording the actors' dialogue superseded virtually all other sound or music recorded for the film. It wasn't until the early 1950s that producers discovered they could enhance the overall quality of the moviegoers' experience by adding specialized sounds that were purposely stripped away during filming in favor of an actor's spoken lines.

The profession's namesake, Jack Foley, was asked by his sound engineer to improve the quality of the audio by introducing a series of "studio clips." Foley discovered that in order to enhance the sound, three categories of sound were required, starting with "footsteps." Each actor executing a scene in a movie walks or runs with their own gait, on a variety of surfaces. By watching raw footage of the film, a Foley artist attempts to replicate and record the actor's pace and sound by walking on the most suitable surface, for instance, cement, gravel, or sand.

The second sound category that must be captured is the "moves." Moves accompany footsteps and include the sounds of skirts swishing, pants rustling, or leather jackets squeaking. Finally, all of the other sounds required to make the experience more believable must be either pulled from thousands of computer-generated archives or shot especially for the film.

# The Life of a Foley Artist

Foley artists are natural-born scavengers. When they're not actively involved in producing sound effects for films and television, you'll often find them scrounging around garage sales and piles of trash looking for anything that will generate a particular sound. A fertile imagination is key. What may sound like a couple passionately kissing in a movie may actually be a Foley artist sucking on his or her own forearm.

When Foley artist Marko Costanzo began freelancing for C5, Inc., he needed to come up with a variety of new sounds to use on his projects. Since most clips weren't available, he invented the following ingenious additions to his audio library:

• For a two-minute sequence of a dragonfly in *Men in Black*, Costanzo clipped off the ends of the blades of a simple plastic fan and replaced them with duct tape. When the fan was turned on, he could control the quality of the resulting flapping sound by brushing his fingers against the duct tape.

• For a knifing scene in the crime drama *Goodfellas*, Costanzo tried stabbing raw chickens, beef, and pork roasts with the bones intact.

• To achieve the sound of walking on freshly fallen snow, he walked on kosher sea salt covered with a thick layer of cornstarch.

• To emulate the sound of a dog walking across a hardwood surface, Costanzo glued press-on nails onto work gloves and clickity-clacked the nails on wood. The size of the dog could be indicated by the thickness of the nails used.

The motion picture industry thrives on creating fantasies. From the moment that the actor steps onto the soundstage, nothing is what it seems. Without Foley artists, our moviegoing experience would be a lackluster one.

# How Can Celebrity Tabloids Get Away with Publishing Obviously Untrue Stories?

Supermarket tabloids thrive on publishing outlandish celebrity rumors and innuendo. You'd think that the subjects of their articles would be suing them all the time.

How in the world could the tabloids survive the legal fees and multimillion-dollar judgments? The truth is, if tabloids are good at one thing, it's surviving.

There are two kinds of tabloids: the ridiculous ones that publish stories nobody really believes ("Bigfoot Cured My Arthritis!") and those that focus on celebrity gossip.

The ridiculous stories are easy to get away with. They're mostly fabricated or based on slender truths. As long as they contain nothing damaging about a real person, there's no one to file a lawsuit. Bigfoot isn't litigious.

Celebrity gossip is trickier. To understand how tabloids avoid legal problems, we need to learn a little bit about the legal definition of "libel." To be found guilty of libel, you must have published something about another person that is provably false.

Moreover, the falsehood has to have caused that person some kind of damage, even if only his or her reputation is

harmed. If the subject of the story is a notable person, such as a politician or a movie star, libel legally occurs only if publication of the falsehood is malicious. This means that the publisher knows the information is false, had access to the truth but ignored it, and published the information anyway.

Tabloids generally have lawyers on staff or on retainer who are experts in media law and libel. By consulting with their lawyers, tabloid editors can publish stories that get dangerously close to libel but don't quite cross the line.

A defense against libel is publication of the truth: You can't sue someone for saying something about you that's true, no matter how embarrassing. Tabloids know that if they print something close to the truth, a celebrity is unlikely to sue because a trial could reveal a skeleton in the closet that's more embarrassing.

Libel lawyers also know that a tabloid is in the clear if it publishes a story based on an informant's opinion. Opinions can't be disproved, so they don't meet the criteria for libel. This explains headlines such as this: "Former Housekeeper Says Movie Star Joe Smith Is a Raving Lunatic!" As long as the tabloid makes a token effort to corroborate the story—or even includes a rebuttal of the housekeeper's claims within the article—it is fairly safe from a legal standpoint.

Of course, legal tricks don't always work. Some movie stars, musicians, and other celebrities have successfully sued tabloids for tens of millions of dollars. That tabloids continue to thrive despite such judgments shows just how much money there is to be made in the rumors-and-innuendo business.

## PREHISTORIC HOLLYWOOD

If a stroll along Rodeo Drive lined with Beverly Hills housewives isn't enough to convince you, Hollywood was once home to a vast array of Pleistocene ice age creatures.

The La Brea Tar Pits, located near the Miracle Mile district of Los Angeles, have yielded the largest repository of fossils from the last ice age, including plants, insects, and mammals.

Despite the name, the La Brea Tar Pits are actually a series of asphalt deposits that bubble up from the ground. Over the centuries, oil has oozed to the surface to form sticky bogs that have trapped all manner of animals, condemning them to premature deaths but preserving their skeletons. Since paleontologists began excavating the tar pits in 1908, remains have been discovered that date back as far as 40,000 years. These include saber-toothed cats, short-faced bears, dire wolves, and even an American lion. In early 2009, as workers began excavating an underground parking garage next to the tar pits, they found a stunning collection of fossils, including a nearly intact mammoth dating back to the last ice age.

Curators from the George C. Page Museum, which houses fossils collected from the site, estimate that the mammoth—whom they named Zed—was between 47 and 49 years old, which is young for a mammoth. Zed's three broken ribs indicate that he'd likely been injured fighting with other male mammoths, a precursor to the back-biting that is so common in Hollywood these days.

The La Brea Tar Pits are no stranger to the limelight, having been featured in several movies, including *Last Action Hero* (1993), Steven Spielberg's *1941* (1979), and the disaster movie, *Volcano* (1997), in which a volcanic eruption originates from the largest tar pit and spews lava on the streets of Hollywood.

# BLACKLISTED!

During the Red Scare, hundreds of film and television careers were destroyed by a vindictive hunt for communists in Hollywood.

In September 1947, Dalton Trumbo was at the height of his career as a screenwriter. He was highly acclaimed, well paid, and still basking in the accolades he received for his work on two patriotic war films: *A Guy Named Joe* (1943) and *Thirty Seconds Over Tokyo* (1944). That month, an FBI agent delivered Trumbo a subpoena from the House Un-American Activities Committee (HUAC), a special investigative committee of the U.S. House of Representatives. Trumbo, along with 42 other film industry professionals—actors, directors, producers, and writers—were named as key witnesses in HUAC's probe into Communist subversion in Hollywood. The good times were about to end for Dalton Trumbo.

## The Hunt for Reds in October

HUAC was created in 1937 to "investigate disloyal or subversive activities in America," such as the Ku Klux Klan and organizations sympathetic to Nazi Germany. HUAC also worked diligently to ferret out American Communist Party (ACP) members and supporters in the U.S. government and media. HUAC cooled its heels during World War II, when the Soviet Union was an ally, but ramped up its pursuits with the postwar onset of the Second Red Scare, which later gave rise to a similar but totally unrelated Red-baiting phenomenon: Joseph McCarthy and the notorious Senate Committee hearings of the 1950s. But in 1947, HUAC had turned its attention to Hollywood.

Citing Soviet-sympathetic war films such as *Mission to Moscow* (1943) and *Song of Russia* (1944), HUAC announced formal hearings to determine if Hollywood filmmakers were undermining U.S. security and freedom by covertly planting

Communist propaganda in American films. Those subpoenaed by HUAC were expected to provide details of Communist activity in Hollywood and, more importantly, name names.

On October 20, 1947, the hearings opened with testimony from several "friendly" witnesses. One of them was Walt Disney, who readily fingered several individuals as Communists, claiming that they were agitators inciting labor unrest in Hollywood. Ronald Reagan, then-president of the Screen Actors Guild, also testified and claimed that Communist intrigue was rampant in Tinseltown.

## The Hollywood Ten

Disney and Reagan were followed by 10 individuals (including Trumbo, Samuel Ornitz, and John Howard Lawson—screenwriters who were also members of the Writers Guild of America, which Lawson founded) who refused to cooperate with the investigation, which they considered a modern-day witch hunt. These "unfriendly" witnesses condemned the hearings as unconstitutional and invoked their Fifth Amendment rights when asked about their relationship with Communist organizations.

For their defiance, the Hollywood Ten, as they were dubbed, were cited for contempt of Congress on November 24. They were also fired by their respective studios and the Motion Picture Producers and Distributors of America barred them from working in Hollywood until they were acquitted or purged of contempt and declared under oath that they were not Communists.

The 10 remained unrepentant, and in early 1948, they were convicted of contempt. In 1950, after failed appeals, they began serving six-month to one-year prison sentences. Trumbo and his cohorts also became charter members of the now-notorious Hollywood blacklist.

## The List That Ate Hollywood

During the next several years, the blacklist grew into a monster that devoured Hollywood careers—a monster that was willingly fed by numerous anticommunist organizations. In 1949, the American Legion presented Hollywood execs with a list of 300 film industry members that they suspected of Communist affiliation. Fearing Legion-organized film boycotts, the studios adopted it as their de facto blacklist. In 1950, a pamphlet known as Red Channels pegged 151 TV and radio professionals as Communist sympathizers. Those named were blacklisted from their respective industries to avoid boycotts of products sponsored by the shows.

From 1951 to 1952, HUAC launched more hearings in which witnesses sold out others in an effort to save their own careers. Among them was director Edward Dmytryk, a guilt-ridden member of the Hollywood Ten, who betrayed 26 colleagues in exchange for an early jail release and the resumption of his directing career.

HUAC reports produced another blacklist of 212 Hollywood professionals who soon lost their jobs. Most were writers who were relatively unknown outside Hollywood. But several prominent actors, producers, and directors landed on the list, including Charlie Chaplin, Lee Grant, Zero Mostel, Orson Bean, and Larry Parks.

Many on the list also had earlier screen credits omitted. Unable to earn a living, dozens of blacklisted professionals left Hollywood (and even America) to continue their careers elsewhere. Approximately 90 percent of those blacklisted never worked in Hollywood again.

## Breaking the Blacklist

Open resistance to the blacklist began to emerge in 1956, when TV and radio personality John Henry Faulk sued the group Aware Inc. after its erroneous labeling of him as a

Communist supporter kept him from getting a job at a radio station. Faulk's court victory in 1962 put an end to the blacklist altogether. Soon afterward, several television productions began hiring and crediting blacklisted artists.

Even before then, there were signs that the blacklist was losing strength. In 1960, director Otto Preminger named Dalton Trumbo as the screenwriter for his upcoming film *Exodus*. That same year, Universal Pictures announced that Trumbo would be similarly credited on *Spartacus*, having been hired two years before by the film's executive producer and star, Kirk Douglas. Dalton Trumbo's 13-year nightmare was coming to an end.

Few knew it then, but Trumbo had already trumped the blacklist. During the 1950s, some blacklisted artists, including Trumbo, worked under different names. Trumbo wrote *Roman Holiday* (1953) under the alias Ian McLellan Hunter. He also penned *The Brave One* (1956) using the name Robert Rich as his "front." Both efforts earned Oscars for Best Writing, which meant golden redemption for Dalton Trumbo.

## THE SECRET SIDE OF ELVIS

Being the King of Rock 'n' Roll is not all it's cracked up to be.

Sparkling white jumpsuit, shiny black pompadour, soulful eyes, and shimmying hips—that's the mythic image of Elvis Presley everyone knows and loves. But although he was a revolutionary recording artist and the King of Rock 'n' Roll, Elvis was also made of darker stuff. From his obsession with guns to his bizarre behavior regarding his mother's corpse and a long fascination with occult teachings, Elvis had a secret side that his publicists preferred to keep under blue suede wraps.

## I Remember Mama

Born on January 8, 1935, in Tupelo, Mississippi, to Vernon and Gladys Presley, Elvis Aaron came into the world along with a stillborn twin brother, Jesse Garon. It was an early tragedy that haunted Elvis for most of his life. The family was poor—a situation made worse when Vernon was sent to prison for forging a check. At age three, Elvis was suddenly the man of the house.

After Vernon's release in 1948, the family moved to Memphis, Tennessee. Even as his recording career began to take off in the mid-'50s, Elvis and his mother remained incredibly close and devoted to one another. She lived with him at his Graceland estate until her death in 1958. To say Elvis did not take his mother's death well would be an understatement, and his grief morphed into often bizarre behavior. Family and friends worriedly noted that he seemed obsessed with his mother's corpse. Later, he talked at length to friends about the technical details of the embalming process.

When Gladys's glass-topped coffin was brought to lie in state at the Graceland mansion, Elvis threw himself on the corpse. Elvis also threw himself on her coffin as it was being lowered into the ground. Recording artist Barbara Pittman said he was screaming and had to be restrained. Afterward, he carried his mother's nightgown everywhere for more than a week.

## Don't Be Cruel

When Elvis began dating 14-year-old Priscilla Beaulieu in 1959, he showed another unexpected side—the control freak. He asked her to dye her hair the same jet black as his own; the couple looked so similar that people believed they were twins.

He chose her wardrobe and once became upset over an imperfect polish job on one of her toenails. He also required her to carry a concealed handgun. Of course, Elvis sometimes carried as many as five guns himself, and was in the habit of shooting objects that irked him. A television with poor reception? Blam! Shattered console televisions were constantly dragged out of the Jungle Room at Graceland. Elvis once even shot his Ferrari after it stalled on the road.

## Got My Mojo Workin'

Elvis continued to feel haunted by the loss of his brother and mother, and he grew desperate for some sort of spiritual answer. For a time, he sought solace in the beliefs of a hair stylist named Larry Geller. Elvis confessed to Geller that as a young child, he often heard a voice and wondered if it was his dead brother. Geller, something of a New Age mystic, introduced Elvis to metaphysical books and to his own philosophy that—as redundant as it sounds—the main purpose of life was to find one's purpose in life. Presley staff member Alan Fortas said Elvis referred to Geller as his guru and to himself as "the divine messenger."

Elvis began carrying a numerology book with him that he consulted to help him decide which gifts to bestow on any given individual. His metaphysical journey ended after he tripped and hit his head in 1967, after which he was "deprogrammed" by his manager Colonel Tom Parker. In the end, Elvis apparently had enough, and his collection of metaphysical books wound up in flames in a burn pit on the grounds of Graceland. But when Elvis was found dead in his bathroom on August 16, 1977, he was wearing the symbols of three religions: an Egyptian ankh, a Jewish Star of David, and a Christian crucifix.

# THE SECRET ORIGIN OF COMIC BOOKS

Today's graphic novels have a long history that stretches back to newspaper comic strips.

In the 1920s and 1930s, comic strips were among the most popular sections of newspapers and were often reprinted later in book form. Generally, these were inexpensive publications that looked like newspaper supplements, though other formats were tried (including "big little books" in which the comic panels were adapted and text was added opposite each panel).

These so-called "funny books" were often given away as premiums for products such as cereal, shoes, and even gasoline. Then, in 1933, a sales manager at the Eastern Color Printing Company in Waterbury, Connecticut, hit on a winning format: 36 pages of color comics in a size similar to modern comics. *Famous Funnies: A Carnival of Comics*, considered the first true comic book, featured reprinted strips with such cartoon characters as Mutt and Jeff. It was still a giveaway, but it was a hit.

The next year, Eastern Color published *Famous Funnies #1* and distributed the 68-page comic book to newsstands nationwide with a cover price of 10 cents.

As the demand for reprinted strips outpaced supply, publishers began introducing original material into comic books. One publisher, searching for features to fill the pages of a new book, approached a young creative team made up of writer Jerry Siegel and artist Joe Shuster, who had been trying for years to sell a newspaper strip about an invincible hero from another planet. Siegel and Shuster reformatted the strips into comic book form, and Superman debuted in *Action Comics #1*. It was an instant smash hit. The "Golden Age" of comics followed, introducing many of the popular heroes who are still with us today, including Batman, Wonder Woman, Captain America, and The Flash. In the 1960s, the "Silver Age" introduced new, more emotionally flawed heroes such as Spider-Man, Iron Man, and the Hulk. The comic book has certainly come a long way since Mutt and Jeff.

# FREQUENCY MODULATION (FM RADIO)

A fearless innovator's marvelous invention is tarnished by betrayal.

Fame and riches are supposed to go to those visionaries that build the better mousetraps. But with the invention of frequency modulation (FM radio), things didn't quite work out that way. Edwin H. Armstrong (1890–1954) invented a new transmission medium that left the former giant, amplitude modulation (AM radio), quivering in its wake. For most people, such a lofty achievement would bring a degree of satisfaction– not to mention a stack of cash. For Armstrong, it would bring mostly heartache.

Before this underappreciated genius found his way to FM, he made other contributions. Two of Armstrong's inventions, the regenerative circuit of 1912 and the superheterodyne circuit of 1917, would set the broadcasting world on its ear. When combined, they would produce an affordable tube radio that would become an American staple. Armstrong was on his way.

Soon afterward, the inventor turned his attentions to the removal of radio static, an inherent problem in the AM circuit.

After witnessing a demonstration of Armstrong's super-heterodyne receiver, David Sarnoff, the head of the Radio Corporation of America (RCA) and founder of the National Broadcasting Company (NBC), challenged him to develop "a little black box" that would remove the static. Armstrong spent the late 1920s through the early 1930s tackling the problem.

Sarnoff backed the genius by allowing him use of a laboratory at the top of the Empire State Building. This was no small offering—in the broadcasting game, height equals might, and none came taller than this 1,250-foot giant, which has since been named one of the seven wonders of the modern world.

In 1933, Armstrong made a bold announcement. He had cracked the noise problem using frequency modulation. With a wider frequency response than AM and an absence of background noise, the new technology represented a revolutionary step in broadcasting.

Armstrong's upgraded system had the ability to relay programming from city to city by direct off-air pickup. But without knowing it, the inventor had effectively boxed himself in. NBC, and by extension Sarnoff, was the dominant force in conventional radio during this time. With America mired in an economic depression, NBC wasn't interested in tooling up for a new system. Even worse for Armstrong, television loomed on the horizon, and NBC was pouring most of its resources into that technology. Instead of receiving the recognition and financial rewards that he so rightly deserved, Armstrong was fired unceremoniously by his "friend" Sarnoff. It seemed like the end of the line—but Armstrong's battle was only just beginning.

In 1937, a determined Armstrong erected a 400-foot tower and transmitter in Alpine, New Jersey. Here, he would go about the business of perfecting his inventions.

Unfortunately, without Sarnoff's backing, his operation found itself severely underfunded. To make matters infinitely worse, Armstrong became embroiled in a patent battle with RCA, which was claiming the invention of FM radio. The broadcasting giant would ultimately win the patent fight and shut Armstrong down. The ruling was so lopsided that it robbed Armstrong of his ability to claim royalties on FM radios sold in the United States. It would be hard to find a deal rawer than this.

To fully appreciate Armstrong's contribution, compare AM and FM radio stations: The difference in transmitted sound will be pronounced, with FM sounding wonderfully alive and AM noticeably flat in comparison. Even "dead air" sounds better on FM because the band lacks the dreaded static that plagues the AM medium. Without a doubt, FM technology is a tremendous breakthrough. But it came at a terrible cost. On January 31, 1954, Armstrong—distraught over his lack of recognition and dwindling finances—flung himself from the 13th-floor window of his New York City apartment.

## THE GAME OF KINGS

Chess is a game where protecting the king is key. So it should come as little surprise that it may once have been a favorite of royalty.

Often called the "royal game," chess is one of the world's most popular games and is enjoyed by millions. It is played informally by friends, in clubs, in tournaments, and even in international tournaments. In its design and strategy, chess delightfully meshes simplicity with complexity and has attracted players the world over; by phone, by mail, and online, players carry on long, thoughtful games that can last years.

Chess has its roots in India and dates to the sixth century AD. It arrived in Europe in the tenth century, where it soon became a court favorite of the nobility. Europe is the likely origin of the modern pieces, which include a king and queen and other notable ranks of the Middle Ages—eight pawns, a pair of knights, a pair of bishops, and a pair of rooks. The latter pieces were called chariots in the Persian game before transforming to the castle pieces in the Westernized version.

The game is played on an eight-by-eight board of 64 squares. Players take alternating turns, and the game continues until one player is able to "checkmate" the opponent's king, a strategic move that prevents the king from escaping an attack on the next turn. The game can also end in a draw in certain scenarios. Each piece moves according to specific rules that dictate how many squares it can traverse and in what direction. The queen is generally considered the most powerful piece on the board—perhaps a nod to the power the queen wielded when the game arrived in Europe.

The first modern chess tournament was held in London in 1851 and was won by Adolf Anderssen, who would become a leading chess master. Since then, computer programmers have developed game strategy using artificial intelligence, and for years there were attempts to create a computer that could defeat the best human players. This finally happened in 1997 when a computer defeated world champion Garry Kasparov.

# Chapter 9
# TOO WEIRD FOR TRUTH?

## SATANIC MARKETING

What's behind the vicious rumor that put mega-corporation Procter & Gamble on many churches' hit lists?

Procter & Gamble, one of the largest corporations in the world, manufactures a plethora of products that range from pet food to potato chips. The company takes pride in its reputation as a business that can be trusted, so it came as a huge shock when, starting in the 1960s, Christian churches and individuals around the country spread the rumor that P&G was dedicated to the service of Satan.

### The Devil Is in the Details

How the rumor got started remains a mystery. According to one of the most popular versions of the story, the president of P&G appeared on *The Phil Donahue Show* in March 1994 and announced that, because of society's new openness, he finally felt comfortable revealing that he was a member of the Church of Satan and that much of his company's profits went toward the advancement of that organization. When Donahue supposedly asked him whether such an announcement would have a negative impact on P&G, the CEO replied, "There aren't enough Christians in the United States to make a difference."

There's one problem with this story—and with the variations that place the company president on *The Sally Jessy Raphael Show*, *The Merv Griffin Show*, and *60 Minutes*: It didn't happen.

## Lose the Logo

Adding fuel to the fable was the company's logo, which featured the image of a "man in the moon" and 13 stars. Many interpreted this rather innocuous design to be Satanic, and some even claimed that the curlicues in the man's beard looked like the number 666—the biblical "mark of the Beast" referred to in the Book of Revelation. By 1985, the company had become so frustrated by the allegations that it had no choice but to retire the logo, which had graced P&G products for more than 100 years.

## Speaking Out

Procter & Gamble did all it could to quell the rumors, which resulted in more than 200,000 phone calls and letters from concerned consumers. Company spokespeople vehemently denied the story, explaining in a press release: "The president of P&G has never discussed Satanism on any national televised talk show, nor has any other P&G executive. The moon-and-stars trademark dates back to the mid-1800s, when the "man in the moon" was simply a popular design. The 13 stars in the design honor the original 13 colonies."

In addition, the company turned to several prominent religious leaders, including evangelist Billy Graham, to help clear its name, and when that didn't work, it even sued a handful of clergy members who continued to spread the off ending story.

Talk show host Sally Jessy Raphael also denied the allegations, noting, "The rumors going around that the president of Procter & Gamble appeared on [my] show and announced he was a member of the Church of Satan are not true. The president of Procter & Gamble has never appeared on *The Sally Jessy Raphael Show*."

## Senseless Allegations

Of course, like most urban legends, this story falls apart under scrutiny. Foremost, one must ask why the CEO of an international conglomerate (especially one that must answer to stockholders) would risk decades of consumer goodwill—not to mention billions of dollars in sales—to announce to the world that his company was run by Satanists. And even if that were the case, he needn't bother announcing it, since any deals made with the devil would be a matter of public record.

In 2007, a jury awarded Procter & Gamble $19.25 million in a civil lawsuit filed against four former Amway distributors accused of spreading false rumors about the company's ties to the Church of Satan. The distributors were found guilty of using a voicemail system to inform customers that P&G's profits were used to support Satanic cults.

# Magnetic Hill Phenomenon

It has taken researchers hundreds of years to finally solve the mystery of magnetic hills, or spook hills, as they're often called. This phenomenon, found all over the world, describes places where objects—including cars in neutral gear—move uphill on a slightly sloping road, seemingly defying gravity.

Moncton, in New Brunswick, Canada, lays claim to one of the more famous magnetic hills, called, appropriately, Magnetic Hill. Over the years, it has also been called Fool's Hill and Magic Hill. Since the location made headlines in 1931, hundreds of thousands of tourists have flocked there to witness this phenomenon for themselves.

## Go Figure

Much to the disdain of paranormal believers, people in science once assumed that a magnetic anomaly caused this event. But advanced physics has concluded this phenom-enon is due "to the visual anchoring of the sloping surface to a gravity-relative eye level whose perceived direction is biased by sloping surroundings." In nonscientific jargon, it's an optical illusion.

Papers published in the journal of the *Association of Psychological Science* supported this conclusion based on a series of experiments done with models. They found that if the horizon cannot be seen or is not level then people may be fooled by objects that they expect to be vertical but aren't. False perspective is also a culprit; think, for example, of a line of poles on the horizon that seem to get larger or smaller depending on distance.

Engineers with plumb lines, one made of iron and one made of stone, demonstrated that a slope appearing to go uphill might in reality be going downhill. A good topographical map may also be sufficient to show which way the land is really sloping.

## I Know a Place

Other notable magnetic hills can be found in Wisconsin, Pennsylvania, California, Florida, Barbados, Scotland, Australia, Italy, Greece, and South Korea.

# THE MYSTERY OF MONTAUK

Montauk, a beach community at the eastern tip of Long Island in the state of New York, has been deigned the Miami Beach of the mid-Atlantic. Conspiracy theorists, however, tell another tale. Has the U.S. government been hiding a secret at the former Camp Hero military base there?

In the late 1950s, Montauk was not the paradise-style resort it is today. It was an isolated seaside community boasting a lighthouse commissioned by George Washington in 1792, an abandoned military base called Camp Hero, and a huge radar tower. This tower, still standing, is the last semiautomatic ground environment radar tower still in existence and features an antenna called AN/FPS-35. During its time of air force use, the AN/FPS-35 was capable of detecting airborne objects at a distance of more than 200 miles. One of its uses was detecting potential Soviet long-distance bombers, as the Cold War was in full swing. According to conspiracy theorists, however, the antenna and Camp Hero itself had a few other tricks lurking around the premises, namely human mind control and electromagnetic field manipulation.

## Vanishing Act

As detailed in the previous article, the USS *Eldridge* was allegedly made invisible to human sight for a brief moment as it sat in a naval shipyard in Philadelphia in 1943. The event, which has been sworn as true by eyewitnesses and other believers for decades, is said to have been part of a U.S. military endeavor called Project Rainbow.

Studies in electromagnetic radiation had evidenced that manipulating energy fields and bending light around objects in certain ways could render them invisible. Since the benefits to the armed forces would be incredible, the Navy supposedly forged ahead with the first experiment.

There are many off shoots to the conspiracy theory surrounding the alleged event. The crew onboard the USS *Eldridge* at the time in question are said to have suffered various mental illnesses, physical ailments, and, most notably, schizophrenia, which has been medically linked to exposure to electromagnetic radiation. Some of them supposedly disappeared along with the ship and relocated through teleportation to the naval base in Norfolk, Virginia, for a moment. Despite severely conflicting eyewitness reports and the navy's assertion that the *Eldridge* wasn't

Too Weird for Truth?

even in Philadelphia that day, many websites, books, a video game, and a 1984 science fiction film detail the event.

But what does this have to do with Montauk right now?

## What's in the Basement?

Camp Hero was closed as an official U.S. Army base in November 1957, although the Air Force continued to use the radar facilities. After the Air Force left in 1980, the surrounding grounds were ultimately turned into a state park, which opened to the public in September 2002. Yet the camp's vast underground facility remains under tight government jurisdiction, and the AN/FPS-35 radar tower still stands. Many say there is a government lab on the site that continues the alleged teleportation, magnetic field manipulation, and mind-control experiments that originated with Project Rainbow. One reason for this belief is that two of the sailors onboard the *Eldridge* on October 24, 1943–Al Bielek and Duncan Cameron–claimed to have jumped from the ship while it was in "hyperspace" between Philadelphia and Norfolk, and landed at Camp Hero, severely disoriented.

Though Project Rainbow was branded a hoax, an urban legend continues to surround its "legacy," which is commonly known as the Montauk Project. Theorists cite experiments in electromagnetic radiation designed to produce mass schizophrenia over time and reduce a populace's resistance to governmental control, which, they say, would explain the continual presence of the antenna. According to these suspicions, a large number of orphans, loners, and homeless people are subjected to testing in Camp Hero's basement; most supposedly die as a result. Interestingly, some conspiracy theorists believe that one outcropping of the experiments is the emergence and rapid popularity of the cell phone, which uses and produces electromagnetic and radio waves. Who knew that easier communication was really an evil government plot to turn people into mindless robots?

# RED EYES OVER POINT PLEASANT:
## THE MYSTERIOUS MOTHMAN

In 1942, the U.S. government took control of several thousand acres of land just north of Point Pleasant, West Virginia. The purpose was to build a secret facility capable of creating and storing TNT that could be used during World War II. For the next three years, the facility cranked out massive amounts of TNT, shipping it out or storing it in one of the numerous concrete "igloo" structures that dotted the area. In 1945, the facility was shut down and eventually abandoned, but it was here that a flying creature with glowing red eyes made its home years later.

## "Red Eyes on the Right"

On the evening of November 15, 1966, Linda and Roger Scarberry were out driving with another couple, Mary and Steve Mallette. As they drove, they decided to take a detour that took them past the abandoned TNT factory.

As they neared the gate of the old factory, they noticed two red lights up ahead. When Roger stopped the car, the couples were horrified to find that the red lights appeared to be two glowing red eyes. What's more, those eyes belonged to a creature standing more than seven feet tall with giant wings folded behind it. That was all Roger needed to see before he hit the gas pedal and sped off. In response, the creature calmly unfolded its wings and flew toward the car. Incredibly, even though Roger raced along at speeds close to 100 miles per hour, the red-eyed creature was able to keep up with them without much effort.

Upon reaching Point Pleasant, the two couples ran from their car to the Mason County Courthouse and alerted Deputy Millard Halstead of their terrifying encounter. Halstead couldn't be sure exactly what the two couples had seen, but whatever it was, it had clearly frightened them. In an attempt to calm them down, Halstead agreed to accompany them to the TNT factory. As his patrol car neared the entrance, the police radio suddenly emitted a strange, whining noise. Other than that, despite a thorough search of the area, nothing out of the ordinary was found.

## More Encounters

Needless to say, once word got around Point Pleasant that a giant winged creature with glowing red eyes was roaming around the area, everyone had to see it for themselves. The creature didn't disappoint. Dubbed Mothman by the local press, the creature was spotted flying overhead, hiding, and even lurking on front porches. In fact, in the last few weeks of November, dozens of witnesses encountered the winged beast. But Mothman wasn't the only game in town. It seems that around the same time that he showed up, local residents started noticing strange lights in the evening sky, some of which hovered silently over the abandoned TNT factory. Of course, this led some to believe that Mothman and the UFOs were somehow connected. One such person was Mary Hyre of *The Athens Messenger*, who had been reporting on the strange activities in Point Pleasant since they started. Perhaps that's why she became the first target.

## Beware the Men in Black

One day, while Mary Hyre was at work, several strange men visited her office and began asking questions about the lights in the sky. Normally, she didn't mind talking to people about the UFO sightings and Mothman. But there was something peculiar about these guys. For instance, they all dressed exactly the same: black suits, black ties, black hats, and dark sunglasses. They also spoke in a strange monotone and seemed confused by ordinary objects such as ballpoint pens. As the men left, Hyre wondered whether they had been from another planet. Either way, she had an up-close-and-personal encounter with the legendary Men in Black.

Mary Hyre was not the only person to have a run-in with the Men in Black. As the summer of 1967 rolled around, dozens of people were interrogated by them. In most cases, the men showed up unannounced at the homes of people who had recently witnessed a Mothman or UFO sighting. For the most part, the men simply wanted to know what the witnesses had seen. But sometimes, the men went to great lengths to convince the witnesses that they were mistaken and had not seen anything out of the ordinary. Other times, the men threatened witnesses. Each time the Men in Black left a witness's house, they drove away in a black, unmarked sedan. Despite numerous attempts to determine who these men were and where they came from, their identity remained a secret. And all the while, the Mothman sightings continued throughout Point Pleasant and the surrounding area.

## The Silver Bridge Tragedy

Erected in 1928, the Silver Bridge was a gorgeous chain suspension bridge that spanned the Ohio River, connecting Point Pleasant with Ohio. On December 15, 1967, the bridge was busy with holiday shoppers bustling back and forth between West Virginia and Ohio. As the day wore on, more and more cars started filling the bridge until shortly before 5:00 p.m., when traffic on the bridge came to a standstill. For several minutes, none of the cars budged. Suddenly, there was a loud popping noise and then the unthinkable happened: The Silver Bridge collapsed, sending dozens of cars and their passengers into the freezing water below.

Over the next few days, local authorities and residents searched the river hoping to find survivors, but in the end, 46 people lost their lives in the bridge collapse. A thorough investigation determined that a manufacturing flaw in one of the bridge's supporting bars caused the collapse. But there are others who claim that in the days and weeks leading up to the collapse, they saw Mothman and even the Men in Black around, on, and even under the bridge. Further witnesses state that while most of Point Pleasant was watching the Silver Bridge collapse, bright lights and strange objects were flying out of the area and disappearing into the winter sky. Perhaps that had nothing to do with the collapse of the Silver Bridge, but the Mothman has not been seen since. Or has he?

## Mothman Lives!

There are reports that the Mothman is still alive and well and has moved on to other areas of the United States. There are even those who claim that he was spotted flying near the Twin Towers on September 11, 2001, leading to speculation that Mothman is a portent of doom and only appears when disasters are imminent. Some believe Mothman was a visitor from another planet who returned home shortly after the Silver Bridge fell. Still others think the creature was the result of the toxic chemicals eventually discovered in the area near the TNT factory. And then there are skeptics who say that the initial sighting was nothing more than a giant sand crane and that mass hysteria took care of the rest. Whichever theory you choose to believe, the Mothman Lives website compiles all sightings of the creature from the 1960s to the present.

# GIANT FROGMAN SPOTTED IN OHIO!

For the most part, frogs are rather unintimidating—unless they're more than four feet tall and standing along a dark road in the middle of the night.

## The First Encounter

On March 3, 1972, police officer Ray Shockey was driving his patrol car along Riverside Road toward the small town of Loveland, Ohio. At approximately 1:00 a.m., Shockey saw what he thought was a dog lying alongside the road, but as he got closer, the creature suddenly stood up on two feet. Amazed, Shockey stopped his car and watched the creature climb over a guardrail and scamper down the ditch toward the Little Miami River. Shockey drove back to the police station and described what he'd seen to fellow officer Mark Matthews. Shockey said the creature was approximately four feet tall and weighed between 50 to 75 pounds. It stood on two legs and had webbed feet, clawed hands, and the head of a frog.

After hearing his story, Matthews accompanied Shockey back to the site of the encounter. The pair could not locate the frogman, but they did find strange scratch marks along the section of guardrail the creature had climbed over.

## Frogman Returns

On the night of March 17, Matthews was on the outskirts of town when he saw an animal lying in the middle of the road. Thinking that the animal had been hit by a car, Matthews stopped his squad car. But when the animal suddenly stood up on two legs, Matthews realized that it was the same creature that Shockey had encountered. Just as before, the creature walked to the side of the road and climbed over a guardrail. Matthews simply watched, although some reports say he shot at the animal. Either way, the creature moved down the embankment toward the river and vanished.

## The Aftermath

When news spread of a second Frogman sighting, the town of Loveland was inundated with calls from reporters across the country. Obviously, reports of four-foot-tall froglike creatures are rarely considered newsworthy, but two witnesses had seen the creature on different nights, and both were police officers.

In the beginning, Shockey and Matthews stuck to their stories and even had sketches made of the creature they'd encountered. But over time, the public turned on the officers, accusing them of fabricating the whole thing. In recent years, the officers now claim that what they encountered was merely an iguana. Most seem happy with that explanation. But it doesn't explain how an iguana stood up on two legs and walked across the road. Or why their sketches looked nothing like an iguana.

## So Where Is the Frog Today?

A local farmer also claimed he saw the Frogman lumbering through his field one evening, but there have been no other sightings since the 1970s. Those who believe in the Loveland Frogman claim that after Matthews allegedly shot at it, it became frightened and moved to a more isolated area. Others think that Matthews's shot killed the creature. Of course, there are some who believe that the Loveland Frogman is still out there and has merely become more elusive. Just something to consider should you ever find yourself driving alongside the Little Miami River near Loveland on a dark, moonless night.

# An Underground Mystery

For centuries, people have believed that Earth is hollow. They claim that civilizations may live inside Earth's core or that it might be a landing base for alien spaceships. This sounds like fantasy, but believers point to startling evidence, including explorers' reports and modern photos taken from space.

## A Prize Inside?

Hollow earth believers agree that our planet is a shell between 500 and 800 miles thick, and inside that shell is another world. It may be a gaseous realm, an alien outpost, or home to a utopian society.

Some believers add a spiritual spin. Calling the interior world Agartha or Shambhala, they use concepts from Eastern religions and point to ancient legends supporting these ideas. Many Hollow Earth enthusiasts are certain that people from the outer and inner worlds can visit each other by traveling through openings in the outer shell. One such entrance is a hole in the ocean near the North Pole. A November 1968 photo by the ESSA-7 satellite showed a dark, circular area at the North Pole that was surrounded by ice fields.

Another hole supposedly exists in Antarctica. Some Hollow Earth enthusiasts say Hitler believed that Antarctica held the true opening to Earth's core. Leading Hollow Earth researchers such as Dennis Crenshaw suggest that President Roosevelt ordered the 1939 South Pole expedition to find the entrance before the Germans did.

The poles may not hold the only entrances to a world hidden deep beneath our feet. Jules Verne's famous novel *Journey to the Center of the Earth* supported yet another theory about passage between the worlds. In his story, there were many access points, including waterfalls and inactive volcanoes. Edgar Allan Poe and Edgar Rice Burroughs also wrote about worlds inside Earth. Their ideas were based on science as well as fantasy.

## Scientists Take Note

Many scientists have taken the Hollow Earth theory seriously. One of the most noted was English astronomer Edmund Halley, of Halley's Comet fame. In 1692, he declared that our planet is hollow, and as evidence, he pointed to global shifts in Earth's magnetic fields, which frequently cause compass anomalies. According to Halley, those shifts could be explained by the movement of rotating worlds inside Earth. In addition, he claimed that the source of gravity—still debated in the twenty-first century—could be an interior world.

In Halley's opinion, Earth is made of three separate layers or shells, each rotating independently around a solid core. We live on the outer shell, but the inner worlds might be inhabited, too. Halley also suggested that Earth's interior atmospheres are luminous. We supposedly see them as gas leaking out of Earth's fissures. At the poles, that gas creates the *aurora borealis*.

## Scientists Look Deeper

Hollow Earth researchers claim that the groundwork for their theories was laid by some of the most notable scientific minds of the seventeenth and eighteenth centuries. Although their beliefs remain controversial and largely unsubstantiated, they are still widely discussed and have a network of enthusiasts.

Some researchers claim that Leonhard Euler (1707–1783), one of the greatest mathematicians of all time, believed that Earth's interior includes a glowing core that illuminates life for a well-developed civilization, much like the sun lights our world. Another mathematician, Sir John Leslie (1766–1832), suggested that Earth has a thin crust and also believed the interior cavity was filled with light.

In 1818, a popular lecturer named John Cleves Symmes, Jr., proposed an expedition to prove the Hollow Earth theory. He believed that he could sail to the North Pole, and upon reaching the opening to Earth's core, he could steer his ship over the lip of the entrance, which he believed resembled a waterfall. Then he would continue sailing on waters inside the planet. In 1822 and 1823, Symmes petitioned Congress to fund the expedition, but he was turned down. He died in 1829, and his gravestone in Hamilton, Ohio, is decorated with his model of the Hollow Earth.

## Proof Gets Woolly and Weird

In 1846, a remarkably well-preserved—and long extinct—woolly mammoth was found frozen in Siberia. Most woolly mammoths died out about 12,000 years ago, so researchers were baffled by its pristine condition.

Hollow Earth enthusiasts say there is only one explanation: The mammoth lived inside Earth, where those beasts are not extinct. The beast had probably become lost, emerged into our world, and froze to death shortly before the 1846 discovery.

## Eyewitnesses at the North Pole

Several respected scientists and explorers have visited the poles and returned with stories that suggest a hollow Earth. At the start of the twentieth century, Arctic explorers Dr. Frederick A. Cook and Rear Admiral Robert E. Peary sighted land—not just an icy wasteland—at the North Pole. Peary first described it as "the white summits of a distant land." A 1913 Arctic expedition also reported seeing "hills, valleys, and snow-capped peaks." All of these claims were dismissed as mirages but would later be echoed by the research of Admiral Richard E. Byrd, the first man to fly over the North Pole. Hollow Earth believers suggest that Byrd actually flew into the interior world and then out again, without realizing it. They cite Byrd's notes as evidence, as he describes his navigational instruments and compasses spinning out of control.

## Unidentified Submerged Objects

Support for the Hollow Earth theory has also come from UFO enthusiasts. People who study UFOs have also been documenting USOs, or unidentified submerged objects. These mysterious vehicles have been spotted—mostly at sea—since the nineteenth century.

USOs look like "flying saucers," but instead of vanishing into the skies, they plunge beneath the surface of the ocean.

Too Weird for Truth?

Some are luminous and fly upward from the sea at a fantastic speed—and without making a sound.

UFO enthusiasts believe that these spaceships are visiting worlds beneath the sea. Some are certain that these are actually underwater alien bases. Other UFO researchers think that the ocean conceals entries to a hollow Earth, where the aliens maintain outposts.

## The Search Continues

Some scientists have determined that the most likely location for a northern opening to Earth's interior is at 84.4 N Latitude, 141 E Longitude. It's a spot near Siberia, about 600 miles from the North Pole. Photos taken by *Apollo 8* in 1968 and *Apollo 16* in 1972 showed dark, circular areas confirming the location. Some scientists are studying seismic tomography, which uses natural and human-made explosions as well as earthquakes and other seismic waves to chart Earth's interior masses. So far, scientists confirm that Earth is comprised of three separate layers. Strangely, some images could suggest a mountain range at Earth's core. Could what seems like a fantasy from a Jules Verne novel turn out to be an astonishing reality? Hollow Earth societies around the world continue to look for proof of this centuries-old legend. Who knows what they might find?

# WICCA: THAT GOOD OL' TIME RELIGION?

Until Wicca grew more popular in the 1990s, many people had never even heard of it. Even among Wiccans the debate continues to percolate: How old is this, really?

## Definitions

To study the genesis of the religious and magical practice of Wicca, one must be sure not to confuse "Wicca" with "witchcraft." Not all witches are Wiccan; Wicca is a nature religion that can involve the practice of witchcraft.

## Antiquity

Throughout human existence, most cultures have had populations that might be considered "witches": esoteric specialists, such as midwives or herbalists, or people claiming spiritual contacts or divinatory skill. To believe someone a witch is to believe that person is able to foresee or change outcomes. Some cultures fear and hate witches; others embrace them. We might call them folk practitioners, shamans, or witch doctors. Wicca cannot demonstrate descent from such folk practitioners, but it draws much inspiration from old Celtic and English folk practice and religion.

During the worst medieval persecutions, Christian leaders slew thousands of Europeans over witchcraft accusations. Many of that era's popular definitions of witchcraft were hardly credible because the persecutors themselves wrote them. They equated witchcraft with diabolism simply because if it wasn't Christian, it had to be Satanic.

Evidence suggests that the persecutions had little to do with witchcraft but much to do with vendettas, estate seizures (especially of affluent widows), and the governmental need for a group enemy on which to focus public anger. Some Wiccans claim that Wicca endured in secret among the most skilled survivors of these persecutions. Unfortunately, there's no evidence that recognizable Wicca existed during "the Burning Times" in the first place, so survival is moot.

Too Weird for Truth?

# Victorian Renaissance

Interest in secret societies and the occult grew in Europe in the nineteenth century. With admiration of ancient Greco-Roman philosophy grew admiration of ancient divinity concepts—including a feminine divine presence or, more bluntly, the idea of God as a woman. While that notion revolted many Judeo-Christian traditionalists, others found it appealing.

By the early 1900s, several British occult organizations and movements drew upon and combined pre-Christian religious ideas and magical theory. Some groups were simply excuses to party, whereas others were stuff y study groups. Others blurred the distinctions or went back and forth. While none were visibly Wiccan, they would later help to inspire Wicca.

## Gardner

During the 1930s, an English civil servant named Gerald B. Gardner developed a strong interest in the occult. Some sources claim that socialite Dorothy Clutterbuck had initiated him into a witches' coven, but that's doubtful because Mrs. Clutterbuck was widely known as a devout Anglican. More likely, his initiation came from a woman known only as "Dafo," who later distanced herself from occultism.

Wherever Gardner learned his witching, he definitely ran with it. In the early 1950s, Gardner began popularizing a duotheistic (the god/the goddess) synthesis of religion and magic that he initially called "Wica." Why then? Well, in 1951, Parliament repealed the 1735 Witchcraft Act, so it was now legal. Wicca borrowed all over the place, creating a tradition of eclecticism that thrives today.

## Buckland

When Wicca came to America with Gardner's student Raymond Buckland in 1964, its timing was impeccable.

For Wicca, the 1960s counterculture was rich soil worthy of a fertility goddess. Today, self-described "eclectic Wiccans"—Wiccans who essentially define their own Wicca to suit themselves—probably outnumber Gardnerians, a group one might fairly call "orthodox Wiccans."

Rough estimates place the number of Wiccans in the United States today between 200,000 and 500,000.

# THE COTTINGLEY FAIRY HOAX

It was a story so seemingly real that even the creator of the world's most intelligent literary detective was convinced that it was true.

## Pixie Party

It was summertime in the English village of Cottingley in 1917 when cousins Elsie Wright and Frances Griffiths borrowed Elsie's father's new camera. When he later developed the glass plate negatives, he saw a photo of Frances with a group of four tiny, winged fairies. A prank, he figured. Two months later, the girls took another photo. This one showed Elsie with a gnome. At that point, her father banned them from using the camera again.

But a few years later, Wright's wife mentioned her daughter's fairy photos within earshot of theosophist Edward Gardner, who was so taken with them that he showed them to a leading photographic expert. After studying them extensively, this man declared the photos genuine. They caught the attention of spiritual believer Sir Arthur Conan Doyle, author of the *Sherlock Holmes* series, who published a magazine article announcing the Cottingley fairies to the world.

## A Delusional Doyle

In 1922, Doyle published *The Coming of the Fairies*. The book argued for the existence of fairies and contained the original photos along with three new pictures that Elsie and Frances had produced. Both the article and book ignited a pitched battle between believers and doubters. Many thought Doyle's fertile imagination had finally gotten the better of him.

## Fairy Tale?

As years passed, people remained fascinated by the story. In 1981, Elsie admitted that the whole thing was a hoax taken too far, and that the fairies were actually paper cutouts held up by hatpins. Frances, however, maintained the fairies were authentic even up to her death.

# EVERYTHING VENTURED, NOTHING GAINED (YET)

Some people consider Oak Island, a small island off the coast of Nova Scotia, Canada, the repository of one of the world's most fantastic treasures. Others, however, think that it's a natural monument to the gullibility of man.

## Stay Away

It's only a short boat ride across the channel (and an even shorter walk across the causeway) between the Nova Scotia mainland and Oak Island. Aside from the oak trees that give the island its name, there's little to distinguish the 140-acre island from the nearly 400 others that dot Mahone Bay. Nevertheless, boats are not permitted to land here, and the causeway is fenced off with a "No Trespassing" sign.

If the casual visitor could set foot on the island, however, they would find its surface permeated by hundreds of mine shafts. Thanks to plenty of folklore and gossip, for over two centuries Oak Island has been the focus of spectacular digging operations, with excavators using everything from pick and spade to modern industrial boring equipment. To date, these exertions have consumed millions of dollars.

## Why All the Fuss?

Depending on the source (and there are many), Oak Island is the final resting place of any number of precious objects, including:

• Captain Kidd's pirate treasure

• Manuscripts proving that Sir Francis Bacon wrote Shakespeare's plays

• South American gold

• Marie Antoinette's jewels

• The Holy Grail

• The accumulated wealth of the Knights Templar and/or the Freemasons

## The Legend Begins

As the story goes, in 1795 a boy named Daniel McGinnis ventured onto the island and gleaned from marks on a tree that rope and tackle had been used to lower something into the ground. The next day, he returned with two companions and initiated the first attempt to recover treasure from what has since become known as the Money Pit—a vertical shaft that by 1897 had already been excavated by a series of individuals and companies. Depths ran to 111 feet with core samples drilled to over 170 feet deep.

## The Problem

Flooding in the shafts, which many believe to be caused by special tunnels built as booby traps to foil treasure seekers, has always thwarted digging operations on Oak Island. Attempts to block these subterranean channels have been unsuccessful and have only revealed that the water from the shafts flows outward to the sea at various locations.

Despite the difficulties, treasure seekers continue to labor on Oak Island because the Money Pit, its auxiliary shafts, and the various features on the island's surface have yielded tantalizing indications that something of value lies beneath. Among the evidence: a stone inscribed with strange markings, a primitive pair of scissors, large amounts of coconut husk, and a piece of sheepskin parchment bearing what appeared to be an inscribed Roman numeral.

## The Skeptics Have Their Say

Naysayers take plenty of issue with Oak Island's supposed treasure. They point out that while it may be likely that at one time pirates or even Freemasons landed on the island, that doesn't necessarily spell buried treasure. And there's nothing weird about sinkholes and subterranean chambers in limestone, they say. In fact, they're all over the region.

Moreover, skeptics note the lack of evidence of any digging on the island before the 1840s. They figure it's much more likely that a story about someone discovering a treasure cave got a few people excited. Legend built upon legend until, like the island itself, the story was muddied and mixed-up by the passage of time. Either way, perhaps Oak Island's greatest treasure is simply the human imagination.